Art, Psychotherapy and Psychosis

The history of art therapy as a psychotherapeutic practice is inextricably linked with clients suffering from psychosis. *Art, Psychotherapy and Psychosis* traces the evolution of this specialized and innovative treatment in psychiatric and psychotherapeutic settings and offers an overview of current practice.

Part I identifies specific clinical issues involved in working with psychosis. The theoretical models applied reflect the influence of psychotherapy, psychoanalysis, analytical psychology and psychiatry. Each chapter is written by an experienced practitioner and draws on detailed case material illustrated with examples of clients' art work. The practices described extend existing theory and develop the application of analytical approaches in art psychotherapy in the treatment of borderline states as well as acute and long-term psychotic illnesses. Part II recounts the historical context of art therapy and psychosis, from the early influence of artists, its origins within psychiatric institutions, to the adaptations which have been made in response to recent legislative changes.

Art, Psychotherapy and Psychosis represents the creative diversity of current practice. Its new perspectives are essential reading for all those interested in psychotherapeutic approaches to psychosis.

Katherine Killick is in private practice as a psychotherapist in St Albans. **Joy Schaverien** is a Jungian analyst and art psychotherapist in private practice, an Associate Professional Member of the Society of Analytical Psychology and author of *The Revealing Image (1991)* and *Desire and the Female Therapist (1995)*.

Art, Psychotherapy and Psychosis

Edited by Katherine Killick
and Joy Schaverien

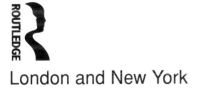

London and New York

First published 1997
by Routledge
11 New Fetter Lane, London EC4P 4EE

Simultaneously published in the USA and Canada
by Routledge
29 West 35th Street, New York, NY 10001

Typeset in Times by
Ponting–Green Publishing Services, Chesham,
Buckinghamshire
Printed and bound in Great Britain by
Biddles Ltd., Guildford and King's Lynn

British Library Cataloguing in Publication Data
A catalogue record for this book is available from the
British Library

Library of Congress Cataloguing in Publication Data
A catalogue record for this book has been requested

ISBN   0–415–13841–8

ISBN   0–415–13842–6 (pbk)

Contents

Illustrations

Editors

Katherine Killick is in private practice as a psychotherapist and clinical supervisor in St Albans, working analytically with individuals. Originally trained as an artist, and then as an art therapist, she is now completing her training as a Jungian analyst with the Society of Analytical Psychology. She worked in adult psychiatry in the National Health Service from 1979–94 and, as head of Art Therapy at Hill End Hospital, she developed an art therapy service which specialised in the treatment of borderline states and psychosis. The principles on which this was based formed the subject of theoretical research which she undertook for her Master's Degree. She has been teaching on this subject, within the art therapy profession and in related fields for many years and has published a number of papers.

Dr Joy Schaverien is a Jungian analyst and art psychotherapist in private practice in Leicestershire. Trained initially at the Slade as a painter, she has worked as an art therapist in the National Health Service, in a therapeutic community, adult psychiatry and out-patient psychotherapy. She was course leader of the Master's programme in art therapy at the University of Hertfordshire and now lectures widely in Britain and abroad on the links between art and psychotherapy. Among her many publications she is the author of *The Revealing Image: Analytical Art Psychotherapy in Theory and Practice* (Routledge, 1991) and *Desire and the Female Therapist: Engendered Gazes in Psychotherapy and Art Therapy* (Routledge, 1995). She is an Associate Professional Member of the Society of Analytical Psychology in London.

Contributors

Fiona Foster MA has a degree in fine art, trained in art therapy and has completed an MA in art therapy. She has worked as a senior art therapist in NHS adult psychiatry and education. Currently she is a practising sculptor and freelance art therapist.

Helen Greenwood qualified as an art therapist in 1978, after graduating in History of Art at Manchester University. Since then she has worked in NHS adult psychiatry, in hospital and community settings, and is currently employed by Wakefield and Pontefract Community NHS Trust. She is a visiting lecturer and tutor on the Art Therapy Diploma Course at Sheffield University, and has been a member of the *Inscape* editorial board for several years.

John Henzell was born in England in 1938, spent his childhood in Australia returning to England after training as an artist. He worked in psychiatric hospitals and centres associated with anti-psychiatry and other radical groups before teaching and research in the 1970s. A founding member of BAAT he developed art and psychotherapy courses in Sheffield where he now lectures and writes.

David Maclagan lectures at the Centre for Psychotherapeutic Studies, University of Sheffield. He is also a member of the London Convivium for Archetypal Studies. He is both an artist and an art therapist and has published many articles on the cultural, aesthetic and ethical aspects of Outsider Art. He is the author of *Creation Myths* (Thames & Hudson, 1977) and is currently working on a book *About the Doodle*.

David Mann trained both as a psychoanalytic psychotherapist and as an art therapist and has experience in both the NHS and private sector. He has published extensively in leading national and international journals and his book, *Psychotherapy: An Erotic Relationship. Transference and Counter-transference Passions* is to be published by Routledge in 1997. He lectures and teaches on various psychotherapy training programmes and runs workshops in the UK and Europe.

Terry Molloy MA is an art therapist and clinical supervisor in private practice and part-time lecturer at the Art Psychotherapy Unit, Goldsmiths College, University of London. He has had extensive clinical experience in adult psychiatry, specialist adolescent services and with children of all ages in special educational settings.

Sue Morter trained as an art therapist in 1972 and 1990. She is working within the NHS and private settings with adults with a wide range of emotional and psychiatric disturbances. Previously she was employed at a large psychiatric hospital for sixteen years during which time her work was predominantly with patients in acute and psychotic states. She has been involved with training students and other professionals in art therapy. Her current interests involve initiating an Arts Community Centre in her own locality, where she intends to develop her private art therapy practice.

Fiona Seth-Smith BA (Hons) works as a senior art therapist in London in a psychiatric unit for adults, in a regional unit for the treatment of disturbed mothers with their babies, and in Parkside Clinic, an NHS psychotherapy clinic in Notting Hill. She also has a private practice.

Claire Skailes MA began working as an art teacher with children who had learning and emotional problems. This led her to become an art therapist, working for many years in Coney Hill Hospital in Gloucestershire, in a wide variety of psychiatric settings. When art therapy became well established she left to work in private practice as an art therapist then took a Jungian training with the West Midlands Institute of Psychotherapy. She now has a practice as a psychotherapist.

Chris Wood is an art therapist working for Community Health Sheffield, often with people with a history of psychosis. She is also currently co-ordinating a post-graduate training course for art therapists at the Centre for Psychotherapeutic Studies of Sheffield University. She is interested in developing helpful methods for training. Her work towards a PhD is concerned with art therapy and psychosis in the public sector.

All the contributors to the book are Registered Members of the British Association of Art Therapists. Katherine Killick, Terry Molloy and Joy Schaverien are also members of Analytical Art Therapy Associates.

Acknowledgements

The inspiration for this book developed from a number of sources which we would like to acknowledge. Several conversations led us to realise that there was a need for a book devoted to this subject. We are grateful to those colleagues in fields other than art therapy who made us aware of what we had to offer to them. From within art therapy Tessa Dalley and Gabrielle Rifkind encouraged us to consider the project. However, we owe our first debt of gratitude to our patients who have taught us so much over the years and to our students, especially those who have linked our theoretical approaches. During the process of producing the book Peter Wilson has generously supported our work in many different ways, which included giving us permission to reproduce his painting *Regal Debate* for the cover.

We gratefully acknowledge the permission given to reproduce the following: The Museum of Modern Art, New York: *The Plague* by Max Klinger. The Adolf Wölfli-Stiftung, Kunstmuseum, Bern: *Waldorf-Astooria: Hotel Windsor in New York* by Adolf Wölfli. The Collection de l'Art Brut, Lausanne: *Le Pays des Meteors* by Le Voyageur Francais and *Train* by Aloise Corbaz. The Bethlem Royal Hospital Archives and Museum: *Cat Paintings* by Louis Wain. Faber & Faber Ltd: *Days* from *The Whitsun Weddings* by Philip Larkin. A version of Chapter 2 'Unintegration and Containment in Acute Psychosis' by Katherine Killick appeared in the *British Journal of Psychotherapy*, Vol. 13, No. 2, January 1997.

Introduction

Joy Schaverien and Katherine Killick

This book traces the theoretical developments and the history of art therapy in the treatment of psychosis. It is intended for an international readership and for all those who are concerned with psychotherapeutic approaches to this client group. We are aware of increasing interest in this subject from within the profession of art therapy and allied professions. Experienced art therapists, as well as trainees, often work with this client group and psychiatrists and psychotherapists who are involved with the treatment of psychosis are increasingly recognising the particular contribution of art therapy. Therefore, this book is addressed to a potentially wide readership: to art therapists, art therapy students and those considering art therapy training; as well as to psychiatrists, psychotherapists, psychoanalysts and Jungian analysts. It is also intended to be relevant to professionals working in the fields of counselling, social work, occupational therapy and nursing.

THE BOOK: RATIONALE

The aim of the book is to offer an understanding of art therapy as a psychotherapeutic approach to patients in psychotic states and patients with a history of psychosis. The material presented comes from work with adults. Although it does not include children or adults with learning difficulties, the book will be of interest to those who work with these client groups. Art therapy with psychotic patients has developed within the wider context of psychiatry and inevitably the changes that have taken place in recent years within the British National Health Service have had an influence on clinical practice. These are reflected directly and indirectly in all the chapters in the book and we are aware that similar, if not identical, issues concern therapists working in many countries. The development of current theoretical approaches to clinical practice, in this specialised area, is traced and can be seen to be intimately related to the growth of art therapy as a profession. The influence of psychoanalytic thinking as well as aesthetic theory is apparent throughout. The book is arranged in two sections: Part I, Art, Psychotherapy and Psychosis and Part II, Context and History. This arrangement is intended to give the reader a sense of the current state of art psychotherapy theory and practice, its history, and also of the potential for its future development. Most of the chapters are illustrated with detailed case examples, including pictures.

It seemed to us that this book was waiting to be written. We decided to invite experienced art therapists to write chapters on their particular area of work to give a sense of the variety of ways in which art therapy contributes to the treatment of this client group. As a professional group, art therapists have a wealth of experience of working with patients who are diagnosed as psychotic. Art therapy is unusual among the professions engaged in psycho-therapeutic work in that students very often begin their careers with place-ments in contexts where such patients are the main client group. In the past, this was in large psychiatric hospitals and, since the move towards care in the community, art therapists are often placed in day centres and other community settings for the clinical component of their training. Psychosis, as described in this book, is a term that has covered many different types of disturbance. Most of the clinical material in the book refers to patients who were diagnosed as schizophrenic within psychiatry, but patients with dia-gnoses of paranoid psychosis and manic-depressive psychosis also feature. The terms 'patient' and 'client' are both used in the book, often reflecting the preference of the writer. However, many of the people discussed in the book were within psychiatric hospitals and are described as patients in accordance with medical custom.

The history of art therapy in Britain, as documented in the book, is inextricably linked with this client group. Relatively little has been published specifically about art therapy with psychotic clients, which is surprising when one considers the amount of contact art therapists have with people in these states of mind. However, there are papers on psychosis in *Inscape* (the journal of the British Association of Art Therapists) by Greenwood and Layton (1987 and 1991), Killick (1991), Greenwood (1994) and chapters which form contributions to books – e.g. Charlton (1984), Wood (1992), Killick and Greenwood (1994) and Killick (1995). Case and Dalley (1992) discuss some of the contexts of art therapy practice with these patients. Theses and dissertations have also been written which address aspects of clinical art therapy practice with psychotic patients. These unpublished works are to be found in the libraries of the institutions where art therapy training takes place. Adamson (1984) described his non-directive way of working, which was almost exclusively with this client group. Similarly other art therapists have, in describing their practice, sometimes written about psychotic clients but without drawing specific attention to the client group (Dalley 1987; Schaverien 1991). Killick's work in the field, which is well known within the art therapy profession, has established the need for a particular approach to psychosis. Her teaching has mainly taken the form of lecturing, supervision and workshops.

C.G. Jung's influence on understanding of both psychosis and art in therapy has been significant. His theories of the collective unconscious, archetypes and his attitude to regression as potentially healing, are threads running through many of the chapters. Early art therapists were influenced by his analysands, Baynes (1940) and Champernowne (1969 and 1971). In particular Champernowne's work at Withymead influenced many art therapists. She considered the art therapist to be a kind of midwife, producing the artwork, while the psychotherapist would interpret its meaning with the patient. This was similar to the attitude held by Adamson (1984) and places the art therapist in a position which defers to the knowledge of the psychiatrist or psychotherapist. Naumberg (1950) linked art therapy and psychotherapy, and although she was working and writing in the USA she was read by art therapists working with this client group in Britain. Since these early days the influence of a wide range of psychoanalytic ideas has permeated the profession. In part this is due to the establishment and increasing formalisation of art therapy training. The art therapy training courses, in Britain, began in the early 1970s and some of the contributers to this book were among the first teachers and students on these courses. Art therapists are now trained to be responsible for their own case load and to understand and work with the dynamics of the transference and countertransference. The nature of psychotic transferences requires specialised understanding and the technical problems encountered are considerable. This has been well documented within the field of psychoanalysis and some of these understandings are now developed in art therapy practice. This is evident in a number of chapters in the book which develop a range of ideas derived from psychoanalysis, analytical psychology as well as art theory.

ANALYTICAL ART PSYCHOTHERAPY AND PSYCHOSIS

The increasing professionalisation of art therapy, which includes awareness of psychoanalytic theory, has led to the point at which there is a debate about the name of the profession. Some art therapists prefer to be called art psychotherapists and it remains a question whether or not this reflects a difference in their clinical practice.

In *The Revealing Image* (1991) Schaverien offered an analysis of the role of the art object as a concrete element in the transference and countertransference in art therapy. She proposed the inclusive term 'analytical art psychotherapy' which offers a way of encompassing the wide varieties of art therapy practice. The term 'analytical' was important as it was intended as a way of establishing and articulating a feature of art therapy, which is the centrality of the artwork and its influence. It acknowledges the 'analytical differentiation', which transforms the psychological state of the artist/client, through the act of making and viewing the artwork itself.

This was further developed in a paper published in *Inscape* (Schaverien 1994) in which she applied this term more widely to articulate some of the differences in the practice of art therapy which she had observed in her own clinical work and in supervision of others. The difference identified in this paper was in the ways in which the understanding of the transference could be applied in certain settings and with particular client groups. Under the headings 'art therapy', 'art psychotherapy' and 'analytical art psychotherapy' there was an attempt to offer a way of talking about similarity and difference within the practice of art therapists. We now propose to attempt to apply this understanding to the chapters in the book which address clinical practice. However, first we need to establish that these categories are a description of already existing practices. They are not intended to be hierarchical or fixed, and as art therapists we need to be flexible and able to move between these different resources in response to particular clients. This flexibility can be observed in the clinical work described in the book which we hope brings the theory alive.

We would suggest that the nature of the practice described by Henzell and Skailes would fit the category of 'art therapy'. These therapists worked within large psychiatric institutions which provide a comprehensive holding environment. The art was the central feature of the interactions and the nature of the setting made working with the interpersonal transference impossible. Therefore the interaction with the artwork was the main feature of the process. Morter, in her chapter, gives a detailed case study of this kind of art therapy and she clearly illustrates the kind of work possible within certain institutional settings even today. A number of chapters describe a psycho-analytically informed approach, which takes account of the psychoanalytic transference and countertransference. These include awareness of the role of the artwork within the therapeutic relationship. It is interesting to note that the authors describe their own approaches in a variety of ways. Killick and Schaverien (in this context) describe their work as 'analytical art therapy'. This term conveys an analytical process which is not psychotherapy in its traditional form. The patients described in their chapters would probably have found psychotherapy impossible without the mediation of the artwork. Although the therapist's awareness of the interpersonal transference informed the way they approached their clients, it was, as both point out, not possible to interpret. This is largely due to the level of disturbance of the patients described. The analytical differentiation was focused in the third area, the picture, at the apex of the triangle of patient–picture–therapist. The transference was enacted and held in the picture and this made it possible for the client to relate to the therapist. Mann, working in an acute setting, and Molloy, working in rehabilitation, both use the term 'art psychotherapy'. Seth-Smith, Foster and Greenwood call the work they describe 'art therapy'. The question is whether these are all different ways of describing a process of the kind outlined above. We think they could all be thought of as examples of different positions on the spectrum of analytical art psychotherapy. They are analytical in relation to the artwork, informed by psychoanalytic concepts, and the therapists are aware of the transference/countertransference dynamics, even when the transference cannot be interpreted.

PART I ART, PSYCHOTHERAPY AND PSYCHOSIS

The first section of the book focuses on issues emerging in the practice of art therapy with psychotic clients. Most of the chapters demonstrate the ways in which a variety of different psychoanalytic as well as aesthetic sources inform art therapy theory and are applied in practice. Each chapter describes some aspect of clinical practice and most are illustrated with pictures made by clients.

In Chapter 1, Schaverien draws attention to the fact that psychotic patients often write words on their pictures and questions why that might be. She elaborates the concept of the transactional object (Schaverien 1989, 1995) and introduces a development of the idea of magical investment in art objects (Schaverien 1991) in relation to the picture as fetish. Drawing on theory from psychoanalysis and analytical psychology, these concepts offer a way of thinking about the particular nature of the object-relating which characterises the psychotic patients' relationship to the artwork. In Chapter 2, Killick uses case material to develop ideas underpinning her approach to psychosis. She articulates some considerations involved in engaging, and forming relationships with patients in acute psychotic states. Applying post-Kleinian psychoanalytic concepts, she suggests that forming and maintaining a container is central to effective work with this psychopathology, and relates this to her work with particular patients in different settings, including private practice. Three-dimensional art materials are rarely given specific attention in the art therapy literature and, in Chapter 3, Foster brings them into focus. Through description of case material she discusses the anxieties, resistances and defences of patients in using art materials with three-dimensional qualities. She proposes links between these and the fragmentation of the body image characteristic of schizophrenic patients. In Chapter 4, Mann uses a case study to show the nature of the relationship which can develop between a patient and his artwork when the patient is in a psychotic state. This is discussed in relation to sexual perversion and the psychoanalytic understanding of the fetish in this context. The term 'fetish' is used by both Schaverien and Mann and applied differently. Mann clarifies the differences in the meaning of the artwork for clients in psychotic states from those with more neurotic psychopathologies. Understanding these issues, in particular the way image-making can serve defensive purposes in psychosis, is crucial to appropriate technique in art therapy practice. Seth-Smith (Chapter 5) uses established art therapy theory to develop an original way of looking at, and thinking about, the images made by patients in different art therapy settings. She applies psychoanalytic theory to outline a set of processes which underlie the creation and meaning of the pictures made in the context of art therapy.

In Chapter 6, the final chapter of Part I, Greenwood proposes a way of thinking about the strengthening of ego functions which therapy might aim to develop. She gives case material from community treatment settings to illustrate this. Thus this chapter reveals some of the changes which have taken place in the settings for art therapy practice and some of the ways in which the practice of art therapy has had to be adapted to accommodate these changes.

PART II: CONTEXT AND HISTORY

The second section of the book offers an overview of the historical context of the practice of art therapy with psychosis. In the first chapter in this section Maclagan (Chapter 7) draws on his knowledge of 'outsider art' to explore ways of looking at the pictures made by people in psychotic states, distinguishing between their 'symptomatic' and expressive, creative aspects. He discusses the artwork made by these patients in the social context of the wider world of art. He questions whether there is a place for 'psychotic art' in the thinking of art therapists and refers to patients living in hospitals who became recognised as artists. Maclagan suggests that a transition of social role from psychiatric patient to artist expresses a healing process for the individual. In Chapter 8, Wood traces the history of art therapy in Britain from 1938 to the present. Her chapter offers a review of the literature as well as describing the practice of art therapy during this period. She discusses the influences affecting treatment approaches to psychiatric patients and traces the growth of art therapy practice within psychiatry. This leads to discussion as well as description by both Henzell (Chapter 9) and Skailes (Chapter 10) of the asylum style large hospital. In common with other art therapists they both began their art therapy careers in such hospitals which have been closing recently in accordance with the move to community care. Henzell offers a personal view; he recounts his own history as an art therapist and his association with the 'anti-psychiatry' movement, in a particular hospital in the 1960s. R.D. Laing's influence on the profession, and on the way art therapists were thinking about psychosis in these years, is drawn out by both Wood and Henzell. Skailes introduces us to some of the inhabitants of a similar asylum-type hospital. The sometimes distressing experiences she describes are characteristic of those of many art therapists who began working with little support and with very disturbed in-patients. In Chapter 11, Morter gives a case study of the process of art therapy with one young man. It is a vivid account and exemplifies the kind of practice which developed over the years in the large asylums described by Wood, Skailes and Henzell. Many of Wood's misgivings about community care, as a setting for art therapy practice, come alive in relation to this patient. It is difficult to imagine how a patient who is as fragmented as this could be engaged and managed in many of the settings in which art therapy is currently practised.

In the final chapter, Molloy (Chapter 12) describes work with people beginning to return to life in the world outside the setting of the institution after psychotic breakdowns. He uses clinical examples to discuss some of the issues which arise in the context of a rehabilitation department. He points to many of the problems of practising art therapy within the current context of community psychiatry and proposes a role for art therapists in this process. Skailes and Molloy both stress the importance of educating fellow professionals about the nature of art therapy practice in order that the work can be appropriately supported.

The way in which the role of the art therapist has evolved with the maturing of the profession as a whole emerges within this section of the book. Hill (1945), Lyddiatt (1971) and Adamson (1984) are seen as early influences holding a belief that art was in itself a healing process. We think this reflected a tendency on their part to undervalue the contribution they, as individuals, made towards establishing the therapeutic setting. Had this attitude prevailed, as Skailes points out, art therapy might well have remained an aspect of occupational therapy. The specialised training which now exists recognises the importance of the therapeutic relationship as well as the healing potential of the art process. The majority of art therapists are artists and are therefore familiar with the vicissitudes of the creative process which, as Henzell suggests, gives a particular perspective on psychosis. The dimension of the relationship within which the art is made has been increasingly acknowledged in the profession over the years. There are now a number of books which address these specific issues, including Case and Dalley (1992) who explore all aspects of the art therapist's role, and Waller (1991) who describes the history.

CONCLUSION

The nature of art therapy as practised by the different therapists who have contributed to the book is diverse, and this reflects the current state of diversity of practice within the profession. Wood in her chapter emphasises the importance of 'care and respect' in approaches to people in psychotic states. We think that both are apparent in the approaches to patients described in all the chapters of the book. It is clear from many of the contributors that the current context of practice in psychiatry is far from ideal. It is also clear that the context offered by the large asylums was problematic. Moreover, we see that 'anti-psychiatry' was not the panacea it was once thought to be. This leads us to consider the nature of psychotic processes which tend to powerfully undermine containing elements in relationships. It may be that difficulties in finding and maintaining viable settings for therapeutic practice with this client group are intrinsic to the work, and the quest for the 'ideal setting' can be thought of as part of working with psychotic processes. At the same time we are aware of many inadequate settings in which art therapists often have to work, and of the social as well as the psychological deprivation which can be suffered by these clients and which may go unrecognised. In part, this book represents an attempt to raise awareness of these issues in the hope that these conditions improve. However, in the chapters which follow it is clear that, despite some very real obstacles to practice, art therapists have nonetheless managed to find 'good enough' settings in which to continue to develop work with people in psychotic states. We hope that this might encourage those feeling overwhelmed or daunted by the difficulties they encounter in their work places. We see this book as a marker which records where we have come from as a profession and the position at the present time. Most of all we hope it forms a foundation on which others can build their theory and their practice.

REFERENCES

Adamson, E. (1984) *Art as Healing*, Boston and London: Coventure.

Baynes, H.G. (1940) *The Mythology of the Soul*, London: RKP.

Case, C. and Dalley, T. (1992) *The Handbook of Art Therapy*, London and New York: Routledge

Champernowne, I. (1969) 'Art therapy as an adjunct to psychotherapy', London: *Inscape* 1 (Autumn).

—— (1971) 'Art and therapy an uneasy partnership', London: *Inscape* 3.

Charlton, S. (1984) 'Art therapy with long-stay residents of psychiatric hospitals', in T. Dalley (ed.) *Art as Therapy*, London and New York: Tavistock.

Dalley, T. (1987) 'Art as therapy some new perspectives', in T. Dalley *et al.* (eds) *Images of Art Therapy*, London and New York: Tavistock/Routledge.

Greenwood, H. and Layton, G. (1987) 'An outpatient art therapy group', London: *Inscape* (Summer).

—— (1991) 'Taking the piss', London: *Inscape* (Winter).

Greenwood, H. (1994) 'Cracked pots', London: *Inscape* 1.

Hill, A. (1945) *Art versus Illness*, London: George Allen & Unwin.

Killick, K. (1991) 'The practice of art therapy with patients in acute psychotic states', London: *Inscape* (Winter).

—— (1995) 'Working with psychotic processes in art therapy', in J. Ellwood (ed.) *Psychosis Understanding and Treatment*, London: Jessica Kingsley.

Killick, K. and Greenwood, H. (1994) 'Research in art therapy with people who have psychotic illnesses', in A. Gilroy and C. Lee (eds) *Art and Music: Therapy and Research*, London and New York: Routledge.

Lyddiatt, E.M. (1971) *Spontaneous Painting and Modelling: A Practical Approach in Therapy*, New York: St Martin's Press.

Naumberg, M. (1950) *Schizophrenic Art: its Meaning in Psychotherapy*, New York: Grune Stratton.

Schaverien, J. (1989) 'Transference and the picture: art therapy in the treatment of anorexia', London: *Inscape* (Spring).

—— (1991) *The Revealing Image: Analytical Art Psychotherapy in Theory and Practice*, London and New York: Routledge.

—— (1994) 'Analytical art psychotherapy: further reflections on theory and practice', London: *Inscape* 2: 41–9.

—— (1995) *Desire and the Female Therapist: Engendered Gazes in Psychotherapy and Art Therapy*, London and New York: Routledge.

Waller, D. (1991) *Becoming a Profession: the History of Art Therapy in Britain 1940–1992*, London and New York: Routledge.

Wood, C. (1992) 'Using art therapy with "chronic" long-term psychiatric patients', in D. Waller and A. Gilroy (eds) *Art Therapy: a Handbook*, Buckingham and Philadelphia: Open University Press.

Part I

Art, psychotherapy and psychosis

Chapter 1

Transference and transactional objects in the treatment of psychosis

Joy Schaverien

In this chapter I develop an idea, initially proposed in *Desire and the Female Therapist* (Schaverien 1995: 215) that, in the treatment of psychosis, the art object mediates as a transactional object. I have argued that the picture, positioned at the apex of a triangle composed of client–picture–therapist, may be unconsciously experienced as a transactional object.[1] In the treatment of anorexia, it mediates in place of the obsession with food and, when acknowledgement of interpersonal relationships is too threatening, it holds the transference (Schaverien 1989, 1994a, 1994b, 1995). There are major differences in the pathologies, and therefore in treatment of psychosis and anorexia, but in both cases the patient experiences difficulties in relating directly with another person. Therefore it is relevant to consider that, when the transference to the therapist is too threatening, a picture offers a neutral and contained area for mediation; it reveals, captures and holds elusive or potentially overwhelming imagery. In considering this I shall identify two distinct ways in which the picture mediates in psychosis – as a fetish and as a talisman, both of which are magically invested transactional objects.

A linked thread relates to a phenomenon which merits closer attention than it has previously received. I have observed frequently that patients who have experienced psychosis, or who are in its midst, write words on their pictures. It seems that consideration of this might reveal some general points about the process of analytical art therapy in the treatment of psychosis. The hypothesis is that, in the juxtaposition of word and image, there is in the first place an attempt to fix experience and communicate with the self, and in the second an attempt to communicate with an Other. This could be understood to be a move towards community through the mediation of a transactional art object.

THE SCAPEGOAT TRANSFERENCE AND PSYCHOSIS

The theory of the *scapegoat* transference, as a way of understanding the role of the art object within the therapeutic relationship, developed out of my clinical work with patients with diverse mental health problems including psychosis, (Schaverien 1987, 1991).[2] As it forms the basis for the ideas in this chapter, I shall briefly review this theory. The scapegoat transference is a form of unconscious transference of attributes and states, through which a picture, or three-dimensional art object, may come to embody otherwise intolerable affect. Fragmented and split off elements in the psyche may be unconsciously externalised and embodied in a picture. Like the scapegoat there may then follow an attempt to dispose of these by disposing of the picture. This is initially an unconscious act, lacking a symbolic dimension. Through the passage of time, and therapeutic interventions, including the safe-keeping of the picture, the 'disposed of' affect is reintegrated. This may then be understood as a symbolic enactment and so the art object serves a positive function as a scapegoat. As a concrete object which embodies the transference it may be understood to be a transactional object. The art object embodied in this way may come to be valued as a fetish or a talisman, consciously or unconsciously, holding elements of feeling 'live' within the therapeutic relationship (see Schaverien 1991: 144).

The scapegoat transference has particular implications when working with psychotic patients. Because of its delusional nature the transference in psychosis is often considered untenable. This has, in the past, caused many psychoanalysts and psychotherapists to consider it to be impossible to work analytically with psychotic patients. However, the scapegoat transference makes it possible to do so. The picture, as a third element in the area in between client and therapist, offers a means of externalising otherwise inexpressible thoughts and feelings. Killick (1993) has shown how, over time, they may acquire meaning which was initially impenetrable. Thus the art object offers an alternative means of mediating the split-off and fragmented elements of the psychotic personality. Here they may be contained until the artist feels ready to acknowledge and own them. The picture permits magical investment, as well as expression of otherwise intolerable impulses, and these may be viewed and acknowledged without injury to any person. As a vehicle which temporarily holds potent feelings 'out there', and so renders them manageable, the scapegoat picture may be understood to be a significant transactional object.

Psychoanalytic theory plays a significant part in the art psychotherapist's understanding of these processes, as I hope to demonstrate. However, I am arguing that there is an element in the patient's relation to the picture which is particular to analytical forms of art psychotherapy and this cannot be fully accounted for by psychoanalytic concepts. It is sometimes argued that the magical investment in artworks, which I describe, is merely a form of projective identification (Klein 1946, Rosenfeld 1965, Ogden 1982, Grotstein 1985). In consideration of this, I turn to Jung whose theories of the collective unconscious and 'participation mystique' (Jung 1963a) have often been compared to projective identification. In recent work Jungian analysts and academics have developed this in writing about communication in the area which they variously call: the area 'in-between' patient and analyst (Schwartz-

Salant 1989), 'the Mundus Imaginalis' (Samuels 1989), 'non-material reality' (Field 1991), 'liminal zone' (Reed 1996). All argue that a term such as 'projective identification', which presupposes that people are fundamentally separate, cannot fully account for the experiences of communication in this mediate area in the analytic situation. I would add that nor does it do justice to the complexity of the interaction when an actual picture exists in the area between the patient and the therapist. There are fundamental connections which underlie all human interactions, and it is relevant to note that psychotic patients are very sensitive to such connections. Furthermore, pictures are not transient like the effects of projective identification; they continue to exist in embodied form and this introduces aesthetic factors into the therapeutic interaction.

THE SETTING

The case material I shall draw upon to illustrate this chapter is from a time when I worked as an art psychotherapist, in a 600-bed psychiatric hospital, with clients suffering from long-term and acute psychotic illnesses. The art room was purpose built; it was large and light with a sink in one corner and shelves for storing paper. Paint and clay were readily available and on one wall was a board where pictures were often displayed. Tables were arranged in such a way that they could be moved according to the needs of the individual and the group. Here I offered open and closed art psychotherapy groups as well as individual sessions. I was a member of a multi-disciplinary team which met weekly to discuss admissions and review the progress of current patients. Patients were referred to group or individual art psychotherapy according to their needs.

In the open, studio group, which was the context for the cases to be discussed below, patients would work alone, sometimes talking to each other, but mostly in silence. The art psychotherapist would move around and speak to individuals within the group. For psychotic patients this is helpful as, in this way, they are able to have as much or as little attention as they seem to require on any particular occasion. The focus of the therapeutic relationship is deliberately centred in the artwork. This is where many of the interactions with psychotic patients are held (Schaverien 1994a). This is rather different from the closed art psychotherapy group where more traditional, group analytic boundaries are established. The formal structure of the closed group means that the frame widens to include attention to the boundaries of the setting in addition to the artwork. Psychotic patients were rarely referred to the closed group and never in the early stages of their admission nor during acute phases.

This setting is evidently different from the current practice of treating people as out-patients in the community and in day centres. However, the need to understand the significance of the artwork in the treatment of psychosis transcends any particular therapeutic setting. In consideration of this it is relevant to make the point that my approach was informed by my previous experience of working in a therapeutic community. Here psychotic processes were accepted as a necessary phase in the treatment of diverse psychiatric states.[3] This fundamentally influenced my view of psychiatric illness and enabled me to understand psychosis as a meaningful process. This continues to influence my approach in my current analytic practice.

PSYCHOSIS

Models for understanding psychosis are numerous and diverse. In psychiatric diagnosis distinctions are made between the organic psychoses which 'are due to demonstrable organic disease' (Rycroft 1968: 132) and the functional psychoses which include schizophrenia and manic depressive illness. In psychoanalysis Freud distinguished psychosis from neurosis and originally considered the psychoses to be unanalysable (Hinshelwood 1989). This was because the transference was unavailable for interpretation; 'such patients occupied themselves narcissistically with their own thoughts and psychic constructions to the complete neglect of the external world, including the analyst' (Hinshelwood 1989: 407). Klein, working with children, observed sadism and persecutory elements in their play and this led her to an understanding of psychotic states in adults (Hinshelwood 1989: 407–12).

It is impossible, in this brief space, to do justice to the many theories of psychosis which have evolved since then but I shall acknowledge those which inform my approach to the clinical material which I will discuss later in the chapter. The philosopher Cassirer, Jung and Lacan[4] are very different theorists who all contribute to my understanding that what is lacking in psychosis is the experience of self as a member of a community. Each, in his own way, advances a view of the move from concrete identification, where there are only signs, through a mediate area towards language and symbolic articulation. Before discussing the use of words in pictures I shall briefly outline my understanding of these theories.

Cassirer (1955a, 1995b, 1957), in his analysis of symbolic form, develops an understanding of the evolution of consciousness in the cultural field. He argues that, ultimately, it is through the experience of the self as a member of a community that the '"I" comes to know it-"self"'. Although it was not his intention, I find this a helpful way of understanding psychosis. The mythical form of consciousness, where 'every manifestation of [the "I"'s] own personal existence and life is linked, as though by invisible magic ties, with the life of the totality around it' (Cassirer 1955b: 175), evokes the undifferentiated state which, very often, appears to dominate in the experience of the psychotic patient. This is similar to 'participation mystique' (Jung 1963a). Cassirer considers that consciousness begins to evolve through the making of artefacts and tools with specific functions. This leads to the investment of magical significance in particular objects which are often associated with rite or cult. Then, as a more symbolic attitude develops, it becomes ritual and religious consciousness. This is a progression from an unconscious state to a conscious, symbolic form of communal act and to language. The meaningful use of language ultimately brings a separate state of consciousness where the '"I" comes to grips with the world' (Cassirer 1955b: 204).

In considering the role played by art objects in the treatment of psychosis, similar processes are observable. It is through actions and symbolic forms, such as art and language, that a sense of self, and of agency, develops. As already stated, I have proposed that pictures in art psychotherapy transform the psychological state in a similar way (Schaverien 1987, 1991). Belonging to a group involves shared rituals and a common language; it is through these that membership of community is confirmed. The psychotic patient suffers because he/she does not experience him/herself as a member of a community. The use of symbolic forms fails and there is no communal understanding. The spoken word cannot be relied upon to mediate. At this point pictures may form a bridge between unmediated experience and the Other. This may be confirmed by words which are written on such pictures often in an attempt to underline meaning (Schaverien 1984).

The origin of Jung's interest in psychosis is described in *Memories, Dreams and Reflections* (Jung 1963b) where he writes of his early work in psychiatry and his encounter with his own psychological crisis. Jung regarded psychotic states as a potential within the psyche of all human beings and used the thermodynamic principle of entropy to elucidate (Jung 1928). He explains that energy is transformed as the result of differences in intensity set up by the attraction, and drawing together, of opposite elements – extremes of heat and cold, for example. This sets up intense conflict which, if overcome, gives way to an equilibrium – a sense of security and calm which is not easily disturbed – a genuine resolution. However the intensity is so great that it may result in 'a brokenness that can hardly be healed' (Jung 1928: 26). This is the fragmentation so characteristic of psychosis.

The patient who has been overwhelmed by psychosis may appear calm, with rather flattened affect – 'the so-called "dulling effect" of schizophrenia' (Jung 1928). If the conflict of opposites is pacified prematurely there may be closure – a false resolution – which results in stasis. At this point the vital feeling disappears and in its place 'the psychic value of certain conscious reactions press to the fore' and the patient, who was flooded by the unconscious, may compensate with an over-emphasis on consciousness (Jung 1928: 32). The effect of psychosis may be that the defence against a repeat of such intensity results in flatness of affect. What is missing is the 'transcendent function' (Jung 1916: 67). This is the bridge between the conscious and unconscious in which dreams, art and myth are central. In the mediating function of the image there is a link between Jung's writing and that of Cassirer.[5] I find that both contribute to an understanding of the psychotic patient's transference as it is revealed in pictures.

Lacan's writings are derived from Freudian drive theory and so are rather different in origin from Jung's, which are based on instincts and archetypes. This difference was a factor in the split between Jung and Freud. Despite this I continue to find both to be useful in developing a theoretical framework for analytical art psychotherapy (Schaverien 1994a, 1995). Similarly, both are helpful in attempting to understand why psychotic patients write on their pictures and Lacan, in particular, is significant in this regard because he was influenced by the linguist Saussure (Culler 1976).

In Lacan's writings (1955–6: 179), psychosis is characterised by an undifferentiated state which he calls 'the Real'. The real is the state where the object sought or desired no longer exists and yet there is a continual search. The 'real' is located in the gap between the object and the wish; it is not itself, the object of desire, but rather it is the desire. It is in this area that the 'lack-in being' of the psychotic state resides. This has been criticised by feminists as it relates to Freudian 'castration theory'.[6] However, Ragland-Sullivan (1992) has suggested that Lacan's 'lack' may be understood to be a 'lack-in-being', common to both sexes (Ragland-Sullivan 1992: 423). The 'dulled state' of psychosis, described by Jung, could be understood to be such a 'lack-in-being'.

The 'lack', the state of identification, is outside the Symbolic Order. It cannot be symbolised and so there is no social link. Between the Real and the Symbolic Order, is the Imaginary which is impossible in psychosis. The Imaginary is not imagination in the accepted sense but, 'the world, the register, the dimension of images, conscious or unconscious, perceived or imagined' (Sheridan 1977: ix). The Symbolic is community which is associated with 'the figure of the law' and the phallic qualities which bring difference (Lacan 1953: 67). These include boundary setting, law giving, and the entry into language. Separation from identification, and so entry into the Symbolic, is represented by 'the name of the father' (Lacan 1953: 67). 'It is in the *name of the father* that we must recognise the support of the symbolic function' (Lacan 1953: 67). If this is interpreted in gender specific terms, as Lacan's language indicates, it too causes problems for the feminist. However, if we comprehend the meaning without necessarily adhering to the limits of gender specificity, it is a helpful means of understanding the state in which the psychotic patient is trapped. We might understand it thus; unable to speak about and so conceptualise experience the psychotic patient remains in a state of identification.

The desire of the person trapped in psychosis may sometimes be understood to be an unconscious search for a return to some pre-natal state of oneness. The physical act of incest is not, as we know, impossible but what is impossible is a return to the undifferentiated psychological state of the unborn, 'Sexual incest is possible . . . but psychic incest – where two identify as one – produces the structure of psychosis' (Lacan, quoted in Ragland-Sullivan 1992: 375). It is in this unconscious desire that the 'lack' and so the madness of psychosis resides. This is an atrophied state from which there is no growth and no movement, very often 'a dulled state' (Jung 1928). An intervention which brings difference is needed and the boundary setting, law giving paternal function may be facilitated in a number of ways. These include interpretations by female or male analysts. In the context of analytical art psychotherapy the difference may be understood to be provided by the mediation of the artwork. This may bring the patient into the realm of the symbolic and so into community in the following way.

The Imaginary is linked to the mirror phase. Here the first stages of separation from identification are evoked by the perception of the body image in a mirror. This usually takes place between the ages of 6 and 18 months and brings alienation and the realisation of the self viewed by an Other (Lacan 1949). It is in this perception that fragments of sensation cohere into a whole-body image. This is the beginning of difference, the perception of self and other heralds the realisation of an inner and an outer view of self. This is the beginning of self-consciousness, and very often associated with it come separation and shame.

In considering the clinical processes involved in the treatment of psychosis we might understand the aim to be to achieve movement from a state of identification to consciousness of inner and outer – self and other. I am suggesting that the picture, as a transactional object, may facilitate this. It is not a mirror but it may have a similar effect. It is self-created but none the less in its physical presence it introduces the viewpoint of the Other. Like the mirror of the mirror-phase it enables a sense of the self as a whole to begin to cohere. Thus, in the way the psychotic patient relates to her or his pictures, we may observe the beginning of the move to the Symbolic Order and so to community (Lacan 1953: 67). The patient begins to be able to separate and experience self-in-relationship.

THE FETISH AND THE TALISMAN

I now turn to consider the pictures made by patients who have experiences classified as psychotic. The continuous existence of the picture introduces a temporal element into the therapeutic interaction which enables the trans-actions surrounding it to alter over time. A distinction can be made between two different ways their pictures are related to by patients who have psychotic experiences; these I identify respectively as the fetish and the talisman. I have written in detail about the talisman elsewhere (Schaverien 1987, 1991) but the fetish is an additional category.

The origins of the term 'fetish' are derived from sorcery. A fetish is a doll or an object made with the intention of conveying some desired effect. It may be experienced as 'live' with influence for good or ill. Since the advent of psychoanalysis the term fetish has come to be commonly associated with sexual perversion. The fetish, in psychoanalysis, is an object of attachment which is linked to the person's sexuality in some fundamental way (Freud 1928). 'A sexual fetish is either an inanimate object or a non-sexual part of a person in the absence of which the fetishist is incapable of sexual excitement' (Rycroft 1968: 50). The link with sorcery is that 'fetishists can be said to regard their fetish as being "inhabited by a spirit". Its "magical powers" give the person potency they otherwise lack' (Rycroft 1968: 50–51). In sexual perversion fetishisation is a 'dehumanising of objects out of fear' (Stoller 1975: 124). The transformation of the object into a fetish is a way of dealing with desire and it might be understood to be a substitute for relating.

In returning to the original, magical sense of the fetish I am arguing that the picture made by the patient in a psychotic state may be similarly invested; it may be attributed magical powers of influence. The image may be a substitute for thought – an enactment out of the unconscious state – and so it stands for 'the thing' in a magical sense. Furthermore, in art theory the term fetishistic is sometimes used to describe repetitive marks in a painting and this too is sometimes a feature of the patient's picture. Kris and Kurz (1979) describe incidents where works of art have been taken for 'living beings' and they also link the magical empowering of art objects with aesthetic experience. Therefore, when the art object is experienced as a fetish, it is not necessarily, nor solely linked to sexuality (although this is not excluded). The fetish, associated with a part of a person, is a sign; it stands for something outside of itself. The picture, invested as a fetish, offers an opportunity for enactment of part-object relating. The temporary attribution of 'life' in a picture may offer a means through which the non-human element may become embodied and then conscious.

The fetish is described as: 'an inanimate object which is believed to have magical powers – any object that is involved in fetishism – any object or activity to which one is excessively devoted' (*Collins Concise English Dictionary*). The talisman is described as: 'A stone or other small object, usually inscribed or carved, believed to protect the wearer from evil influences. Anything thought to have magical and protective powers' (*Collins Concise English Dictionary*). From these descriptions there is very little to distinguish them and the common factor is that they are both magically invested. However, in the way that I shall apply them, the fetish is an object which indicates a self-referential state; it is 'an object or activity to which the patient may be excessively devoted' and so the relationship to it has an obsessional quality. It may, as in sorcery, influence others, but it is not relational; it does not expect a response. The talisman, on the other hand, involves a form of relatedness. It has protective powers, and is valued and kept for this purpose. It holds a magical investment and carries it between people.

In association with the Lacanian mirror phase, the fetish might be understood to be an example of the state of identification where 'two identify as one'. The fetish art object is experienced as 'live' and associated with some form of private or unconscious rite. This is like the 'centrifugal retracing' of the transference – a perpetual retracing, a returning to the first absence – to the point at which 'the mother moved away' (Lacan 1977: 62). (See Schaverien 1995: 147–89 for a more detailed discussion of this.) Another way of understanding this is that the patient who is suffering psychosis is arrested in a self-referential loop which constantly turns in on itself. It seems to be a search for something lost – the 'ideal' state of oneness perhaps – and what is needed is some way out of this state.

Thus, for my purpose here the distinction between the fetish and talisman art object is taken to reflect ways in which clients relate to themselves and also to the therapist as a person. It reveals the state of the transference. I intend to demonstrate, through case examples, an observable change in the psychological state when relating to the picture-as-fetish is transformed to relating to picture-as-talisman. Words written in pictures may echo this and reveal the beginning of the distinction between internal and external experience. This is often absent in psychotic states.

WORDS IN PICTURES

Contrary to the traditionally held view (i.e. that psychosis produces powerfully inspired imagery), the pictures of psychotic patients are often repetitive, rudimentary and apparently devoid of 'meaningful' imagery. Furthermore, words written in the pictures seem to be a substitute for pictorial eloquence. Through my own experience, and supervision of colleagues, I have observed that the art psychotherapist may feel guilty and sometimes confesses a sense of near boredom when working with such patients. I suggest that this could be understood to be a significant countertransference response to pictures which embody the 'dulled state' of entropy or the 'lack in being' of the undifferentiated state. The absence of a sense of self, as a member of a community, means that, in the transference, the patient relates in a way which leaves the therapist outside. The therapist may be bored because, in the countertransference, she or he experiences disconnection and feels excluded from the relationship.

In considering the words written on pictures, such as those to be shown below, it is important to distinguish the written from the spoken word; both are methods of communication and so reveal movement towards an 'other'. The spoken word is usually spoken to a listener, but this is not necessarily the case with words written on pictures. These make a pattern which, as part of the overall design, may appear incoherent or as signs referring directly to some experience or fixed idea. To the therapist the pictures may seem to indicate some coded or private language. Wittgenstein (1953: 94) discusses how a private language is pointless; like the right hand giving the left hand money, the transaction is without symbolic meaning. The picture may be like this. In failing to communicate it reveals the inability to make meaningful links. As a transactional object it reveals the repetitive activity which apparently leads nowhere. The state of the patient may be self-absorbed, circular and self-referential, and so neither word nor image offers a way into community. Alice's picture exhibits an aspect of this.

Alice

Alice, a 40-year-old woman, was an in-patient suffering from a severe psychotic illness. Her psychosis had been exacerbated by the toxic effects of the medication which was prescribed to control her mania. This had led to bizarre behaviours which were acted out on the wards. Pictures she had made during the acute phase of her illness included words scrawled at different angles in pen on the paper. Sentences and pictorial imagery carried complex messages which apparently had meaning for Alice but I found them impossible to decipher. Alice had been overwhelmed by the unconscious but now she was in a stabilised state; however, she still spoke rather incoherently.

Her picture (Figure 1.1) shows apparently disconnected objects drawn in a rather rudimentary way and labelled. There are oven chips, bread, cat food, milk, flour, cakes, the local paper, marmite, chocolate biscuits, toothpaste, cola, tights, stationery and a TV. Drawn in charcoal, some of the objects are splashed with colour. The words underline the images and give them a

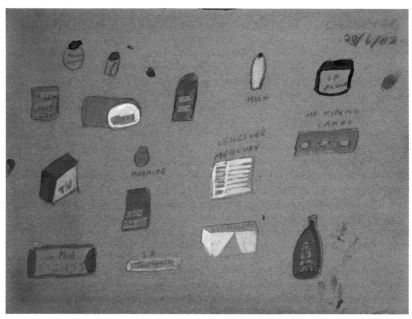

Figure 1.1 Alice's picture

meaning which would not have been communicated by the pictured objects alone. Visually the impact of the picture does not convey its meaning and so it is a 'diagrammatic' rather than an 'embodied' image.[7] I listened as Alice spoke about her picture, but very soon I became confused by the narrative which began in the object but took paths in all directions. The baffling tale meant that I was left feeling uncomprehending, unused and even useless. Yet Alice came regularly to the art room, apparently pleased to have the opportunity to draw, and she seemed to value my attention.

What is happening here? Why does Alice, heavily medicated and suffering from an apparent dislocation, write the names of these objects on her pictures? What is she is telling and to whom? And why are the objects and stories of such patients frequently repeated in apparently meaningless fashion? Does this relate to Jung's description of 'entropy' or to Lacan's 'lack in being'?

I suggest that it does; and that what is missing in Alice's experience is a sense of being linked to others in a meaningful manner. 'The "I" feels and knows itself only insofar as it takes itself as a member of a community, insofar as it sees itself grouped with others into the unity of a family, a tribe, a social organism' (Cassirer 1955b: 175). It is this, it is community, which Alice's account seems be struggling to find and yet somehow she keeps missing the point. Rochester and Martin (1979) analyse the discourse of schizophrenic speakers and attempt to ascertain the point at which the listener, often the clinician, gives up on the patient. When the patient's discourse is considered to be incomprehensible, the diagnosis of psychosis is often made but they suggest that this may be the result of a failure in the listener rather than in the speaker. When regarding the pictures made by such patients it may be similar. When we fail to understand the significance of the visual and written communication from Alice, and others like her, perhaps the incomprehension is to be regarded as a failure in the viewer rather than in the artist.

In common with other psychotic patients, Alice's rather chaotic use of spoken language made little apparent sense and yet the words in this picture do convey meaning. Through the cataloguing of everyday objects we might understand Alice to be attempting to organise her experience. It would seem that the items depicted are ones which Alice might need to buy when she is not in hospital. The picture is like a shopping list and the purpose of such a list is both to organise, and to fix in mind, something which might otherwise be forgotten. Alice's picture might be understood similarly as an attempt to organise her experience as well as to retain a link with the outside world. We might understand it thus: trapped in the undifferentiated state where 'two identify as one' she was unconsciously searching for the link, *the law of the father* maybe, which would make the 'difference'.

The meaning of words written on pictures, such as this one, is easily missed by the therapist because they do not appear to have symbolic meaning. They are signs which refer directly to things outside themselves, like maps. Yet, for Alice, suffering from the multiple effects of psychosis, they may be like an anchor in a storm. The ego, flooded with unconscious material as she had been, may be grasping at words in a desperate attempt to fix something in a moving universe; perhaps to affirm, for herself, her place in the world. Her relationship to the picture appears to be fetishistic, the engagement with the artwork circular rather than triangular, because the therapist is not included. Instead of the triangle client–picture–therapist, described in the beginning of the chapter, there is a dyadic movement which is composed of client–picture–client–picture. Apparently unable to enter into relationship with another person, Alice remains locked into a set of self-engaged actions which leaves her outside community.

I propose that it is when, in the transference, awareness of the therapist as a person begins to develop that the words written on pictures begin to reveal a symbolic attitude. This is the move, in psychoanalytic theory, from two-person relating of the pre-Oedipal stage to three-person relating of the Oedipal stage. The picture mediates and reveals this. For Alice the therapist-as-person did not really exist at this time, a connection was missing, the symbolic function was absent. Thus, although the pictures seem to signal a move out of the self-referential state and towards the Other, this is only just beginning. In Lena's pictures which follow we see the move from this to a more differentiated state.

THE TALISMAN

The empowering of a picture as a talisman involves a more complex set of processes than the fetish. In differentiating diagrammatic and the embodied image I discussed the difference between the token and the talisman and introduced the fetish (Schaverien 1991: 137–153). In this chapter I am further differentiating between the roles of the picture as a fetish and as a talisman. Both are magically invested, but whereas in the fetish the transference excludes therapist as person, the talisman embodies the transference to the therapist and carries it over time. I have classified the artist's relation to the picture into five stages (Schaverien 1991: 106, 1994a: 44). In psychosis these are activated in particular ways.

Immediately after the picture is made there may be an unconscious *identification* with the image, magical thought processes may dominate and the picture is often related to as a fetish. The psychotic patient often is arrested at this stage which might be considered similar to the 'lack-in-being' (Lacan 1953). If words are written on the picture, they are often like musings or transient written thoughts rather than intended to communicate. In the next stage, *familiarisation*, the picture begins to become familiar and the unconscious begins to become conscious. We might consider this in relation to the 'mirror phase' (Lacan 1949). The picture is 'outside' and offers a reflection of some aspect of the self. There is a dawning of consciousness and the beginning of differentiation. A conscious attitude begins to consolidate in the phase of *acknowledgement* and the artist may begin consciously to acknowledge the implications of the picture and to speak of it to the therapist. Pictures may contain words intended to communicate, so language, *the law of the father* (Lacan 1953), comes into play. The move towards the symbolic order is facilitated. In the fourth stage, *assimilation*, integration of elements which are held in the picture continues. The material which has become conscious is owned and the implications assimilated. This could be understood as a further movement into the symbolic order. It is at this stage that the picture may be valued as a talisman.

If there is a concrete object some form of *disposal* will take place. This may be a conscious and fully differentiated decision after the stage of acknowledgement. However, with the psychotic patient it may be an unconscious and premature act – an attempt to be rid of something unacceptable. The disposal of the artwork is always significant and the therapist may intervene to keep the work and value it until the client is in a psychological state to make a conscious decision about its disposal. Furthermore, the development of a conscious attitude to disposal is an important element in the resolution of the transference. The series of pictures by Lena show how these stages apply in clinical practice.

Lena

Lena's first picture was a fetish but, while we might understand Alice's picture to be evidence of the 'dulled state' of 'entropy' (Jung 1928) Lena's first picture seems to show the 'brokenness that can hardly be healed' (Jung 1928: 26). Throughout the time that I knew Lena, anti-psychotic medication was necessary and whenever it was reduced she became paranoid and even, at times, violent. I shall present five of Lena's pictures, selected from more than 300, from different phases in her treatment. They demonstrate the change in her psychological state as it was mediated through the pictures. In the conjunction of image and written word the move into community is evident.

Lena was 27 when she was admitted after a serious suicide attempt. She first came to the art room as a member of an open studio group. Her face was pale, she was evidently tense and her demeanour was such that it was clear that she did not wish to be approached. So, having given her some art materials and explained the length of the session to her, I left her alone. She immediately began to paint and was engrossed when Dr X, the doctor who was responsible for her care, came into the art room. He had previously made an arrangement, with me, to visit during this open studio session. It was only after he had gone that I noticed what Lena had done to her picture. The picture was now covered with a black wash and the image she had been painting was completely obliterated. A huge, painted, black hand covered most of the paper

Figure 1.2 The hand

which was very wet (Figure 1.2). In places, she had scrubbed the brush into the paper making holes and tearing it.

She was to explain to me some time later that, when Dr X had entered the art room, she had become terrified because, as she put it: 'He was "out of his box".' She explained that, for her, everyone belonged 'in a box' – that is, a certain place – and as long as she knew where they were she could cope. However, if someone of significance to her appeared unexpectedly, she felt overwhelmed. The fear generated by her inability to control her inner-world objects is evident in this; the act and the picture embodied the fragmentation which she experienced.

The doctor's visit is the sort of intrusion that is very often unavoidable; even so, this incident highlights the importance of holding the frame and maintaining the boundaries. In Lena's world the doctor belonged in the room on the ward where they had met and she could not cope with this unexpected change. Similarly, I belonged in the art room, and when Lena saw me on the ward she became petrified by the experience of me 'out of my box'. 'Out of one's box' is a colloquial expression for madness and eventually, after many months had passed, we were able to use this term to understand the feelings evoked by these situations. This was only possible when Lena had moved to the stage of *acknowledgement*. She could then speak to me and the feelings became conscious and so manageable – most of time. Once such a metaphor can be used, a degree of symbolisation is available and a relationship is possible.

This picture was an embodiment of the scapegoat transference in its true sense and it was also a magical fetish. It was a potent externalisation of an unconscious state which reveals the stage of *identification*. The hand with which Lena wished to cover her picture was painted on to it, obliterating the original image. This literal rendering of the gesture reveals the lack of differentiation of psychosis. There was no distinction between her body and the paint and paper; she was it and it was her.

At the time this picture was made, I suggest that neither the art therapist nor the doctor was experienced as a person but, rather, each assumed the proportions of persecutory elements of Lena's inner world. Her internal relationship was exclusively with her picture. The intrusion, experienced when the doctor entered the room, impinged on this. Lena felt exposed and the picture, which was experienced as 'live', was activated to protect her magically.

There are no written words in Figure 1.2, but, in the lower right corner are three J's, two crossed by a third. The seeds of relationship are hinted at in this. It was again much later, when she was able to speak to me, that Lena was able to tell me that this was a sign that she had previously carved into her arm with a blade. She also told me that the J's stood for Jesus and a previous social worker. My initial is also J, and it is possible that, in the transference, I already played a role. The fact that Lena had previously carved these initial into her flesh is significant; it seems that this picture mediated as a transactional object in a practical manner. Whereas, in the past, Lena would cut herself when experiencing persecutory feelings evoked by a stressful situation, on this occasion she painted. The undifferentiated state was acted out in the picture, so instead of cutting her own body, Lena painted the initials and tore the paper. It is unlikely that, at this stage, Lena was able to make a clear distinction between her body and the picture. We might understand her as being arrested in the Lacanian 'real' and she is identified totally with her picture. The lack of separation means that she was not capable of *thinking* that it was 'as if' she had cut herself, which would be a symbolic act. This was not a symbolic act but a concretisation of the impulse. However, despite the 'as if' being, at the time, unthinkable she enacted it in the picture. She did not cut herself but it was 'as if' she had done so. In this the beginning of differentiation is evident. The picture is a substitute for thinking when thinking is impossible. We saw, with Alice, that in the fetish object a connection is missing; in a different way this was the case here. The symbolic or the transcendent function was not activated. As a transactional object this picture was a fetish; it was a result of acting out of the unconscious state rather than a conscious enactment. The relationship to the picture was the dyadic client–picture–client–picture.

This is different from the talisman which holds the feeling for another person in a conscious or semi-conscious manner and it is 'an enactment in a culture' (Schaverien 1991: 152). Although it was associated with another person, the doctor, the picture did not *hold* a feeling state in relation to him.

Figure 1.3 Arrows

However, it is important not to underestimate the therapist's role during this phase. The therapist is a necessary and even significant witness but the relationship is either actively denied or merely remains unacknowledged. This could be understood to be a form of pre-Oedipal, part-object relating as a result of which the therapist may feel that there are no *people* present and so, in the countertransference, feels unused. Two more of Lena's pictures indicate the beginning of movement out of the state of identification and into the symbolic.

Figure 1.3, painted on green sugar paper, was made when Lena was beginning to trust and talk to me. There is a black outline of a transparent body with a pin figure in the centre and black arrows attacking it. Behind are green, vertical lines with arrowheads which indicate directional movement and imply that this is a puppet. Within the body are disjointed elements, painted white and overlaid with red lines – a blood supply perhaps. The whole body is encircled with a yellow line which appears to hold the parts together. The face is despairing and from the eyes fall tears. There are no words in this

picture which graphically and wordlessly embodies Lena's state. It reveals
the pain of the potential fragmentation of psychosis in a way which no words
could convey. There are times when words can add nothing to an image: the
picture says it all – it is its own vivid and powerful interpretation.

When presented with an image such as this the therapist can say little that
will not diminish its power; all the therapist can do is acknowledge it.
However, I was very moved by this picture and so I think it indicates the
beginning of a relationship. Lena was able to communicate her state to me
through the vehicle of the picture. Thus, although the concrete nature of the
artwork is highly significant, even in the early stages of work with psychotic
patients, the imagery is equally important. This picture is an embodied image
and a scapegoat; it symbolises a state not yet consciously known. The process
of *familiarisation* begins when it 'feeds back'. Like the 'mirror stage' (Lacan
1949), here is the perception of herself as a boundaried or embodied being.
Lena realised that it both confirmed her feeling and conveyed it to me because
I took the picture very seriously. Lena then began to value her pictures as
both an expression of her state and a way of communicating. To speak directly
to anyone was to lose herself, but the picture made this possible; it mediated,
holding the space in-between us. As we spoke Lena's gaze was firmly fixed on
the picture and most of the time I, too, looked at the picture rather than at
her, and in this way we began to develop a way of relating through the
pictures. They were transactional objects.

Painted in blue and black on light brown sugar paper, the words written on
Figure 1.4 are an integral part of it. The figure shows a face crossed with
chains and with tears flowing from the eyes. A large circle indicates a huge
open mouth, in which the word 'NO !' is painted in large letters and
underneath, in smaller lettering, is the word 'YES?' The scale of the 'YES?',
with its question mark, seems to undermine the bold 'NO!'. The ambivalence
conveyed by the words is also evident in the face, which appears to be
shouting or crying out, but yet is constrained by chains and padlocks. Viewed
in conjunction with the previous picture we might surmise that, boldened by
its reception, Lena gains confidence to make a more definite image of her
feeling state. This is emphasised by the pattern of the assertive words which
communicate directly with the viewer. This, too, is an embodied image; there
is nothing to add. To speak about such an image directly or to attempt to
analyse it at this stage would rob it of its potency. It is important when
working with such pictures to remember Wittgenstein's well-known aphor-
ism: 'What we cannot speak about we must pass over in silence' (Wittgenstein 1922: 74). Lena was now beginning to trust me a little and so the words
communicate her feeling state. She wanted to let me know how it was for her
and she used the picture as a vehicle. This became a pattern in our
relationship; she wrote words on many of her subsequent pictures and, later
when I asked her 'Why words?', she replied that the image was not enough.
This is often the reason given for writing words in pictures and indicates the

Figure 1.4 NO! Yes?

need for relationship. Lena was beginning to separate from the state of unconscious *identification*, 'the lack in being' and to move to the more conscious stage of *acknowledgement* which, in turn, we could understand as leading to the 'symbolic order'. The relationship to the picture was beginning to become triadic, client–picture–therapist.

When the therapist exists as a person in the mind of the patient, the picture may be related to a talisman and it may even symbolise the relationship. A year after Lena's admission, Dr X had left and had been replaced by Dr Y. In psychiatry it is common practice for junior doctors to move departments on six-monthly rotation. When this change took place I had encouraged Lena to make a picture to express her feelings of loss. In this way I affirmed the significance of the relationship and gave her permission to own her feelings. As with Dr X, it was the task of Dr Y to see all the people on the ward at regular intervals to monitor their progress and so he, too, became important for her. Lena was still unable to discuss her feelings directly and so Dr Y and

Figure 1.5 Freeze!

I developed a way of working with her; she was able admit her feelings for Dr Y to me and her feelings for me to him. A split transference inevitably developed and, although this is usually considered a disadvantage, it worked very well. This worked because the analytic process was adapted to the setting and neither of us attempted to interpret the transference; instead it was used as a symbolic holding. We made it clear to her that we communicated with each other, and so she was aware that the 'parents were together'. This enabled her to feel safely held.

Figure 1.5[8] Dr Y is depicted seated at a desk and a wall-chart shows his record of interviews with patients; he ticks off their names after seeing them. Lena found this mechanical and evidence that she meant nothing to him. He is behind a thick brick wall, through which a phallic double line penetrates to a seated stick figure. On it is written 'ANSWERS ONLY'. She was terrified of him, and of her feelings about him, and has written FREEZE! and, under the chair in which the figure representing herself sits, USELESS ME! At the top left of the picture is a figure which represents me with my name above it: JOY. The brick wall seems to separate me from the doctor but between her and me there is a table on which a piece of paper – a picture – is placed, and instead of a brick wall there is a cracked, glass one. A phallic object penetrates in her direction from this one too, but on it is written MORE TWO WAY, and the words seem to bend towards her. This is perhaps related to gender; Dr Y was a man and this may have added to her fear of him. The line between herself and me is less directly penetrating and so may indicate that, as a woman, I was less feared. It seems that this reveals the Oedipal dimension and perhaps the difference associated with the male doctor was an important factor in enabling her to differentiate from the mother/therapist.

The picture as a transactional object is clearly illustrated here. Between the figure, which represents Lena, and Dr Y is a brick wall. If it was not there there would be nothing to keep them separate. On the other hand, between herself and the art psychotherapist there is a table with a picture on it. It is the picture which maintains a distance and a space between us. It seems to follow that she is able to relate to me because we are also kept separate by the picture. If we refer back to Lacan's location of psychosis in a form of psychic incest, where 'two identify as one', we may understand that the fear of relationship is the fear of regression to this state. The art object, in the therapeutic space, holds the area in-between and permits a symbolic relationship to emerge. The symbolic function is brought about, in part, through the safety provided by the art object.

It is notable that this picture, in contrast to Figures 1.2, 1.3 and 1.4, is drawn in charcoal and crayon. The paintings were embodied; the pictures themselves brought about a change in state. They were also pictures to which spoken words could not be added without diminishing the image. This drawing is different, it is diagrammatic, it describes relationship and seems to invite comment. In this sense it indicates a change in Lena's psychological state. This shows how both diagrammatic and embodied images play a role in the treatment of the same person. With the less disturbed patient, who may be over controlled, diagrammatic pictures may lead to the ability to make embodied images. For such people it may be a positive development when the pictures become embodied (Schaverien 1987, 1991); however, with the psychotic patient, such as Lena, it is a positive development and indication of relationship when she makes a diagrammatic image.

Lena chose to display this picture on the wall on the ward for all the patients and staff to see. Thus the words written on this picture are intended to communicate. The transference is clearly exhibited and *acknowledged*. Later, further acknowledgement of relationship was possible when Dr Y moved on after six months. Lena spontaneously made a picture on which she wrote 'Thank you Dr Y'. She placed this too, on the ward in a prominent position, where he and everyone else would be able to see it. In this way she was able to fully *acknowledge* the loss associated with his leaving. The picture was a talisman; it was consciously valued, and embodied the significance of the therapeutic relationship.

The last two pictures that I shall show here were made in the same session many months later. In Figure 1.6 a figure in the sky sits, surrounded by stars, on a moon. The whole is painted in white on bright blue paper and contains the words 'FANTASY WORLD'. Figure 1.7 is painted in black on orange paper and shows a figure sitting at the bottom of a mountain-like structure in a pool of tears. The tears come from two eyes which look down from the sky, in which is written 'REAL WORLD'. The contrast between the two pictures is

Figure 1.6 Fantasy world

Figure 1.7 Real world

notable; the figure in the clouds seems to be an idealisation while the other seems to be facing a sad reality.

I propose that these two pictures mark separation and differentiation as well as the ability to symbolise. In painting these on different pieces of paper Lena is distinguishing her 'fantasy' world from the 'real' world and differentiating between inner and outer. Figure 1.7 could also be understood to be evidence of the mourning stage of the depressive position (Klein 1935). This is when the reality, which has so long been denied through psychotic defences, modifies and the underlying sense of loss becomes conscious. If we compare these pictures with Figure 1.2, her first picture made two and half years earlier, there is an evident change in her state. Lena now feels herself to be a member of community. The undifferentiated state of psychosis has given way and this is reflected in the pictures and her ability to speak about herself and to communicate. The first picture was undifferentiated and a magical fetish while these two pictures are talismans; they hold the relationship of self to other.

The disposal of Lena's images is of note. During the process of the work I kept her pictures in the art room, symbolically placing a value on them. When the hospital closed Lena was offered the opportunity of keeping all her pictures or of selecting a few. She did not wish to keep any of them; it seems that her identification with the pictures ended with the therapy. With some people pictures continue as talismans, valued and empowered long after termination (see Schaverien 1991 and 1995 for examples of this). It was not so with Lena; she had truly finished with them and perhaps this demonstrates a healthy resolution of the transference. Some years later I contacted her to ask permission to write about her pictures and she was pleased to tell me that she had recently married. Lena continues to need medication to stabilise her condition and maintains out-patient contact with the consultant who was responsible for her treatment. However, she can now live as a member of the community in the outside world rather than in the protected world of the hospital.

CONCLUSION

In this chapter the intention has been to extend the clinical application of the scapegoat transference and develop an understanding of the transactional role of pictures in the therapeutic relationship with psychotic patients. I have argued that the patient may relate to the pictures as fetish objects or as talismans, and this reflects the transference. In the interactions surrounding the pictures, as well as in the imagery they embody, they offer an opportunity for complex investments. As concrete objects within the therapeutic setting they mediate in the actual space in-between client and therapist. With the psychotic client the mediating function of the art object is especially significant. Relating directly to another human being may be experienced as far too threatening to a fragile personality, but to relate through a mediating object may be possible.

The words written on pictures also reflect the transference. They could be understood as controlling the irrational expressive function. Words written on pictures may be employed as a decoy; they may mystify, mislead or confuse or set a false trail in order to preserve the self. The picture offers the advantage that, whatever the feelings or thoughts attributed to it, they may be safely contained 'out there', separate from the artist. The words and images exist in space and time and remain within the picture until the artist is ready to own the rejected element. Pictures which contain words in addition to images might be understood to exhibit the perpetual interplay between the need to change and the need to remain the same. Thus the picture mediates in the therapeutic relationship, creating a space where none at first exists. It plays a significant part in bringing the unconscious to consciousness and in facilitating relationship. The picture is a multi-faceted transactional object.

NOTES

1 For a distinction between the transactional object, 'the transitional object' (Winnicott 1971) and 'the transformational object' (Bollas 1987), see Schaverien (1994b, 1995).
2 See Duane (1991: 55–8) and Lena (1991: 130–6). Other pictures by Lena are shown in this chapter.
3 The unit opened in 1962 and was closed in the early 1980s. This indicates something of its philosophy and its place in the politics of the NHS in Britain as outlined in other chapters in this book.
4 It is interesting to note that Jung and Lacan both began their careers by working with psychotic patients – as do many art therapists.
5 Some of the links between Jung and Cassirer have been pointed out by Avens (1980).
6 This presents a problem for feminist theorists which cannot be ignored in this context. In Freudian/Lacanian theory, the lack is linked to the female state where women are viewed as castrated men because they do not have the visible sex organ. When this is transposed to culture, women could be considered to be outside the symbolic order; a further implication of this might be that all women are psychotic. Much feminist psychological theory has centred around this debate, for which I do not have space here. (For a more detailed discussion of these issues, see Schaverien 1995.)
7 For a detailed discussion of the distinction between diagrammatic and embodied images, see Schaverien (1987, 1991)
8 This picture is discussed in an earlier paper (Schaverien 1982).

REFERENCES

Avens, R. (1980) *Imagination is Reality*, Dallas: Spring Publications.
Bollas, C. (1987) 'The transformational object', in *The Shadow of the Object*, London: Free Associations.
Cassirer, E. (1955a) *The Philosophy of Symbolic Forms*, Vol. 1: *Language*, Yale University Press.

—— (1955b) *The Philosophy of Symbolic Forms*, Vol. 2: *Mythical Thought*, Yale University Press.

—— (1957) *The Philosophy of Symbolic Forms*, Vol. 3: *The Phenomenology of Knowledge*, Yale University Press.

Culler, J. (1976) *Saussure*, London: Fontana Modern Masters

Field, N. (1991) 'Projective identification: mechanism or mystery', *Journal of Analytical Psychology* 36(1): 93–109.

Freud, S. (1928) 'Fetishism', in *Standard Edition* Vol. xxi, London: Hogarth Press (1968 edition)

Grotstein, J. (1985) *Splitting and Projective Identification*, New Jersey: Aronson.

Hinshelwood, R. (1989) *A Dictionary of Kleinian Thought*, London: Free Associations Books (1994 edition).

Jung, C.G. (1916) 'The transcendent function', in *Collected Works*, Vol. 8, London: Routledge & Kegan Paul (1960).

—— (1928) 'On psychic energy', in *Collected Works*, Vol. 8, London: Routledge & Kegan Paul (1960).

—— (1963a) *Mysterium Coniunctionis*, in *Collected Works*, Vol. 14, Princeton: Bollingen.

—— (1963b) *Memories, Dreams and Reflections*, London: Fontana.

Klein, M (1935) 'A contribution to the psychogenesis of manic-depressive states', in *Love Guilt and Reparation*, London: Hogarth (1985).

—— (1946) 'Notes on some schizoid mechanisms', in *Envy and Gratitude and Other Works*, London: Hogarth Press (1975).

Killick, K. (1993) 'Working with psychotic processes in art therapy', *Psychoanalytic Psychotherapy* 7(1): 25–38.

Kris, E and Kurz, O. (1979) *Legend, Myth and Magic in the Image of the Artist*, New Haven: Yale University Press (first published 1934)

Lacan, J. (1949) 'The mirror stage as formative of the function of the I as revealed in psychoanalytic experience', in *Ecrits: A Selection*, London: Tavistock/Routledge (1977).

—— (1953) 'The function and field of speech and language in psychoanalysis', in *Ecrits: A Selection*, London: Tavistock/Routledge.

—— (1955–6) 'On a question preliminary to any possible treatment of psychosis', in *Ecrits: A Selection*, London: Tavistock/Routledge.

—— (1977) *Four Fundamental Concepts of Psycho-analysis*, London: Penguin.

Laplanche, J. and Pontalis, J.-B. (1988) *The Language of Psychoanalysis*, London: Karnac and the Institute of Psychoanalysis.

Ogden, T.H. (1982) *Projective Identification and Psychotherapeutic Technique*, London: Maresfield.

Ragland-Sullivan, E. (1992) 'The Real' entry in E. Wright (ed.) *Feminism and Psychoanalysis*, Oxford: Blackwell.

Reed,H. (1996) 'Close encounters in the liminal zone: experiments in imaginal communication'. Part 1, *Journal of Analytical Psychology* 41(1).

Rochester, S. and Martin, J.R. (1979) *Crazy Talk*, New York and London: Plenum Press.

Rosenfeld, H. (1965) *Psychotic States*, New York: International Universities Press.

Rycroft, C. (1968) *A Critical Dictionary of Psychoanalysis*, London: Penguin.

Samuels, A. (1989) 'Countertransference and the Mundus Imaginalis', in *The Plural Psyche*, London: Routledge.

Schaverien, J. (1982) 'Transference as an aspect of art therapy', London: *Inscape*.

—— (1984) 'Word and image in art psychotherapy', unpublished Master's thesis, University of Central England. (Formerly Birmingham Polytechnic.)

—— (1987)'The scapegoat and the talisman: transference in art therapy', in T. Dalley *et al.* (eds) *Images of Art Therapy*, London and New York: Tavistock/Routledge.

—— (1989) 'Transference and the picture: art therapy in the treatment of anorexia', London: *Inscape* (Spring).

—— (1991) *The Revealing Image: Analytical Art Psychotherapy in Theory and Practice*, London and New York: Routledge (1992 edition).

—— (1994a) 'Analytical art psychotherapy: further reflections on theory and practice', London: *Inscape* 2.

—— (1994b) 'The transactional object: art psychotherapy in the treatment of anorexia', *British Journal of Psychotherapy* 11(1): 46–61.

—— (1995) *Desire and the Female Therapist: Engendered Gazes in Psychotherapy and Art Therapy*, London and NewYork: Routledge.

Schwartz-Salant, N. (1989) 'Archetypal foundations of projective identification', in *The Borderline Personality: Vision and Healing*, Wilmette, Illinois: Chiron.

Sheridan, A. (1977) 'Translator's note', in *Ecrits: A Selection*, London: Routledge.

Stoller, R. (1975) *Sex and Gender*, Vol. 11: *The Transsexual Experiment*, London: Hogarth Press

Winnicott, D.W. (1971) *Playing and Reality*, London: Penguin.

Wittgenstein, L. (1922) *Tractatus Logico-Philosophicus*, London: Routledge & Kegan Paul (1981 edition).

—— (1953) *Philosophical Investigations*, Oxford: Blackwell (1981 edition).

Chapter 2

Unintegration and containment in acute psychosis

Katherine Killick

INTRODUCTION

This chapter draws on material from six years of psychotherapeutic work which I undertook with a schizophrenic patient in the environment of an art therapy department in a large psychiatric hospital. I shall discuss the material with particular reference to the work of Bick, Bion and Meltzer. I propose that the analytical art therapy setting came to constitute a containing object for the patient's unintegrated state of mind. This enabled a shift from intrusive identification to projective identification to take place in his use of the therapist and the setting. The substances and objects in the setting helped to absorb the violence of intrusive identifications which defended against the catastrophic anxieties overwhelming his capacity to think when he was acutely psychotic. Over time images emerged which he used to communicate with me, and the evolution of one particular image is traced. I propose that this work was helpful to the patient, and I question whether work of this kind is possible in current psychiatric settings.

My interest in these issues grew through working as an art therapist with patients in acute psychotic states who were in-patients in a large NHS psychiatric hospital. I have described the process of developing this interest elsewhere (Killick and Greenwood 1995). Before leaving full-time work in the hospital, I developed an art therapy service which specialised in the treatment of psychotic and borderline psychopathology, and this setting is also described in detail elsewhere (Case and Dalley 1992). My experiences in this setting have informed my subsequent work with patients who have a history of psychosis in the NHS out-patient service in which I worked until 1994 and in my private practice. They continue to inform my analytic work with psychotic areas in non-psychotic individuals in private practice. The material presented here comes from six years' work with one young man, whom I met first when he was acutely psychotic. I shall discuss this state of mind in terms of a failure of containment at the level of 'unintegration', as proposed by Bick (1968), with particular reference to the patient's use of 'intrusive identification', as defined by Meltzer *et al.* (1986), as a defence against catastrophic anxiety. I shall outline some aspects of my approach to this in the art psychotherapy setting, and trace the patient's developing capacity to use myself and concrete aspects of the setting to contain his projected material. I shall end by questioning the viability of this kind of work in current psychiatric settings and in private practice.

UNINTEGRATION AND CONTAINMENT

I shall begin with a discussion of theoretical issues relevant to the material. Bick (1968) has presented ideas relating to very early infant experience which I find convincing in thinking about the nature of the issues being negotiated between therapist and patient in these states of mind. She writes about an 'unintegrated' state in which 'the parts of the personality are felt to have no binding force amongst themselves and must therefore be held together in a way that is experienced by them passively, by the skin functioning as a boundary'. This depends initially on the introjection of an external object which is 'experienced as capable of fulfilling this function', and later, on identification with the containing function of the object. She suggests that the 'containing object is experienced concretely as a skin' and describes a 'frantic search' for such an object, such as the nipple in the mouth, in infantile unintegrated states. Until the containing object is introjected 'the concept of a space within the self cannot arise' and the infant, or patient in this state of mind, is vulnerable to catastrophic anxiety. This is the quality of anxiety which the therapist working with acutely psychotic patients encounters.

In the absence of 'a space within the self', Bick writes, '. . . the function of projective identification will necessarily continue unabated and all the confusions of identity attending it will be manifest'. I shall now discuss this statement with reference to some more recent thinking about the nature of what Bick is referring to here. Meltzer *et al.* (1986) distinguished between two forms of projective identification: 'projective identification' which is characterised by a need to communicate and a wish to be contained, to enter 'the chamber of maiden thought'; and 'intrusive identification' characterised by invasion for the purposes of evacuation and control. The latter is employed as a mechanism of defence against extreme anxiety. Bion's work offers a way of thinking about the process of containment whereby the internal space referred to by Bick becomes established (Bion 1962). I am assuming here that the reader is familiar with Bion's concept of 'containment', in which 'beta elements' are rendered bearable and meaningful by 'alpha function'. The capacity to use projective identification as distinct from intrusive identification depends, at least in part, on the degree to which containment has been experienced.

Colman (1995), working with Winnicott's (1965) ideas of 'gesture' and 'recognition' in relation to the ideas I have discussed, offers a way of thinking about the meaning of containment at the unintegrated level. He writes, 'projective identification is not a possibility at first, since there is no secure sense of the inside to be projected out of'. He describes how, in this state, beta elements are simply evacuated and the mother, responding to the infant, confers meaning on the raw experience, the 'gesture', by 'recognising' it as a 'potential communication'. He goes on to propose: 'We need to think of this early form of communication not as projective identification from ego to containing object, but as an interactional field.'

Intrusive identification develops when 'potential communications' are not contained by the mother's recognition of the infant's gesture. Colman (personal communication) writes, 'when gestures (which I equate with beta elements) are not contained by being given meaning within the interactional field – the emotional experience within them becomes intolerable and has to be evacuated'. He then makes an important distinction between the mother in relation to the infant and the therapist in relation to the psychotic patient. 'The mother is predominantly responding to gestures whereas the therapist is predominantly having to manage intrusive identifications . . .' due to the patient's 'legacy of failed communications'. The patient whose material I shall present was initially attempting to get rid of an experience that *could* be communicated, and which, as his anxieties lessened, became more communicable. The infant's gesture, on the other hand, is *not yet* a communication.

Bion (1967a: 108) describes an internal object, which in its origin was 'an external breast that refused to introject, harbour and so modify the baneful force of emotion' which is destructive of all links, and linking functions, from projective identification (as defined earlier), to 'the most sophisticated forms of verbal communication and the arts'. In particular, the linking function of emotion is hated and attacked. This offers a helpful way of thinking about the state of mind which is contingent on a failure of containment at the level of unintegration. It seems to me that the nature of this internal object is modified through the process of therapy with a patient in an acute psychotic state by containment of the kind proposed earlier. In the case material which follows, the therapist's interventions aimed to establish the possibility of a container which could be used for projective identification, by recognising the potential communicative meaning of the patient's intrusive identifications. The concreteness of materials, objects and transactions within the analytical art therapy setting helped to establish an 'interactional field' in which the patient's intrusive identifications could constitute 'gestures' and be recognised as potential communications.

Balint and Little have both written about the value of regression, in analysis, to an undifferentiated state, called 'basic unity' by Little (1981) and 'the harmonious interpenetrating mix-up' by Balint (1968). Both suggest that regression can enable the patient to assimilate the new experience necessary to work through the primitive anxieties and defences which I have described. This requires that the analyst make a particular kind of object relationship available to the patient, which corresponds to the interactional field described by Colman (1995). Balint (1968) describes this as an 'environment–patient relationship' which he links to Winnicott's (1965) 'facilitating environment'. He writes,

> the only thing that the analyst can do is to accept the role of the primary substance, which is there, which cannot be destroyed, which *eo ipso* is there to carry the patient, which feels the patient's importance and weight but still carries him, which is unconcerned about keeping up proper boundaries between the patient and itself, etc., but which is not an object in the true sense, is not concerned with its independent existence.

The patient whose material I shall present was gradually able to use the analytical art therapy setting as an object of this kind, and I think that this experience was significant in enabling a 'skin container' (Bick 1968) to form.

THE SETTING

The art therapy department in which my earlier work took place no longer exists in the form which I shall now describe, having changed in accordance with the move to the current pattern of psychiatric service provision known as 'care in the community'. It was adjacent to the acute in-patient facilities of a large psychiatric hospital, which made it possible for patients in acute psychotic states to attend art therapy consistently, often for two two-hour sessions per day, five days per week. They could continue their involvement after discharge. The department was a converted ward, with a large main room, kitchen and toilet facilities, store rooms, an administrative office and two individual therapy rooms. Each patient would spend the majority of his time engaged in self-directed activities in the main room of the department, and would meet his therapist individually for one hour a week in one of the individual therapy rooms. He would be given a space, with large wooden table and chair, within the main room, which could be organised as he wished. The main room would often have up to twelve patients using it, with two or three therapists, and sometimes a student or volunteer helper, in attendance. It included music-playing equipment, books and an area where patients could sit together. Patients were able to use the milieu in whatever way they wished, provided essential boundaries regarding the survival and maintenance of the setting, and of the objects and people within it, were maintained. Regular community meetings contributed to establishing the nature and function of these boundaries.

The patient's table, and the activities in which he engaged while in that space, formed a potential space for thinking through the activities of painting, drawing and modelling. This was maintained as a private space for the patient, and therapists would disengage from invitations to get involved in what happened there. Each patient was given a folder in which two-dimensional art objects could be kept, and a notebook in which thoughts could be written or drawn between individual sessions. If models were made, a box to hold them was provided. The folder formed part of the weekly session with the therapist, regardless of whether it held objects or not. The patient could decide what, if anything, to place in the folder, and might place objects outside it. They could be placed out of the therapist's sight, on walls, window ledges and other spaces.

Every patient's internal compromises emerged in relation to the way this space was used. A patient with a compliant 'false self' organisation might attempt to seduce the therapist into prescribing the activities in which he was to engage at the table. One patient insisted for months that he was failing to meet the expectations of the therapist because he was not producing artwork. Gradually the distinction between the demands of his internal world and the absence of demand in the external world became sufficiently apparent to enable him to draw his first picture. A patient with a more paranoid organisation might tend to avoid using the table at all in the 'knowledge' that to do so would constitute getting into a trap of one kind or another. One patient who 'knew' that his artwork would be taken away and shown to an organisation which was persecuting him, eventually made an object which, he felt, the therapist would be unable to resist picking up, and he laid a trap that would enable him to catch her in the act. This would prove to the therapist that he 'knew what she was really up to'. Again, the fact that the expected invasion did not happen helped to establish the distinction between the internal persecution and the external state of affairs. A patient with an ambivalent organisation might invite the therapist to look at his work outside session time, then say that his work was 'rubbish' and try to throw it away.

When patients were acutely psychotic, I would refrain from ways of relating to the artwork which addressed content and meaning. It seemed to me that, if the patient made art in this state, the object made could not be related to as a communication. The making of the art was an aspect of the 'attacks on linking' described by Bion (1967a) and therefore attempts on the part of the therapist to relate to the art as if it had communicative meaning would therefore fail to recognise its actual defensive meaning. I would suggest that the art is used by the patient experiencing catastrophic anxiety as a means of intrusive identification, i.e. as a way of forcibly evacuating unbearable anxieties into the art object, and that accordingly it holds evacuated beta elements. The patient's relation to the artwork needs to be handled in a way which takes account of his extreme anxiety – that what has been projected out will be forced back into him. This is conveyed by the way in which the therapist handles the material. As Balint (1968), Little (1981) and other analysts have noted, the therapist's way of being with the regressed patient holds more significance than what is said. Tone of voice, gesture, and the emotional atmosphere conveyed by the therapist through these actions, are often being attended to with great sensitivity.

In these states, I think the concreteness of the substances and objects available to and made by the patient in the art psychotherapy setting enables the violence of the intrusive identifications to be absorbed without damage to the patient or the therapist. Via the art objects, an intrusive identification can once again become a potential communication. Schaverien (1991) has described this sequence in her discussion of the 'scapegoat transference'. As Colman (personal communication) points out, 'it is one which will include not only the original emotional experience which was not contained but also the trauma of nonrecognition'. The art objects can hold projected material until the patient is ready to bring it into relation with the therapist's mind. I have discussed this elsewhere (Killick 1993). The patient will indicate if and when he is ready to bring back that which has been projected out. Bion (1967b) writes of the heroic effort which is involved in this: 'If he wishes to bring back any of these objects in an attempt at restitution of the ego . . . he has to bring them back by projective identification in reverse and by the route by which they were expelled.' This is experienced as 'an assault', and only the patient can decide whether, if ever, he is able to undertake this.

BOUNDARIES

Negotiation of rules and boundaries in the setting over time is often the first way in which distinctions between inner and outer realities are established between therapist and patient. When working with psychotic patients, I would introduce a boundary preserving the survival of the patient's artwork within the setting. Whereas tearing up a painting or smashing a model might constitute an important step in the evolution of an internal image, and needs to be tolerated, I think the removal of the object from the setting altogether has a different meaning. When the necessity for intrusive identification predominated in the patient's way of being, attempts to remove art objects from the setting could be seen as the patient's attempt concretely to evacuate from the mind the material held in the object. I would ask patients not to remove their artwork, in order to set limits to this destructiveness, which would inevitably increase their anxiety.

I developed a practice of offering a separate folder, or box, to hold work of this kind, which could be placed anywhere in the setting – under the rubbish bin, for example, 'as if' in the bin. One patient titled this folder 'Things I would throw away if she let me'. Once this limit was set with a patient, the violence of the evacuative act would often erupt into the setting at this point in the form of tearing up or smashing the work. The apparent destruction of the first object might then create a new object, often a broken or torn one – a potential link to the patient's fragile sense of self which might in time be communicated to the therapist. The individual session with the therapist and the folder, which might or might not hold images, constituted a space within which the patient could experience varying degrees of relatedness with the therapist. The images might not be shown at all during the session. They might be used as things whose disposal was discussed. One young woman in a manic state spent her sessions deciding how the vast quantities of work which she produced could be organised into different groupings, which were then placed in folders, each of which was given a title which resonated with the contents. In time this formed the foundations of a metaphorical language for her feeling states.

Over time, repetition of experiences which enable internal and external realities to be felt as different seems in itself to lessen catastrophic anxiety. It is a profoundly moving experience for the therapist when the patient begins to use the session to communicate. After months of ritualised use of the sessions which maintained the status of his pictures as lifeless things, a man sighed, wearily, 'I think I've had enough of this speech therapy. Can we talk today?' He looked me in the eyes and I felt that he was in the room with me. At a later stage the art object might assist the patient in the effort to convey experience to the therapist. When the patient is ready, pieces of artwork which have remained hidden for months, even years, may all of a sudden be brought into the session and spoken about. The art may begin to hold the potential for communication. Schaverien (1994) writes of similar experiences in her work with anorexic patients. This shift can happen within the space of a session, but may take years to become established. In order to keep my own mind open to the possibility that a patient might at any time be ready to make this leap, I found that I need actively to remind myself, often with the help of supervision, that part of the patient welcomes my attempt to make contact. In my experience of both working in these areas and working with students and supervisees, the therapist's faith in the process can be subtly eroded by countertransference feelings of despair and futility.

CLINICAL MATERIAL

I shall now share some material from long-term individual work with a patient within the setting I have described. Mr X, a young man in his early twenties, diagnosed schizophrenic, was referred to full time attendance on the day of his first admission to hospital. I worked with him for approximately six years, initially as an in-patient on his first admission to hospital, which lasted about eighteen months, and, after discharge, as an out-patient. Although I was eventually able to better understand what his experience was on the day I first met Mr X, this was not possible at the beginning. He appeared as a dishevelled presence, flitting about the room, making no eye contact, and occasionally muttering words that were difficult to hear and difficult to understand, such as 'voodoo', 'balancing angle' and 'out of focus'. He seemed to me to be in a state which another patient had once described as 'a body without skin', in which any contact pained him. I understood more of his experience at this time after the work described later had taken place, and I shall now summarise this using his own words as far as possible:

> He was dead, and had been ever since he was made aware of the existence of the 'out of focus', an invisible civilisation which is permanent and composed of gods and spirits. This civilisation is more reliable than the 'mortal world' in which his body exists, but uses this world to manifest itself. He was a 'hostage' of the out-of-focus, who were controlling his thoughts and demanding that he perform the acts they dictated in the mortal world. If he failed to be a 'good model' and perform these acts perfectly, he would be sadistically punished, but if he succeeded he would have glory in the mortal world and immortality in the other. In order for this to be possible his 'cybernetics' had to be perfectly 'tuned' with the 'focus' that would enable him to 'balance' the demands of the two worlds. The out-of-focus had, however, played a cruel trick on him by designing his body in such a way that his functioning interfered with his 'cybernetics'. He was troubled by 'aliens in the system', 'voodoo', 'hallucinogen' and other experiences which comprised the workings of his embodied self. His mortal substance had interfered with his immortal focus to such an extent that he lost his 'balancing angle' and became so 'poverty stricken' that he resorted to behaving in such a way as to warrant hospital admission. He was seeking a means of restoring his cybernetics through the acquisition of a 'balancing angle' which would enable him to 'advance focus'.

I now understand that Mr X's early involvement in art psychotherapy was driven by the concrete quest for this 'angle', which overwhelmed all boundaries within the setting for some time. This had the quality of 'frantic search' for the containing object, described by Bick. He broke into the room out of hours, took over several tables, stole my bicycle, and so on. His relationship to the setting and the art process was absolutely concrete. He spoke entirely in the language which I have explained, demanding that I provide him with the 'balancing angle', and dismissing me as 'useless' when I failed instantly to comprehend and comply. His state of unintegration was apparent in his use of several tables, appropriated from other patients, at each of which he made artwork in a different style. His paintings, and what he said, seemed rich in symbolic meaning to me, but they were not experienced as such by him. He brought various objects into the setting and ceaselessly worked to create designs for 'models' which, I came to understand, constituted blueprints for future human beings in his mind. He was enraged by my apparent inability to grasp the importance of his mission, and to make the setting available to him 24 hours a day.

Mr X initially produced enormous numbers of drawings of a head, which he called 'Sleeping Muse'. He was driven to create a perfect image which would in some way help him to secure his 'balancing angle', but none of his drawings reached the required degree of perfection. He sought to throw away his work. I think that the discrepancy made him feel he was continually failing and this filled him with dread. Throwing the drawings away seemed to be an attempt to evacuate the pain of this experience. In accordance with the ideas and practice presented earlier, I negotiated with him to keep his drawings, simply telling him that this is the way things are done in this place because we think everything he does has meaning and value, that he may think differently about his work in time, and that when he leaves he can decide what he wants to happen to it. I suggested that he use a folder for the things he wanted to throw away. He would walk away as soon as I began to speak to him, telling me I was 'hallucinogenic' or putting 'voodoo' into his system. I imagine that he was warding off his dread that I was trying to push projected material back into him.

I think that Mr X was trying to evacuate the 'imperfect model' – the 'voodoo' beta elements constituting a link to his own 'imperfect' embodied sense of self – by destroying his work. It may be significant that the image was one of a head – the head containing as it does the wherewithal for symbolic thought. After a few weeks he told me that I could be of use to him if I would have a sexual relationship with him or if I paid him money to do his artwork. I commented that he was trying to find some kind of connection with me. I think that he was at this point experiencing me as a breast with something to offer which could be of some use, as well as a source of 'hallucinogen'. He seemed, as usual, angered by my response but afterwards was able to listen to me speaking without walking away, as had been the case before. He then told me with tremendous aggressive force that the artwork was not his, that it did not belong to him and that he had not made it. The out of focus had prescribed it and now that it had failed they demand that it be thrown away. Otherwise, it would be a blueprint for an imperfect human being. I told him that I was not prepared to be dictated to by the out of focus without understanding why. I hoped that he might help me understand more about this world but that we were at that moment in the world of the art therapy room and accordingly had to follow its rules.

At this stage his defensive organisation seemed 'hell bent' on annihilating any and every such rule or boundary which he encountered. He was menaced by the experience of limits. It was as if he was the setting and the rules were my attempt to annihilate him. At times I experienced his rages as threatening me with annihilation. I struggled with feeling that I was destroying the connectedness between us as I tried to present him with aspects of the reality of the setting in as digestible a form as possible. Any separation experience which represented breakage, or loss, of the connectedness between us felt like a physical attack. It was an exhausting time – as is any experience of bearing this degree of intrusive identification in the countertransference. Following the interchange around the 'Sleeping Muse' drawings, Mr X took a quantity of plasticine and pounded it with his fists. The substance, plasticine, absorbed an explosive discharge of primitive affect, which persisted for around 15 minutes. Then the quality of his relating changed as he began to form a head. He kept the head close to him on his table for a further two sessions, during which he repeatedly destroyed and recreated the form of a head in relation to similar heated exchanges between us.

One day, after many bruising encounters he came to me and asked me if I knew where his lost trilby hat was. For the first time I felt him to be vulnerable, frail, appealing. There was a sense of an 'I' present, which could experience loss. He had lost an object which was linked to his head, and which he thought I might be able to find. Then he told me, in a bewildered way, 'I keep losing things' and for the first time there was a moment of contact between us as his distress was experienced. I was able to identify with his experiencing of the pain of loss which I think referred to his internal situation, the poverty-stricken state of his sense of self, fragmented and depleted by violent splitting and projective processes.

Bion (1967b) suggests that the ego is never wholly withdrawn from reality, that a non-psychotic personality exists, 'parallel with, but obscured by, the psychotic personality'. The ego's contact with reality is never entirely lost, rather '... masked by the dominance ... of an omnipotent phantasy that is intended to destroy either reality or the awareness of it ...'. These contacts with Mr X's non-psychotic personality suggested that the more containing aspects of the setting were emerging, and that accordingly the experience of emotion was more bearable. I was able to explain that some of the rules which I had tried to convey to him were intended to help people to keep things. He then laid the head on its side on a shelf in the room where it remained for two years. He periodically took it down and remodelled it. I think he was initially using the art materials for evacuative purposes. Then the object he created helped him to learn from the experience, over time.

Having placed his head securely on my shelf Mr X followed me around, walking exactly behind me. As I walked up the corridor on my way to a case conference he followed, silently. I asked him what he was doing, and he said, 'I am listening to my own thoughts. I didn't know I had my own thoughts.' I think the 'Sleeping Muse' image both emerged from and gave form to an aspect of the interactional field of the transference/countertransference, in which I as an early breast/mother was containing Mr X's dead or sleeping non-psychotic infant self. The experience of the containing breast seemed to be enabling him to experience his own capacity to think. Around this time he wrote a note to me, stating:

I love beautiful women, not necessarily for sex, yet not entirely without. Inside this place, we are introduced once all the spiders and cockroaches are swept away, beauty holds the fort, fearless of debauchery and hate. We humans are one step away from mindless diesels and two steps into buckled symbolism.

The interactional field between us, 'this place', now had an inside and an outside. A 'beautiful' object withstands the onslaughts of the spider/cockroach objects. There is a distinction between a state of 'mindless diesels' and a state of 'buckled symbolism', inside which we are 'introduced'. Mr X brought an egg box into the room and began to use the image of an egg box in his pictures, and the egg box image seemed to me to constitute a container for his egg/self. The egg can be thought of as a symbol of wholeness in potential. I think that, in Bick's (1968) terms, a 'skin-container' was beginning to form in the transference/countertransference field at this stage. Two months later, he built himself a kind of nest out of cardboard boxes and overalls in the corner of the room, to which he retired when full of 'voodoo', and lay still. The possibility of containment for those elements was developing, and his nest building seemed to me to be a significant shift in his use of the containment offered by the setting. Previously, he had left the room to retire to his bed on the ward when in this state of mind, evacuating himself from the setting.

One day, Mr X looked at the head and said affectionately, 'She's in a mess. Needs sorting out.' He remodelled the features to include eyes and a mouth. This is an example of the use of art for projective, as distinct from intrusive, identification. He was now, I think, projecting his 'mess' into the model/therapist for the purpose of 'sorting out'. His affectionate 'sorting out' of the 'mess' the head was in part reparative. The model was then put to rest again for another eighteen months or so. During this time he was discharged from the hospital and attended art therapy less frequently, developing relationships outside the hospital, and often telling me he would prefer to get rid of our relationship and his link to psychiatry altogether. Many of his experiences became more speakable at this stage, and he altered the relationships between the features on the head. The concreteness of the substances he used, and of the image itself, allowed the object to persist as it did over time, and not only to survive his physical attacks on it, but also to be transformed by them into a symbolic image. It seemed to me that this contributed to this growth in ego strength. Several months later he painted a series of heads which he described as 'Self Portraits', which suggested that there was then an experience of 'self' to do a 'portrait' of. A year later, for the first time, he brought a self portrait (Figure 2.1) into an individual therapy session, and said:

> I don't know whether to put it sideways or upwards – lying down muse or standing. It's just the head – no neck or anything . . . I felt it was me as a kind of monster – dying in my sleep. It wrecked my life . . . This picture sums it up. . . . They're just about a crisis in my life and how I coped with it at the time.

Figure 2.1 Sleeping muse

He was now able to use the picture to communicate with me. That which had previously been unspeakable and unthinkable was now viewed as something that he, Mr X, had experienced, that could be thought about, and that he could tell me about. At this point I, as the therapist, might begin to be able to develop a conversation with him within which the images serve the purposes of symbolic forms. Until this point it was unnecessary for me to explore the content and meaning of his images in order to be of service to a therapeutic process, and I think that an attempt to do so would have been experienced as extremely persecuting by Mr X. At the same time it was essential that I be active in creating and maintaining a setting within which the symbols could be born, experienced and eventually shared. It is my experience that, once the patient feels contained, 'object use' as described by Winnicott (1974) becomes a possibility, and the art process can begin to serve the purposes of play. As I have said elsewhere (Killick 1993), at this stage the patient can be assessed for analytic work in which the primitive transferences present in these states of mind can be worked through.

CONCLUSIONS: THE NEED FOR SANCTUARY

My work with a number of patients, like Mr X, in the setting I have described, continued after they had been discharged and were no longer acutely psychotic. Regular weekly sessions would often continue for several years. I began to work exclusively on an out-patient basis in 1989, and I eventually stopped working within the NHS in July 1994. Within the NHS setting in which I was employed, there was no possibility of working with these patients at a frequency greater than once per week. As far as I am aware, through my supervisory work and conversations with colleagues, this is generally the case in out-patient art therapy and psychotherapy departments. Effective work with the psychotic transference in my opinion requires a greater frequency of sessions in order that containment can be mediated through the experience of continuity.

One man with whom I began to work in the setting I have described when he was an in-patient, continued in weekly therapy sessions with me as an out-patient for three years, until I left the NHS. He had a long history of acute psychotic episodes, with bouts of destructive acting out which had involved attacks on his own body and others. The out-patient setting in which I worked with him was a multi-purpose room in which things could not be left, thereby limiting the possibilities for placing objects in the setting. One day he commented: 'People like me need places like that art room. Places which allow the mind to heal.'

He said that had he been very ill he could not have started work with me in this setting, and I agree with this. Because he had introjected the image of the art therapy room at the hospital, and knew that it was held in my mind as well, our shared memories were a resource which helped to contain some of the painful experiences which developed in his therapy. Thinking about the meanings of the possibilities offered by 'places like that art room' enabled us to develop different compromises in the new setting. He would take some pictures home with him; others would be left in his folder; and others in a little niche inside a cupboard which, we agreed, would probably be sufficiently secure. In many ways the change of setting offered us a new opportunity to think about the meaning of the old, and to translate those meanings into the context of his network of relationships within the community. However, at times the levels of despair in the transference would obliterate his experience of the continuity of our relatedness and this was difficult to manage within the once-weekly out patient setting.

At the time of writing I continue to work privately with patients with whom I started when they were in an acutely psychotic state within the setting I have described. This work is well supported by the local community psychiatric services. Some principles of the approach which I have described can be continued within a private practice setting, and the fact that the contract for therapy is essentially between myself and the patient makes resistance to increased engagement more containable than it would be in a setting where this is not a possibility. However, many patients who might be able to use a psychotherapeutic approach such as the one I have outlined are not in a position to finance themselves, and the nature of their psychopathology often precludes the possibility of earning a living. The NHS art therapy service in which I used to work is now based in an out-patient community setting, which means that sustained daily work with acute psychotic in-patients is no longer possible. Moves like this have happened and are happening throughout the country, and I consider this to be a great loss. If a patient is acutely psychotic, a setting which can bear and contain the unintegrated state of mind over time is needed, and it seems to me essential that settings which foster the experience of containment offered by 'places like that art room' continue to exist within the NHS.

REFERENCES

Balint, M. (1968) *The Basic Fault* London: Tavistock
Bick, E. (1968) 'The experience of the skin in early object relations', *International Journal of Psycho-Analysis* 49: 484.
Bion, W.R. (1962) *Learning from Experience*, London: Heinemann.
—— (1967a) 'Attacks on linking', in *Second Thoughts*, London: Heinemann.
—— (1967b) 'Differentiation of the psychotic from the non-psychotic personalities', in *Second Thoughts*, London: Heinemann.
Case, C. and Dalley, T. (1992) *The Handbook of Art Therapy*, London: Routledge.
Colman, W. (1995) 'Gesture and recognition: an alternative model to projective identification as a basis for couple relationships', in S. Rusczczynski and J. Fisher (eds) *Intrusiveness and Intimacy in the Couple*, London: Karnac.
Killick, K. and Greenwood, H. (1995) 'Research in art therapy with people who have psychotic illnesses', in A. Gilroy and C. Lee (eds) *Art and Music: Therapy and Research*, London: Routledge
Killick, K (1991) 'The practice of art therapy with patients in acute psychotic states', London: *Inscape* (Winter).
—— (1993) 'Working with psychotic processes in art therapy', *Psychoanalytic Psychotherapy* 7(1): 25–38. A slightly amended version appears in Ellwood, J. (ed.) (1995) *Psychosis: Understanding and Treatment*, London: Jessica Kingsley.)
Little, M. (1981) *Transference Neurosis and Transference Psychosis*, Northvale, New Jersey Jason Aronson.
Meltzer, D. *et al* (1986) *Studies in Extended Metapsychology: Clinical Applications of Bion's Ideas*, Perthshire, Scotland Clunie Press.
Schaverien, J. (1994) 'The transactional object art psychotherapy in the treatment of anorexia', *British Journal of Psychotherapy* 11: 1. Also in Schaverien, J. (1995) *Desire and the Female Therapist*, London: Routledge.
Winnicott, D. W. (1965) *The Maturational Processes and the Facilitating Environment*, London: Hogarth Press.
—— (1974) *Playing and Reality*, London: Pelican.

Chapter 3

Fear of three-dimensionality

Clay and plasticine as experimental bodies

Fiona Foster

It has long been observed (Bleuler 1950; Arieti 1974) that people suffering from schizophrenia tend to have profound difficulties in engaging in inter-personal exchange relationships. This seems to be based, at least in part, in their psychotic fears of direct, emotional connecting and often leads them to radically avoid ordinary and therapeutic interactions.[1]

These difficulties were very apparent in the large psychiatric hospital in which I worked as an art therapist. The overriding approach to understanding and treating schizophrenic patients in the institution was in line with a traditional, medical model. All patients were prescribed anti-psychotic medication and were sent for 'rehabilitative activities', including art therapy. Psychotherapy was considered to be neither suitable nor vital 'in these cases'; indeed it was often portrayed as 'dangerous', very similar to the 'culture' described by Killick and Greenwood (1995). Professionals thus seemed to view art therapy as not dangerous and, interestingly, patients often preferred to come to the art therapy department in favour of other prescribed activities. Cynically, one might conclude that not much was happening in art therapy and that it accommodated both patients' and professionals' anxieties. Yet, art therapy was offered to schizophrenic patients as an active, psychotherapeutic approach, in which many managed to engage.

In overcoming the initial engagement problem of schizophrenic patients, one essential aspect of art therapy could be seen as offering a non-demanding setting. Here a primary engagement with art materials/objects is encouraged, as opposed to primary engagement with another person (Killick 1993; Killick and Greenwood 1995). While most patients seemed to engage initially in the art therapy process, I often observed that patients got stuck in repetitive productions of rather lifeless, schematic imagery. Also, patients' production of more complex and 'powerful' imagery often evoked a lot of feelings and symbolic associations in *me*, but seemingly not in the patients, and thus certainly did not lead to progressive, emotional ways of relating and working through. These observations have also been made quite frequently by other art therapists with whom I discussed my work. Killick (1991) writes: 'The psychotic patient's imagery – if he or she produces imagery at all – can often appear seductively rich in symbolic meaning to the therapist wishing to "organise" the material into "knowledge"'. (Killick 1991: 4).

As a sculptor by background, I was struck by how rarely schizophrenic patients made spontaneous use of the sculpting materials (clay and plasticine) available in the art therapy setting. Indeed, they seemed actively to avoid engaging with them other than for the making or copying of familiar decorative or utilitarian objects such as ashtrays. While this might be seen as a personal disappointment to the sculptor in me, which has no relevance to therapy, I noticed that those patients who eventually got to work with three-dimensional substances, seemed to progress more in their self-development. Later they more easily moved into a traditional, directly and affectively interpersonal therapy relationship.

I thought that there might be something about making three-dimensional objects which evokes psychotic anxieties of a similar kind to that observed regularly when schizophrenic patients are facing direct, emotional and interpersonal contact with a therapist. In this chapter I am going to discuss my investigation into this perceived avoidance of clay and plasticine. This led me to appreciate the levels at which schizophrenic patients struggle with psychotic anxieties and how these may find expression in art-making. I developed some ideas of how to overcome some of those psychotic anxieties and to use the full therapeutic potential of clay and plasticine for a dynamically structuring (Pankow 1981; Schuff 1982) form of art therapy with schizophrenic patients.

To begin, I shall explore the differences between two- and three-dimensional art-making. In particular, I shall discuss this in relation to touch experiences and their possible consequences for schizophrenic experience and behaviour. My patients, usually in a state of severe, psychotic frag-mentation, rarely seemed to create imagery containing 'bodies' of three-dimensional quality – that is, bodies with depth, substance and firm outlines. Often they drew or painted in a way which emphasised a flat two-dimensional appearance, seemingly showing little differentiation between background and foreground (see Figure 3.1). This way of creating images was usually not due to a lack of skill in drawing or painting, for I often observed that the same patient who appeared to lack 'the skill' at one time suddenly had it at another.

In drawing or painting on a flat surface, tools are generally used such as a pencil, crayon or paintbrush to make contact with the surface. One might see these 'tools' as 'separators' or 'distancers' between the hand and the material. The actual touch experience of hand and tool is uniform and only variations in pressure sensations of hand, wrist or arm movement seem to create a difference. This is in marked contrast to the infinitely variable visual experiences produced. There may be more varied tactile experiences in finger painting – for instance, the sensation of something wet, sticky, cold or watery. However, the action of smearing paint across paper remains a fairly constant experience, in that the surface is flat and the forms or marks made remain

Figure 3.1 Untitled 1

physically flat to touch, whatever colours are used. In addition, in finger painting, the end product often has a blurred, undefined and non-descript form.

In painting, three-dimensional forms can be made to 'disappear' or be 'blurred' by being painted over. With clay and plasticine, however, one starts with an already existing three-dimensionality, with a body in space. The form may be changed, but the three-dimensional substance cannot be made to 'disappear' or to be 'blurred'. Whatever one does with it, one cannot fully get rid of the three-dimensional quality and an awareness that there is an inside, a rearside and a front.

As bodies in space, clay and plasticine seem to invite touch and physical interaction. Depending on the degree of physical force used in handling them, one can get a range of tactile sensations including gentle touch, stroking of a firm but soft surface and substantial resistance to pressure applied. They can provide a feeling that one's finger is *in* something, that one has entered into the inside of a body-like form and/or that the substance engulfs one's finger. Even with the use of modelling tools, the experience of body-likeness is largely preserved, e.g. when smoothing over a three-dimensional body, digging, stabbing, cutting, going into and out of a substantial body.

In terms of direct touch experience, clay in its malleable state tends to stick and cling very firmly to the skin, thus giving a continuous sensation of contact with a substance even when one has stopped physically handling it. Both the response by my psychotic patients to the initial, wet stickiness and to the subsequent drying up, hardening and cracking states of clay on the skin, was usually one of distress and necessitated urgent removal of the clay from the skin. One psychotic patient screamed that his 'hands were cracking up'. Another was frightened by 'the sticky stuff getting under his skin'. Similarly, but less dramatically, those few psychotic patients who engage in finger painting seem to limit their physical contact with the wet, sticky paint to a very short time and usually hurry to wash the paint from their hands. It is as if the substance is experienced as continuing to interact with the psychotic patient's body, even when he or she has discontinued handling it.

I suggest that those 'physically alive' qualities of experiences made by a human being in using clay and plasticine are connected not only with 'body-likeness', but also with 'life-likeness' of these substances. I am not claiming that either the handling of 'dead' three-dimensional materials provides the same experience as the handling of live bodies, or that the semblance is so close that one could easily be fooled into believing them to be the same. In addition to rational cognitive differentiation between live and dead materials, there are other unconscious and conscious irrational processes of cognition which enhance the similarity aspects of the materials. Langer (1979) pointed out that sculpture (and therefore sculptural substances) may 'embody the appearance of life in non-representational shapes' (Langer 1979: 89) which constitutes the perception of a 'life-like' quality in sculpture. An interesting development of these ideas for an understanding of transference phenomena in art therapy has been proposed by Schaverien (1987, 1991).

In the context of my investigation here I would like to propose that the 'life-likeness' and affective aspects of object relations with three-dimensional bodies are of major importance for an understanding of many psychotic patients' avoidance of working with three-dimensional substances. It seems that those patients who, for whatever reason, do get involved with clay and plasticine, often do so only once or make only intermittent contact with the materials. Such contact is often terminated with expressions of distress or sudden disinterest. Physical distancing is occasionally accompanied by verbal statements which refer to the material or the object as 'disgusting, awful, rubbish, no good for me'. Equally, these patients often express a wish to destroy the object, squash it or throw it away.

The most striking and regular behaviour during contact with clay or plasticine is the squashing of it into a flat, pancake-like form. For some this is the only interaction they let themselves in for. Others hesitantly make a few dents in the material, followed by a quick action of flattening the whole piece. Yet others take only tiny bits, which, almost automatically in the process of picking up, they tend to press into flat, coin-like shapes, thus clearly reducing the three-dimensional body qualities of the material. This phenomena of reducing and eliminating depth appearances is similar to that mentioned in the context of picture making by schizophrenic patients, but it is even more pronounced when handling three-dimensional materials.

My efforts to explore the patients' minimal involvement with these substances led me to various behavioural, cognitive and psychoanalytic theories. Among these, I found that the Kleinian concept of projective identification, as a defence mechanism against psychotic anxiety, and of psychotic object relations (Segal 1989) provided me with a particularly helpful understanding as to why my patients should avoid three-dimensional substances in particular. Projective identification starts with the splitting of constructive and destructive aspects of the self and leads to projection of the destructive parts into external objects. It is important to stress that Klein conceptualised the bad parts as comprising both destructive impulses and parts of the primitive self which are associated with emotionally highly charged body parts and body products, e.g. breast, penis, faeces, urine, etc. She stressed in her descriptions the body part quality and destructive aliveness of those projected parts. Equally she described the receiving external objects in terms of bodies with an inside, *into* which the projected parts can be located. The destructive powers were experienced as now operating in an 'alive' fashion inside the external object, emanating from it, and thereby identifying it as a destructive object. Eliminating the destructively experienced impulses and parts of the body from one's inside was seen as a means of reducing the powerful anxiety of destructiveness from within. Yet, anxiety is not totally eliminated, as the receiving external object is perceived as threatening insofar as that contact and interaction with it could lead to re-entry of the bad parts into the self. This anxiety can be reduced by avoiding contact and interaction with the threatening external object.

Interestingly, schizophrenic people who hear hallucinatory voices or feel influenced bodily by (delusional) forces from the outside world, generally describe the presumed source of such influencing powers as three-dimensional objects, for example a TV set, black box, human or monstrous bodies. In the art therapy setting, I suggest that it is the corporal three-dimensionality of clay and plasticine which makes them likely to be chosen as external objects for projective identification. The substances themselves are objects with an inside into which bad parts of the self can be projected, which thus become bad objects threatening to re-enter the self.

Klein suggested that the quality of badness thus perceived in an external object, or body, is closely connected to the assumed quality of the projected body part or body product. Clay and plasticine in their visual and tactile properties bear a close semblance to faeces in particular, which also bear cultural connotations of badness. Thus there is not only the often described internal preoccupation of psychotic patients with faeces (Segal 1989), but also an actual confrontation with faeces-like substances in the external environment of the art therapy setting. How this presence and semblance might be processed in the mind of a psychotic person can be understood in terms of Segal's concept of symbolic equation (Segal 1989). In psychotic perception clay may not be seen as clay, or clay looking *as if* it was faeces, or *as if* contaminated by one's own thoughts and feelings, but as faeces *de facto*.

I propose that it might be the convergence of these two aspects of psychotic object relations, projective identification and symbolic equation, which:

(a) single out clay and plasticine as likely persecutory objects in the art therapy setting;
(b) motivate psychotic patients' avoidance of using them.

Another aspect of the joint workings of projective identification and symbolic equation can be illustrated with the (already mentioned) patient who did work with clay and then became very frightened when he experienced it drying and cracking on the skin of his hands. I assume that in his case the actual body sensations of pulling and tightening might have signalled concretely the attempt of the substance to get under his skin. This, in connection with a visual image of cracks, might have been experienced by him as announcing the cracking up of himself. I might be accused here of wildly imposing my own fantasies on a much more mundane, behavioural motivation. I cannot answer this other than by referring to patients who, when recovered from psychosis, recall exactly such experiences.

The previously described flattening of clay and plasticine might now be understood as an attempt to reduce the three-dimensional body qualities of the material and its likelihood of becoming a container for persecutory forces and of semblance with bad body parts. Apart from the defensive process of eliminating the potential danger to self, it also provides a concrete sense of control over a body and its (affective) content.

In the confusing and disturbing world of psychotic experience, which goes along with powerful fears of losing even the most basic structure of self, patients desperately tend to eliminate fear and build some more reliable structure at the same time. Elimination is partly achieved by avoidance behaviour and structuring by basic, concretised ways of functioning, e.g. rigid and repetitive, delusional thought and ritualised actions.

This striving for control and reliable structures, inside themselves and with external objects, is of major importance for the understanding of psychotic patients' behaviour in the art therapy process. It can be observed in the flattening of three-dimensional materials and even more so in repetitive drawing and painting of geometrical patterns which allows for the controlled making and handling of reliable structures. This activity often only extends into experimentation with size, variety of shapes and the colouring in of relatively anxiety-free, two-dimensional shapes. The narcissistic aspect of this controlling behaviour is vital for both the stabilisation of a fragile self-structure and for the potential development of positive project identification (Segal 1989).

My explorations so far allow me now to link up clinical observations in a more coherent form: there seems to be a hierarchy of diminishing anxiety/ avoidance behaviour from direct interaction with human beings through three-dimensional to two-dimensional art objects. Equally, there seems to be a line of progression from experimentation with two-dimensional to three-dimensional materials and objects and then to direct, interpersonal forms of an emotional relationship with another human being. Thus, a whole range of destructive and constructive aspects of basic object relations can be observed in how psychotic patients make and avoid contact and interaction with art materials. The most important aspect for me as an art therapist is that these observations may help me to gauge roughly the level of functioning at which a patient's self-reorganising processes towards higher levels get stuck. It also may suggest ways in which to facilitate the development of more and more substantial and emotionally connecting forms of relating through art therapy. This aspect of art therapy has been extensively described by Killick (1987, 1993; Killick and Greenwood 1995).

Within the field of psychoanalytic psychotherapy with psychotic patients, Kleinians strongly favour psychoanalytic transference interpretations (Rosenfeld 1982; Segal 1989). Many other psychoanalysts see major modifications of classical, psychoanalytic technique as necessary for therapy with psychotic patients (Little 1986; Pankow 1961, 1981). I cannot review this extensive debate here, but I want to draw attention to the importance of a highly structured setting for therapy that all approaches seem to agree upon. It is recognised that schizophrenic patients need a very containing, reliable structure in the therapy setting in order to be able to work on the extremely frightening psychotic phantasies aroused.

Among all these different approaches, I would like to refer briefly to a psychotherapy approach with psychotic patients proposed by the psychoanalyst Gisela Pankow (Pankow 1961, 1981; Schuff 1982). Very early in the therapy, Pankow asks a patient to make objects for her. Not unlike Klein, she sees the patient's made object as a container for fragments of his or her body-self. But, unlike Klein, she does not interpret the supposed phantasy meaning and nature of unconscious object relations to the schizophrenic patient, nor does she initially interpret them in terms of how the patient unconsciously might want to involve the therapist. Instead, she explores with the patient the form and possible functions of the object, as an object in its own right – for instance, whether the object is hard or soft, female or male, etc.

Pankow sees it as important to create initially a setting in which the made object is clearly placed and dealt with as a body that is *not* directly connected with either 'the person'-therapist or 'the person'-patient. Therapist and patient 'study' together the object 'over there' which creates a less threatening alliance between therapist and patient and also a distance from the object. Distance from the object, its status as an object for study and exploration, and the active alignment of the therapist with the patient *vis-à-vis* the separate object, reduces the fear about the object and whatever dangerous fragments it might contain.

This exploration of fragments of body-self becomes possible in the guise of exploring *it* (the external, self-made object). *It* can be concretely handled, deformed and reformed. *It* can be given all sorts of fantasy functions and relations with other bodies while remaining an *it*.

Pankow sees this technique as concretely facilitating the building up of a body image for the patient via an external object which contains body-self-fragments and which can be more and more differentiated and gradually (in an acknowledged way) more and more identified with.

Once sufficient structuring of the patient's body image is achieved, Pankow invites the patient to connect the made object with her own body. This can be in the form of asking the patient what *it* (the made body-object) could do to Pankow's body, what the result of that action might be, and how Pankow might respond. In these explorations *it* is now not only a modified or new concrete object, but an object with lots of live functions. *It* can now be explored by the patient in its potential relationship with an actually present human being (body), the therapist, without having to bring his or her own body into the interaction in an acknowledged, concrete way. *It* now contains a lot of the patient's self, has helped the patient to introduce himself/herself via unconscious identification with his or her positive and negative aspects of him/herself, united in a more and more whole external object.

Once this has been achieved, Pankow describes the patient's gradual conscious acknowledgement of his or her identification with aspects of the made object, which can now be communicated and interpreted by Pankow in a more traditional, psychoanalytic way, i.e. in interpersonal terms of the here-and-now therapeutic relationship.

Killick has written about this approach in some detail in the context of presenting her original art therapy model of understanding and treating psychotic patients (Killick 1987, 1991; Killick and Greenwood 1995). I, too, find this approach fascinating in terms of how it uses object making and object experimentation. It organises the patient–therapist relationship around the concrete structuring of a third body which reduces psychotic anxiety about direct interpersonal forms of relating. By doing this it respects the need of the schizophrenic patient to preserve his or her threatened self via narcissistic control, yet furthers, with the support of the therapist, the narcissistic self-structuring process of the patient without disengaging from work on the frightening issues. The latter can be worked on by both patient and therapist via the created object at a safe enough distance. Yet, it is also Pankow (1961) who remarks that: 'The principal difficulty is to make the patient touch the modelling clay' (Pankow 1961: 162). She does not, however, suggest how to overcome this difficulty. My own approach to this problem and to other issues of art therapy with psychotic patients is illustrated in the following case study.

CASE STUDY

A 32-year-old female patient, whom I shall call Mary, was diagnosed as suffering from schizophrenia. She had been in and out of mental health institutions for 10 years, oscillating between severe withdrawal behaviour, self-neglect and highly excited states with severe fragmentation of thinking and feeling. On one occasion she set fire to herself, but did not sustain physically disabling injuries. Throughout the past ten years there had been no episode of her functioning in a non-psychotic way, despite medication and strenuous efforts to rehabilitate her.

In the beginning Mary would sit opposite me in silence, staring at me endlessly with a fixed, frozen smile. When she spoke, which was rare, she mostly repeated single words like: '. . . alright? . . . All-right?' My invitations to use the art materials or to talk with me were ignored. I hypothesised in my mind that she had adopted a very radical, defensive avoidance behaviour to counteract psychotic anxiety, and I therefore stopped trying to pull her into direct interaction with me or with the art materials. Instead, while sitting opposite her, I made some casual drawings and played with some plasticine in a deliberately absent-minded fashion. After some considerable time she seemed to start watching my activities, and one day surprised me by telling me: 'I like doctor B . . ., I really do . . . don't hate her . . . love her . . . she is lovely . . . can't disturb her.' When I tried to enquire further into what she was talking about, she interrupted me quickly, and staring at me said: 'I saw a beautiful painting . . . a beautiful one . . . a really beautiful one . . . someone is going to give me a present.' I was not sure whether this sequence was making a meaningful link between my drawings and a doctor (me in disguise?). There seemed to be no possibility to engage her in an exploration of 'the drawing', or a conversation about the meaning of her words. Each time I directly communicated with her, she interrupted me with less and less coherent statements. But, my arrangement of the setting seems to have given her an opportunity to observe me from a distance, to engage with my objects (drawings, plasticine), and to use them as idealised object representations: 'lovely doctor', 'beautiful painting'.

When Mary talked she referred to relationships in which something can be exchanged interpersonally ('can't disturb her', 'someone is going to give me a present'). Yet, when I tried to meet and exchange with her in direct interpersonally connecting communication, the connecting aspect of it disintegrated. She filled and structured the space around her with strings of sentences and verbally prevented my communications from 'touching or entering' her. My function as an object thus shifted from being a container for positive, idealising projective identification to an object of negative projective identification. Her frantic space-filling subsided when I returned to my casual drawing activity.

A few sessions later, Mary placed herself immediately opposite me, covering her face with her hands and expressed, in a muffled voice: 'I am not sure . . . whether . . . I might kill you . . . or . . . he kills me'. She then looked up and stared at me, saying: 'My father says such horrible things.' Suddenly, screwing up her face she appeared to burst into tears, but although uttering little sobs, no tears appeared. I found myself to be surprisingly and strangely untouched by this outburst. It seemed as if Mary was going through the motions of crying, but not the emotions. Putting her head in her hands, she made louder sobbing sounds. Suddenly she looked up at me with a fixed smile, and took some clay, which I had put nearby. She pressed it into a flat pancake form on the table and announced: 'Looks like a gun.' She squashed it up, manipulated it again and said: 'It's a speedboat' (see Figure 3.2). She then began to fiddle with an almost invisible, tiny piece of clay, saying that it was 'the driver'. While fiddling with 'the driver', she started to speak of her past travels: 'I spent six months in Greece, working on a farm. It was hard work, I had to get up very early. I met some nice people there. Then I went to Canada for three months with some friends to look for some work. After that we travelled to France. . . . I used to be a laboratory technician. I enjoyed that and I would like to go back to work.' I occasionally asked a few questions regarding her travels to which she responded appropriately, and I felt as if I was having an everyday conversation with a non-psychotic person.

The rapid changes of levels of functioning were stunning. From the frightening confusion over 'who was killing whom', father seemed to emerge as a persecutory image. It was not clear whether Mary actually hallucinated

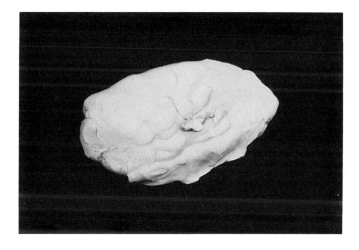

Figure 3.2 Speedboat

his abusive words at the time, or just associated a killing issue to a memory fragment of father. The whole-person image of father, with horrible words coming out of him, seemed to mobilise psychotic anxiety in Mary, and a response of dissociation of feeling and movement functions (e.g. crying, but not really crying). I was surprised when she suddenly picked up the clay. This could be interpreted as a means of turning away from whole person images (me, her, him, father) with dangerously persecuting powers (killing, horrible things said), and as a turning to a substance which we could both study. Having reduced the clay object to a flat, almost two-dimensional object, Mary seemed to have enough control over *it* to locate the killing issue in *it* in the form of a gun. Although one cannot be sure, the sudden further flattening of the clay and the transformation of the clay gun into the idea of a speedboat might have suggested that the killing power became too alive in the clay gun. The power and speed of action element of the gun seemed to remain, but became part of an exciting vehicle (speedboat). Interestingly, in the process of creating a powerful body (speedboat) for herself, she added a controller (a driver) and seemed to identify with the image as a whole. The structuring of a (narcissistically) powerful and controlled (travelling) body outside of herself, then seemed to facilitate an identification with her memory self-image as a (travelling) capable person, and allowed her to be in her own full, historical body and to interact with me, for a while, as a capable person to another capable person.

As the session was coming to an end, she placed 'the speedboat' on a shelf allocated to her, put the rest of the clay away, and then suddenly said: 'I'm bad, worthless . . . bad thoughts . . . I'm not going to hurt anyone, haven't hit anyone for ages.' These statements were made when separating from the 'good, controlled vehicle for self'. The bad image of self returned in her body/mind with aggressive impulses, which she defended against. Strikingly, the quality of her communication gave me an experience of being talked to, and she seemed to embody a sense of 'I' who *has* thoughts and feelings and could do something with her body to others, rather than defend herself through splitting and projective identification.

In another session Mary said out of the blue: 'I'm scared in case of being the only one left.' She then turned to me and told me, in an engaging tone of voice: 'I don't think my parents want me to meet anyone . . . may I have a cup of coffee?' She got up and made it herself. Having drawn my attention to the disconnecting wishes of her parents and possibly becoming the only one left, Mary asked permission to connect herself to a cup of coffee and to feed herself. On return with her coffee, Mary expressed a wish to use clay. She immediately squashed and flattened some clay, and while holding it in her hand she said: 'Look! . . . Pockets of love . . . they represent brothers and sisters' (see Figure 3.3). She then counted the dents made by her fingers and, holding the clay firmly in her hands, she said: 'It feels like a mother's bust, not in a sexual way, but in a cuddly, protective way. In fact, it feels so

Figure 3.3 Pockets of love

Figure 3.4 Offertory

like a mother's bust, I think I'll put it down.' Having put it down and seemingly very excited and pleased, she got up to get some more clay. While manipulating it, she announced: 'This could be the offertory, where hard-earned money goes' (see Figure 3.4) . . . 'I like these (pointing to the two clay objects) . . . this one is pockets of love . . . and this one the love offered . . . I'm quite a tender person.'

Having established just before this sequence a rudimentary sense of self, and having fed herself with a cup of coffee, she used the clay to create a concrete body for the projection of love ('pockets of love'). Love was projected as bits (into pockets) which merge into the projection of the good breast (into a *whole* object). It is striking how Mary needed to defend the function of love-giving against the function of sex-giving to intrude into these objects. Firstly, she seemed to stress the non-sexual function of love 'in pockets' by referring to brotherly and sisterly bodies. Secondly, the 'bust' was not only designated as belonging to a mother's body, but was explicitly defined as non-sexual. When she explored the image of cuddly interaction with the 'breast' she seemed to reach a danger point in which the good (non-sexual, protective) breast threatens to switch over into the bad (sexual, aggressive) breast, so she put it down. Distancing from the concrete object seemed to help in the maintenance of the 'good breast' (positive projective identification) and to allow for exploration of further interactive aspects concerning love.

Mary created in a new clay object ('offertory') a container that is capable of *receiving* love. The portrayal of love is highly concretised in that the substance of love is money, and the recipient of love is an offertory – a box within the body of a concrete church. But, a fundamental structuring process can be observed in which there is a rudimentary distinction between whole bodies and part bodies, and distinction between a giving body and a receiving body, which allows for a basic transfer of the vital feeling (love) from one body to another. This structure can be internalised by Mary to identify herself as a whole person with tender (loving) feelings which could be given to somebody else.

During the next session Mary told me that Jill, another patient, 'gave me a hug and it reminded me of pockets of love'. It would be a mistake to assume that this rudimentary structuring would now lead to easy and rapid growth towards normal functioning. The struggle between destructive and constructive forces is a very powerful one which needs to be reworked on many different levels repeatedly.

I want to move on a few weeks in Mary's therapy and describe some other aspects of working with objects. After a very distressing session, I engaged Mary again via modelling some clay in front of her. She commented: 'Looks awful . . . looks like a baby . . . looks like an old man . . . he's so awful', and became very frightened.

At this point it seemed important that the made object was a separate object of study for both patient and therapist or that it belonged to the therapist's body. In both cases distance of the object from the patient's body might reduce anxiety and facilitate further engagement. I therefore made a point of saying that this 'awful' object was *my* object, and then suggested to her: 'You might like to change the shape that I have made.' She took the clay from me, laid it on the table, flattened and smoothed it down, and then commented:

'Looks like my back.' As she seemed to be able to contain the situation, and even dared to personalise the clay object (in its now safe, flat form) as part of her *own* body, I decided to suggest further concrete experimentation, but made a point of depersonalising it. I asked her if there was anything that one might add 'to this object' and 'to the back' (not *her* back). She replied: 'Legs', and pushed her fingers into the clay as if to make 'legs'. These took the form of dents or impressions rather than three-dimensional legs. She then commented that it was 'a baby in swaddling-clothes'. I asked if the baby was lying on its back or front, and she replied that it was lying on its back, then picked it up to look at the back, exclaiming: 'That's interesting! Didn't know that it would look like that.'

The concrete exploration of form and function in the clay objects leads to differentiations: here in terms of 'a baby' having a back and a front. While the beginning of this happens in a flat, two-dimensional form, the turning over action is moving into considering and acting with three-dimensional aspects. Throughout this process she maintained the position of an observer, a handler and a controller of an object, which has internal links to her own body, but is treated just as an external body, independent of her. I think that it was this type of self-structuring in action, on another body, which allowed her to feel safe enough to make the next, unprompted move.

She made what she called 'a house' with another lump of clay. The 'house', a large triangular three-dimensional blob, was made hurriedly. She then put the previous object ('the baby') into the 'house'. As she did this, the 'house' and the 'baby' suddenly became: 'A giant's mouth . . . a horrible, nasty giant whom one would be terrified of . . . one daren't breath a word . . . daren't move . . . it could kill you . . . it could kill a person . . . if they breathed a word.' While saying this, Mary appeared to be terrified. Leaning over towards me and looking into my face, she said earnestly and quickly: 'The giant says, not to tell a word to anyone.'

It seems that putting the 'baby' object into a container suddenly brought up a new and threatening life-like image of another container, 'a giant's mouth', which shares with the 'house' the dimension of being something big and having something small inside. But now the function has changed from protective containment to something 'horrible and nasty'. An interaction between two mouths is implied: the giant's mouth can kill and would do so if the mouth of the baby (Mary) would tell (probably a powerful story). Seemingly, the anxiety of annihilation can only be reduced by curbing even the most fundamental experiences of life, movement and breathing. In the past, Mary often froze in her body. Now she communicates via objects and words with some coherence about this experience, though not without feeling the threatening body sensations which belong to her story.

Although the story actually told in the session sounds like a fairy story, the boundary between telling a fairy story and her feeling to be in it gets more and more blurred. She seemed to talk to me as if she was in direct interaction with the giant and was communicating to me as an outsider to her world, i.e. reporting what the giant says to her.

Even more than before I had an overpowering association in my own mind of her telling me in a fragmented and distorted form about her experience in the past of having been sexually abused by her father. I felt that I was witnessing her psychotic way of handling the 'live' emergence of past sensations in her present body. Again, tempting as it might have been to verbalise my associations in the hope that 'a fact' might be confirmed or disconfirmed, and that a truth shared would dispel the muddle and pave the way towards restitution, I abstained. I felt that not only would it be prudent to be cautious about my own associations but, far more importantly, Mary's mental state was by no means conducive to interpersonal examination of different views and meanings while she was in a state of blurred boundaries between external and internal realities and of increasing psychotic anxieties. If the structuring therapy with her was to work, she would clarify her history and identify the nature of her sexual experiences in it.

In an attempt to hold the escalation and to create a sufficiently secure setting in which to continue the basic structuring process, I asked Mary whether 'the person could draw or write, rather than breath the words'. Again, I did not address my suggestion to her in the form of a 'you' (as a direct personalisation), but used the once-removed term, 'the person', who could find a less life-like (life-breathing) form of expressing herself. If Mary chose to take up my suggestion, it might enable her to continue to explore the issues in a safer form (paper object) rather than to remain in a direct and escalating relationship with the giant. She said: 'Ah . . . yes.' Taking a scrap piece of paper lying next to her, she wrote without speaking: 'The giant opens his mouth and the baby shudders with fear. I'm warning you, breathe a word and I shall kill you. Shut your mouth and keep quiet!'. While showing me the writing, she watched me intensely. Then she took the piece of paper back and hurriedly drew two figures on it. Now Mary 'opened her mouth' and called the drawing: 'My father exposing himself.'

The drawing (Figure 3.5), which was not commented on any more by Mary, does not obviously seem to show 'father exposing himself'. It shows two crude bodies, one having a little stick figure in the head area – maybe it is a two-dimensional version of 'the baby in the giant's mouth'. Immediately after the sentence about father was spoken, Mary squashed up the three-dimensional clay object which had been identified as the giant's mouth. While this might be seen as an unproductive elimination, I let it happen for containment reasons and to allow her to experience power over the threatening object. Also, she did something interesting with the paper when I asked what she wanted to do with it. She decided to put it underneath a dustbin. It seemed to express a concretised condensation of two opposing attitudes

Figure 3.5 My father exposing himself

towards the body (object) that contained the problem issue: the wish to throw away or annihilate (dustbin) and the wish to preserve (put under cover).

Looking back at this and some of the following sessions, there seemed to be a repeated cycle of my being able to introduce three-dimensional material as a facilitator for more personalised embodiment for Mary, which then had to be allowed to be undone, or to be robbed of its three-dimensional qualities. The exploration then continued on a two-dimensional level which, in turn, facilitated the possibility of creating new three-dimensional contact either with another clay body or with Mary's own body.

Now, after having worked with Mary for about a year, she occasionally regresses to psychotic levels of functioning which are reorganised very quickly. Mostly she interacts with me from a position of feeling in possession of a good enough structure of self. Mary is now largely preoccupied with relationship issues between 'whole' people, rather than 'part-objects'. She acknowledges conflicts as being inside herself and between her and me, and tries to draw me into 'childlike', neurotic relations, for example, she 'threatens' me with ending art therapy because I 'make' her talk about her family, which she does not want, yet wants, and complains about me not being there for her often enough. Mary uses clay and plasticine more freely now and she no longer seems to have any need to squash the life-likeness out of three-dimensional objects (see Figure 3.6) or herself.

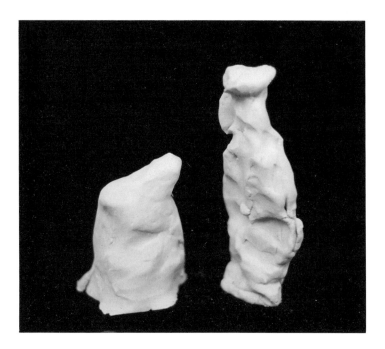

Figure 3.6 Untitled 2

WAYS FORWARD

This case study shows how different levels of functioning and anxiety sometimes necessitate the return to two-dimensional forms of structuring and the potential use of such reworking for progression to higher levels of mental organisation. It also illustrates the importance of facilitating therapeutic experimentation with three-dimensional materials. It fills the gap between a basic structuring process in a safe relationship between patient and two-dimensional materials, and direct interpersonal forms of relating. New and therapeutic experiences with body-like and life-like objects become possible, because the objects are self-made, controllable and concretely changeable in interactions which are 'touching and forming'. The psychotic anxieties about the dangerous *inside* of Self and an Other can thus be worked with dynamically.

I believe that overcoming the avoidance of using three-dimensional materials and objects is an important step in art therapy. I hope to give a few more examples of how this might be done without simply trying to remove avoidance as a 'symptom'.

A patient, who tended to mutilate her body, showed signs of mutilating herself during a session. I took little blobs of clay and put them, one by one, into her already self-hitting hands. She dropped the first few, but then, with some force, stuck the next ones into the picture she had worked on earlier (see Figure 3.7). She stopped hitting her own body and instead hit and squashed the clay pieces more firmly onto the paper. This was the beginning of our work with three-dimensional external bodies in which she could contain and structure the frightening experiences of her own body (self). I would like to suggest that clay could be introduced at that moment because:

(a) the flow of her defensively attacking movements was not stopped, but diverted onto an alternative 'body';
(b) they were more easily controllable by being small and were given in small bits;
(c) they could be put into an already self-created and controlled external body (her painting).

Another patient would often sit in front of a blank piece of paper 'not knowing what to draw'. In one session he walked up to a plasticine model of a 'head and shoulders' which was sitting on a shelf, and exclaimed: 'That's good ... really good ... it's really good.' Making sure I had some plasticine in my hand, I walked up to him, told him that the model had been

Figure 3.7 Untitled 3

made with plasticine, casually handed him a little and turned away. The patient said: 'I don't know what to do with it . . . what shall I do? I know . . . I'll make my own head!', and started to work with the plasticine. I think this is an example of how one might introduce a three-dimensional object into the process of narcissistic self-structuring already in action in a patient. He seemed to project an idealised, narcissistic aspect of his self-representation onto the sculpture on the shelf, but did not dare to touch it or to make a body for himself spontaneously. It seemed as if the fantasy in the patient's head of interacting with such substances created more anxiety than the actual contact with them. My turning away from him, a concrete message of 'You do not need to relate to *me*', might have contributed to his accepting the material.

Handing over of material might be extended into joint handling. For example, the therapist may start making a flat, and therefore safe, clay shape, and while casually working on it ask the patient 'to help' to push or press the therapist's finger into the clay. The therapist's finger then becomes a separator between the patient and the clay, while at the same time the patient is allocated control of the therapist (finger) and the clay.

In another variation, the patient may be asked what the therapist should make with a piece of plasticine. In this way the therapist's body becomes a servant in the production, i.e. 'I will make something – you can tell me what to make . . . and how.' This facilitates an interpersonal interaction which is safe for the patient as it allocates mastery to the patient and a subservient role to the therapist. The therapist, in the making of the object, might say to the patient: 'How might I do this? . . .', or 'I am stuck . . . is this how I do it? . . . what next?' By telling the therapist what to do with the object, the patient makes a relationship with the therapist in order to relate to the object.

My final example illustrates this process well. A male patient consistently ignored all invitations to work with any art materials. One day I took a piece of plasticine and asked him casually what I could do with it. Looking at my hands he suddenly said: 'A hand.' Pretending not to know how to make a hand, I asked him how I might make one. He said: 'Squash it, flatten it . . . flatten it first!' Placing it on the table between us, I again said I was not sure how to do this, and asked him to show me how it could be flattened. With my hand still on part of the plasticine, the patient started to push his thumb into the plasticine, and began to flatten it out. At this point I removed my hand to allow him to continue. Towards the end of the session he had made a flat 'Egyptian man . . . sitting on a park bench'. Both the patient and the 'Egyptian man' continued to sit and look at each other for many weeks before they could dare to move again.

CONCLUSION

I hope to have contributed to some understanding of schizophrenic patients' fear of three-dimensionality and the therapeutic potential of facilitating their engagement with three-dimensional art materials and objects. As body-like and life-like objects they allow for experimentation on an intermediary level of relating between two-dimensional self-structuring and direct, interpersonal exchange relationships with an art therapist, and thus provide a potential bridge for progressive development.

NOTES

1 A great deal of my thinking in this chapter derives from tutorials and seminars on the MA in Art Therapy Course, St Albans (1988–90). I am particularly indebted to Katherine Killick whose original research and art therapy approach with psychotic patients (Killick 1987, 1991, 1993; Killick and Greenwood 1995) has been very influential in my work, and to Heiner Schuff's presentations of Gisela Pankow's work on dynamic structurization (Schuff 1982).

REFERENCES

Arieti, S. (1974) *Interpretation of Schizophrenia*, 2nd edn, London: Crosby Lockwood Staples.
Bleuler, E. (1950) *Dementia Praecox or the Group of Schizophrenias*, New York: International University Press.
Killick, K. (1987) 'Art therapy and schizophrenia: a new approach', unpublished MA thesis, School of Art and Design, University of Hertfordshire.
Killick, K. (1991) 'The practice of art therapy with patients in acute psychotic states', London: *Inscape* (Winter): 2–6.
Killick, K. (1993) 'Working with psychotic processes in art therapy', *Psychoanalytic Psychotherapy* 7: 25–38.
Killick, K. and Greenwood, H. (1995) 'Research in art therapy with people who have psychotic illnesses', in A. Gilroy and C. Lee (eds) *Art and Music Therapy and Research*, London: Routledge.
Langer, S.K. (1979) *Feeling and Form*, London and Henley Routledge & Kegan Paul.
Little, M.I. (1986) 'Transference neurosis and transference psychosis', *Toward Basic Unity*, London: Free Association Books.
Pankow, G. (1961) 'Dynamic structurization in schizophrenia', in A. Burton (ed.) *Psychotherapy of the Psychoses*, New York: Basic Books.
Pankow, G. (1981) 'Psychotherapy: a psychoanalytic approach. An analytic approach employing the concept of the body image', in M. Dongier and E. Wittkower (eds) *Divergent Views in Psychiatry*, New York: Harper & Row.
Rosenfeld, H.A. (1982) *Psychotic States*, London: Karnac.
Schaverien, J. (1987) 'The scapegoat and the talisman: transference in art therapy', in T. Dalley *et al.* (eds) *Images of Art Therapy*, Tavistock.
Schaverien, J. (1991) *The Revealing Image: Analytical Art Psychotherapy in Theory and Practice*, London: Routledge.
Schuff, G.H. (1982) 'Dynamic body building', in papers presented to the two-day conference 'Art and Drama Therapy', School of Art and Design, University of Hertfordshire.
Segal, H. (1989) *Klein*, London: Karnac.

Chapter 4

Masturbation and painting

David Mann

Using the work of one psychotic patient I shall demonstrate how the painting process might be used for masturbation purposes. Psychosis entails the loss of the 'as if' quality of experience, the therapist does not *seem* like the father or mother but is experienced as though he or she *is* the mother or father. I shall suggest that this patient with a sadistic paranoid psychosis treated the painting as though it were a woman. Women, painting and masturbation were all incorporated into his perverse state of mind and denied individual differences. I shall stress that I am not equating painting with a masturbatory activity or that masturbation is a perversion *per se*. I shall conclude with some remarks about masturbation in fine art and its distinction from the perverse psychotic state described here.

Psychosis entails the loss of the 'as if' quality of experience. For example, a neurotic concern might be, 'those people over there *might* be talking about me'; or someone in a neurotic state might say to the therapist, 'You are *just* like my father'. A psychotic response, however, would be, 'those people over there *are* talking about me' or saying to the therapist, 'You *are* my father'. One of the distinguishing features of psychosis is the concrete nature of thoughts. It is as though the symbolic or metaphorical nature of thought and language is in suspension. This chapter seeks to describe a particular patient for whom painting did not merely represent having sex or masturbating: rather, painting was the sexual activity itself.

I have stated in a number of previous publications (Mann 1989, 1990, 1991) that I do not accept the prevailing view in much art psychotherapy literature that the act of painting or producing pictures is an inherently creative process. What I have attempted to demonstrate is how the painting or picture-making process can be used by the individual's psychic defensive strategies. The defensive use of art runs counter to most people's idea of art as a creative activity. Levens (1989) also explores the idea of working with defence mechanisms in art therapy and notes that regressed patients may manifest their regression by smearing paint or other pre-representational styles. Though recognising that the patient's defences may appear in the artwork, Levens is still inclined to consider the picture-making process as essentially being able to bypass verbal defences and therefore less amenable to control. This is not quite my view. I do not believe defences should be equated with the verbal; indeed, many of the more primitive defences are essentially pre-verbal in origin and content. I also take the view that everything an individual does is autobiographical. Everything he or she says, does or believes is expressed in psychological symptoms. Fantasies or feelings find expression in either the most creative acts or the most destructive repetition compulsions, or the greatest of human achievements in art, mythology, science, law or religion. All of these are products of the psyche and therefore reflect the structure and content of their originators. It follows, then, that neurotic or psychotic states of mind will find their structures and contents repeated in a work of art. That is to say, whatever forms of defence the individual habitually deploys to cope with psychological distress and anxiety – such as projection, splitting, projective identification, disassociation, etc. – will find expression in the painting process. Insofar as the individual is resisting change, or is clinging to old defensive manoeuvres, the painting process will embody the various defences the psyche employs. I am not denying the creative potential or use of art. I seek rather to elaborate and explore this defensive side of the image-making process as it is only by working through the individual's old defensive mechanisms that we can liberate him or her from the infantile and childhood repetitions that feed the transference.

I do not wish to imply that this is an either/or process: either painting is creative or defensive. As I shall elaborate below, the individual is constantly held in a tension between the tendency to regress or progress, to go backwards or forwards, to remain the same or undergo change and development. At different times in a person's life one or the other process will dominate. Most people move between these two positions but generally are developing and learning from experience; this is the process we call individuation. The less able we are to learn from experience, the more we may be introduced to the neurotic and psychotic components of the mind.

If the painting process can be utilised by the defences for the purposes of avoiding change (that is to say, avoiding a creative experience), it seems possible, if not probable, that the psychotic's experience, the loss of the 'as if' quality of images, will also find expression in the painting process. The absence of 'as if' connections is particularly apparent with psychoses that make extensive use of projective mechanisms.

At this point it is probably relevant to describe how I work. My perspective in this chapter is psychoanalytic. I particularly work from an object relations viewpoint, drawing on the ideas of Winnicott, Fairbairn and Klein. I am working from the assumption that the first few years of infancy are crucial for all later psychological development and that the psyche contains throughout life a conflict between regression and progression, resistance and change. These processes will manifest in later life. In therapy they dominate the transference. The analysis of the transference and the therapist's counter-transference are seen as the fulcrum on which the therapy turns, and are thus central to the therapeutic transaction. What I find useful in Kleinian theory is the description of certain primitive mechanisms of defence. What follows is consistent with the Kleinian view of projective identification.

Projective identification was first described by Klein in 1946. Since that time it has been developed and expanded by various writers to the extent that it now provides a rich source of ideas and understanding of what transpires between mother and child, therapists and patients. Therapists differ in the weight and importance they give to this mechanism; it is fair to say that projective identification has found validity outside the Kleinian school by some post-Freudians and post-Jungians.

Projective identification is considered a frequent defence amongst infants; it is also used by regressed adults. When something feels intolerable it must be dealt with in order to reduce the sensations of discomfort and anxiety. One method is to try to get rid of the feeling. What is projected is a distressing inner experience, a fantasy or feeling that for some reason the individual needs to expel from his or her interior world. This may be done either for purely expulsive reasons to achieve riddance, or as a primitive form of communication, whereby it is hoped that the recipient of the projected feeling may use it to understand the projector's experience. It is important to note that what is projected is not always something bad. Frequently good parts of the self may be split off and projected into another to protect the positive aspects from being destroyed by the harmful bad feelings/fantasies. This is often found in situations where the patient feels despair yet somehow the therapist remains hopeful of ultimate success.

As a short-term measure such defensive manoeuvres enable the psyche to discharge contents that are too painful to contain. As a long-term consequence such splitting and projections result in inner impoverishment. The psyche becomes split and the individual is unable to function as a whole. What is of particular importance as far as the subject of this chapter is concerned is that, once the psychical contents have been expelled into the external world such as a parent, therapist or a painting, the projected elements are no longer experienced as part of the self; they become ego-alien. The therapeutic task is to facilitate the individual to be able to take back or withdraw the projections from the external world. Whether via a painting or a therapist, the projected contents need to be returned from their container to the projector in a manner that makes the experience more digestible. When projective identification is involved this is done by the recipient (container, e.g. painting or therapist) of the unwanted feelings being able to detoxify the original projection of its distressing component and enabling the patient to introject, take back in, what was previously felt to be too intolerable to keep inside. The painting process is clearly a particularly effective medium to be utilised by projective mechanisms. Painting both promotes projection of psychic contents and provides a container (literally the edge of the paper) for projections, thus beginning to organise psychic toxins that cause anxiety and distress. Even so, art psychotherapy has been slow to introduce the ideas about projective identification into the understanding of the picture-making process. Weir (1987) makes a few passing references but does not develop discussion on this particular mechanism. Some years ago (Mann, 1989) I published an article outlining how projective identification may be thought about in the picture-making process. Though I had been working with these ideas for several years I was stimulated to write as a response to an article by Schaverien (1987) who, it seemed to me, had lucidly described how projective identification works in art therapy but used different terms to describe it, which I thought muddled the discussion and reinvented the wheel when there was already a large and rich body of literature that might usefully inform art psychotherapists. In a later work Schaverien (1991) acknowledges the similarity between projective identification and her theory of the talisman, though she maintains that there is a difference in that projective identification cannot fully account for the investment the patient makes in the painting. I am not convinced by this distinction, as patients and infants who use projective identification to split intolerable psychic contents remain passionately attached, either in love or hate, to the containers of the projections: the projections are still part of the self whether split or not, and as such will always bind the projector into a passionate relationship to the recipient container. This remains true whether the container is a mother, a therapist, an abstract idea (such as a nation or race), and is true also for a painted image. However, the reader has to make up his or her own mind in this debate. Since my article in 1989, a number of other art psychotherapists have sought to demonstrate how projective identification operates in the painting process (Case 1994; Greenwood 1994). It is clearly a useful framework offering a rich area for art psychotherapists to explore.

When distressing elements in the psyche are split off and projected out they are then experienced in a paranoid manner. Rather than being perceived as part of the self, they are felt as external danger. The paranoid psychotic thus considers that he or she is a victim in a dangerous world. What originates as a psychological danger is experienced as external danger that possesses very concrete characteristics.

The patient I wish to describe had a perverse as well as a psychotic state of mind. Before describing our work in detail, something needs to be said about perversions. To the best of my knowledge, perverse states of mind have not been discussed in art psychotherapy. This is in contrast to an extensive literature in psychoanalysis dealing with the subject. In common with the prevalent views within psychoanalysis, I am defining perversion as a state of mind rather than a form of sexual behaviour. It has been frequently noted by Stoller, McDougall and others that many, if not most, of the activities in perversion may also form a part of a 'normal' loving relationship. What makes the perversions distinct is the psychic structure.

Within psychoanalysis, various descriptions are applied to define a perversion. Stoller (1975: xiv) defines it thus: 'Perversion is a fantasy put into action – a defensive structure raised gradually over the years in order to preserve erotic pleasure.' It is both habitual and repetitive in nature. McDougall (1978) also emphasises this last point, the lack of freedom and rigidity of the perverse scenario. Another line of thinking is developed by Khan (1979: 9) who describes how 'the pervert puts an *impersonal object* between his desire and his accomplice: this *object* can be a stereotype fantasy, a gadget or a pornographic image. All three alienate the pervert from himself, as, alas, from the object of his desire'. Bach (1994) also highlights that perversions are inconsistent with whole object love; the ambiguity of relationships cannot be tolerated and people are treated as things.

The following material illustrates some of these issues. Working with perversions generally poses extreme difficulties for any clinician. The transference is invariably affected by the state of mind: transference perversions tend to produce countertransference perversions. (A more comprehensive discussion of transference perversion is to be found in my book, *Psychotherapy: an Erotic Relationship. Transference and Countertransference Passions* (Mann 1997).) My illustration in this communication serves primarily as a way of beginning to think about working with perversions in art psychotherapy. The therapeutic success, as will be obvious in this instance, was negligible. However, often the best lessons are learned from unsuccessful experiences.

I spent some time working on an acute admissions ward in a psychiatric unit. The doors were permanently locked though there was access to the outside via a lift, and some patients took full advantage of this exit. The main treatments were chemical but there was also a fully integrated occupational therapy programme. Art psychotherapy was part of that facility. There was no art room on the ward, so I used a communal day room in which I turned off the radio and shut the door. All ward patients were free to join the group. Usually while the art psychotherapy was in progress non-participating ward patients tended to respect the boundary, which would only occasionally be breached.

Edward was 27 when I worked with him. He had been admitted to the acute admission ward with a paranoid psychosis. He had had several other admissions since his adolescence. His childhood had been in a stormy household with both parents resorting to violence against each other but not towards him. He was brought up by his father after his mother left home when he was about 5; he maintained contact with his mother, which he described as infrequent but exciting as she would take him on trips and visits his father could not afford. Edward described his mother as being very attractive and seductive; promising much but delivering little. Father, on the other hand, was more bland but stable. He took care of all Edward's physical needs but could not provide other supports for his son. Edward described him as a 'dope freak', living in the past of his heyday in the 1960s; he spent all his spare money on cannabis and had been 'stoned' for most of Edward's 27 years of life.

His first sexual experience was at 10 years of age, when he was seduced by the woman next door. At the time he enjoyed it and was grateful to be initiated into sexual pleasures; however, he has since come to regard it as a source of difficulties in his relationships with women. Since that time he has had a succession of brief relationships with women. I gathered they tended to be short-lived as the women grew tired or exasperated by his sexual demands. I do not believe he gave me the full details of his sexual activities, though they featured bondage and anal intercourse; there were also indications that he used violence. Some of the childhood history may be seen in his sexual practices: the violence between parents was re-enacted with his partners; bonding the women reversed his experience of his mother's leaving and represented his wish to tie her up to keep her from going; his sadism was perhaps an attempt to be the master of the sexual encounter after feeling powerless at his mother's and neighbour's seductiveness.

My first encounter with Edward was rather brief but dramatic. I was running my regular art psychotherapy group on the acute admissions ward. Edward arrived halfway through, talking loudly to nobody in particular. He stood at the table and squirted a blob of white paint from a bottle; it looked like semen. He said with a non-humorous laugh, 'I'm giving the table a good time!' A couple of the other group members seemed to think this was quite funny and laughed. He then left. I was inwardly quite angry and felt abused by this intrusion; I also felt intrigued to find out a bit more about him. When I later found out about his sexual behaviour I considered my feeling of being abused to be a similar reaction to that of the women he incorporated into his sadistic enactments. Ward staff told me about his appeal to the women patients, though he was not close to anybody in particular. He had periods of violence and at other times had visual hallucinations; he could be sexually disinhibited, masturbating in public and shouting, perhaps to a hallucination, 'I'm fucking you'.

On the next few occasions I worked with Edward he did not want to paint but told me the bulk of the history outlined above. He would arrive late, speak very little, pay only a mild interest in the paintings made by others and eventually leave. The tone of words had a touch of contempt towards both himself and the listener. He never developed a therapeutic alliance or anything that could be called a reciprocal relationship. I was treated no differently from anybody else insofar as everyone was treated the same; it was as though there was no difference between individuals. Rather than being in a relationship, my countertransference feeling was more of being a spectator to his exhibitionist pronouncements. Although he had a certain charm it was also very difficult to like him. Again, I suspect this to be a typical reaction felt by the women he abused but probably also has origins in his own abuse at 10 and being reduced to a bystander when his mother left when he was 5 and at watching the marital violence before that age.

After this he brought a painting to show me what he had recently done in his dormitory. The picture was of a naked female torso, crudely drawn and distorted: the top consisted of two inordinately large breasts; in the lower half, instead of a vagina and pubis, he had painted buttocks. He told me he had 'fucked this tart' and explained that he had masturbated while painting and mixed the semen into the paint that covered the woman's backside. He then left and I heard him in the corridor making a lewd remark to a female nurse. I could not hear her reply. I was left to analyse my countertransference. As on the first occasion, I was aware of feeling intrigued and abused, but this time there was more. I was left feeling totally impotent by what I felt was a performance designed to shock. His painting had not been done during an art psychotherapy session but between sessions, thus maintaining a relationship with the therapy outside contact time, but which is then distorted and perversely twisted into something sadomasochistic. My feeling of castration was very aptly mirrored by his painting: the procreative sexual organ was removed and replaced with an excretory sphincter. Both the painting and the therapist had been used for massive projective identification. Edward evacuated his feelings of abuse and impotence into the picture and myself, and having safely split off these feelings he left feeling unburdened and humorous. The painting and therapist were thus used identically as though we were one and the same thing, no difference between pigment and myself. In my opinion this represented another instance of his perverse state of mind, which was intended to reduce all objects and people to things with no intrinsic value.

He did not attend the following week. His mother had visited and he had a relapse after she went, perhaps reawakening his feeling of her departure when he was 5 years old. When I next saw him he was very withdrawn. He sat quietly and painted in monochrome. He explained that he had painted a 'stacked hi-fi system'. It looked for all the world like a piece of brown excrement. I told him so. He said he felt like a 'piece of shit' and wanted to 'fuck some bird's arse'. I said he felt like an anal-baby wanting to get back inside his mother. This seemed momentarily to help to clear his thoughts. He said: 'Dad smokes shit, that's what they call dope, mum made us both feel like shit when she left.' He then became confused again. During this session I felt that his communication resembled somethings we might call a more human relationship. It is hard to tell where the change originated. Over all I am sure his mother's visit had left him depressed and less manically exhibitionistic. However, I also wondered if the relatively safe containment of his projective identifications from the previous session (safe in that neither I nor the painting retaliated or rejected him) enabled him to feel that a less perverse relationship with others was possible. In terms of his artwork we can see how difficult it was for him to maintain this contact. A hi-fi system is for music, arguably the most powerful of the art forms for uniting separate individuals in a common rhythm and harmony, to be 'in tune' with each other. Yet Edward's attempt to unite rather than merely have all distinctions obliterated was painfully depicted in his music-making machine, which was more faecal than rhythmic.

He never attended any further art psychotherapy sessions. I saw him around the hospital for a few more weeks. He seemed to become less disturbed and was eventually discharged back to his father's house. It would be colluding with his omnipotent fantasies to think that art psychotherapy affected this change. It was widely considered, probably rightly, that he had been stabilised by his medication, but this would not have changed his perverse fantasies. However, by way of illustrating the difficulty of working with perversions, another hypothesis might be formed: by the law of talion (Racker 1968) the perverse transference would provoke a perverse counter-transference. We might that say the therapeutic potency is perceived to be castrated as an aspect of the denial of the paternal penis, the law of difference.

There is clearly a good deal that can be said about this material. In a previous article (Mann 1994) I discussed the significance of sexual fantasies on the therapeutic process. A more in-depth study of the erotic transference and countertransference will be found in my book (Mann 1997). For now I shall focus on just a few pertinent aspects. It would seem, taking his sexual behaviour as a whole, that he made little distinction between ejaculating when masturbating or with a partner. Either way he was concerned only with his own satisfaction and fulfilment of his fantasy. Coen (1981: 94) writing about sexualisation as a defence, points out:

> Masturbation may enhance illusions of omnipotent ability for magical manipulation. The masturbator's magical manipulation of his own genitals transforms them from a limp, dormant state into an excited, alive, erect, gravity defying one, all under his own control and direction. The image of the genials coming to life may serve as reassurance that the dead, fragmented self or inert or dead maternal imago can be resurrected. For the more disturbed patient, such masturbatory experiences may serve to validate the illusion that the representational world can be omnipotently and pleasurably manipulated and controlled.

In this repect we can see that Edward's masturbatory activities with the table and the picture represented an omnipotent attempt to blur the distinction between his fantasies and external reality; that the latter was subordinated to the former.

His sexual world was an anal-world. In an anal-world everything is ground and mashed up, individual identity is obliterated, all constituent parts reduced to a faecal mess. Chasseguet-Smirgel (1984) has defined this world as an 'anal universe' concerned with the disavowal of difference, and ultimately concerned with the denial of the father's penis and its representations as paternal law. In his psychosis with the absence of 'as if' thinking, to spill white paint on the table *was* the same as masturbating or having sex with a woman (or table), the paint *was* semen. Later, when he masturbated onto his picture there was no line of distinction between painting a woman's buttocks and masturbating over them or actually having anal sex. The distinctions were blurred and had become one and the same. We might say that the concrete, external reality of the painting was erased by the extensive use of projective identification whereby the painting was a continuation of his psychic fantasy.

There are a number of implications for art psychotherapy I would now like to draw out from this vignette. Firstly, the act of painting can be incorporated into the psychotic processes and form part of the delusional system. The painting becomes part of the madness. The painting ceased to be a separate object in the external world, and appeared to be fully incorporated into Edward's perverse and psychotic fantasy system. The painting did not help him to think of himself and others as different; rather it confirmed his omnipotent fantasy that others are just under his control and were extensions of himself and his desires. There was no separateness, only a faecal mess. Sometimes the faecal mess was his, sometimes it belonged to others (mother made him 'feel like shit'): anal zones could thus be interchangeable; the anus and vagina were also interchangeable. In his fantasy he had 'fucked a tart'; a 'tart' being both a derogatory sexual term for a woman and also a kind of sweet food to be incorporated into the digestive system and reduced to faeces.

This raises a number of difficulties for art psychotherapists. The messiness of paint lends itself very easily to a paint/excrement confusion. At the risk of making a sweeping statement we might say that painting largely deals with various kinds of symbols. The thing painted is not the thing in itself, which is so beautifully illustrated in Magritte's painting of a pipe with the words written below, 'This is not a pipe!' Whatever the subject of a painting such as an object (person, vase of flowers, etc.) or feeling, the painting is never the object or the feeling, but an expression of the object or feeling: there are no 'angry paintings' only paintings made in anger or evoking anger. The attributions of the pigment are those of the artist or the spectator. The pigment or the painting is the vehicle for expression. The painting of a pipe is not the pipe any more than a painting of a woman's buttocks are the woman's buttocks. However, this symbolic quality, the 'as if' nature, can be lost with some forms of psychosis.

Most psychotherapeutic procedures, including art psychotherapy, ultimately rest on difference and distinction. For example, an awareness without anxiety of the separateness of another's thoughts; or the distinction through dissolving the transference that the individual is not relating to his or her mother while talking to the therapist. This distinction can prove intolerable to some psychotics. I think this is possibly why psychotherapy and art psychotherapy may often be ineffective with some psychotics. By ineffective I mean something quite specific here, referring to therapeutic procedures and the therapeutic alliance not leading to significant restructuring of psychic processes and enabling the individual to progress beyond his or her infantile defences, ultimately reducing the transference and the repetition compulsions from interfering in everyday life.

We may come to understand Edward's experience of art psychotherapy as follows. Both the painting process and the therapist were incorporated into an anal-sadistic maternal transference. This maternal transference was an anal-universe where there are no distinctions. The sadistic mastery in the transference to women/art/therapist was an attempt to replay and counteract his original feelings of powerlessness and helpless impotence at his mother's seductiveness and departure. His experience of a drugged, ineffectual father not only contributed to the absence of the paternal transference but also the father's passivity meant that there was nothing to mitigate the maternal power which dominated unopposed. With the massive use of projective identification, Edward expelled his intolerable psychic world into the artwork which was then experienced as a concrete participant under the control of his perverse fantasies.

The use of art psychotherapy in such a perverse way brings painting close to a fetish. Stoller (1979: 7–8) defines a fetish thus:

We might best begin by calling it *dehumanization*; the fetish stands for the human (not just, as is sometimes said, for a missing penis). A sexually exciting fetish, we know, may be an inanimate object, a living but not human object, a part of a human body (in rare cases even one's own), an attribute of a human, or even a whole human not perceived as himself or herself but rather as an abstraction. . . .

To fetishize, one must also deal with the excremental. The anatomic closeness of the reproductive and excretory systems, the overlapping of intense sensations between the two, and the tension between dirtiness and cleanliness created by toilet training erotize urination and defecation and give erotics an excremental cast. . . .

The creation of a fetish, then, is made up of several processes (fantasies). (1) A person who has harmed one is to be punished with a similar trauma. (2) The object is stripped of its humanity. (3) A nonhuman object (inanimate, animal, or part-aspect of a human like a breast or penis) is endowed with the humanness stolen from the person on whom one is revenged. In this way the human is dehumanized and the nonhuman humanized. (4) The fetish is chosen because it has some quality that resembles the loved, needed, traumatizing object.

If what I have said so far about the use of a painting in a perverse psychotic state of mind is viable, it is easy to see how a picture may become a fully-fledged fetish, a vehicle for vicarious sexual pleasures. I think, though, that in the case of Edward his painting had not totally become a fetish, if only because he incorporated painting in an incidental manner into his perverse fantasies. That is to say, painting had momentarily been utilised by his perverse fantasies because it happened to be available on the ward. I doubt whether painting would have found its way into his perverse world or been incorporated as part of his habitual fantasy system, which is so characteristic in perversions. However, further research into art psychotherapy with people with perversions may indeed throw more light on how a painting can be transformed into a fetish.

By way of conclusion, I wish to make a distinction between the perverse psychotic use of masturbation in art compared with non-psychotic, though undoubtedly neurotic applications of masturbation in fine art. Two artists in particular seemed to be most interested in exploring the relationship between masturbation and art, Egon Schiele and Salvador Dali. In 1911 Schiele painted himself in *Self Portrait Masturbating* (Whitford 1993); Dali made at least two famous images of other people masturbating, *The Great Masturbator* (1929) and *William Tell and Gradiva* (1931) (South Bank Centre 1994). With neither artist was the object painted confused with the object itself. Both artists are examples of the fact that no simple equation can be made between masturbation and painting or masturbation and perversion. The distinguishing feature is not behaviour but the intent, the content of the fantasy. It seems to me that both Schiele and Dali, while representing masturbation, are not experiencing their brush as a penis, the paint as semen and the act of painting as sexual intercourse (or even if they were it was not the only or even the most important consideration). Dali's painting of William Tell is particularly telling in this respect: Tell is masturbating into Gradiva's armpit. Though her arm is treated as a fetishistic object in the subject of the painting, the painting itself is not a fetish. The 'as if' quality is not lost between what the painter is depicting and how it is depicted. It goes without saying that both artists have introduced their own psychology into their artwork: why else would the usually private activity of masturbation be placed into the public domain of art except for some neurotic, exhibitionist motivation? However, the sexual activity is utilised by the demands of artistic representation (the 'as if' quality of art) and not vice versa. There is not the blurring of psyche and reality as it is encountered in psychosis.

REFERENCES

Bach, S. (1994) *The Language of Perversion and the Language of Love*, London: Jason Aronson.

Case, C. (1994) 'Art therapy in analysis: advance /retreat in the belly of the spider', London: *Inscape* 1(1): 3–10.

Chasseguet-Smirgel, J. (1984): *Creativity and Perversions*, London: Free Association Books.

Coen, S.J. (1981) Sexualization as a predominant mode of defense, in *Journal of the American Psychoanalytic Association*, 29: 893–920.

Greenwood, H. (1994) Cracked pots: art therapy and psychosis, in *Inscape* 1(1): 11–14.

Khan, M.M.R. (1979) *Alienation in Perversions*, London: Maresfield Library.

Levens, M. (1989) 'Working with defence mechanisms in art therapy' in A. Gilroy and T. Dalley (eds) *Pictures at an Exhibition*, London: Routledge.

Mann, D. (1989) 'The talisman or projective identification? A critique', London: *Inscape* (Autumn): 11–15.

—— (1990) 'Art as a defence mechanism against creativity', in *British Journal of Psychotherapy* 7(1): 5–14.

—— (1991) 'Some schizoid processes in art psychotherapy', London: *Inscape* (Summer): 12–17.

—— (1994) 'The psychotherapist's erotic subjectivity' *British Journal of Psychotherapy* 10(3): 344–54.

—— (1997) *Psychotherapy: An Erotic Relationship. Transference and Countertransference Passions*, London: Routledge.

McDougall, J. (1978) *Plea for a Measure of Abnormality*, London: Free Association Books.

Racker, H. (1968) *Transference and Countertransference*, London: Maresfield Library.

Schaverien, J. (1987) 'The scapegoat and the talisman: transference in art therapy', in T. Dalley *et al.* (eds) *Images of Art Therapy*, London: Tavistock.

—— (1991) *The Revealing Image: Analytical Art Psychotherapy in Theory and Practice*, London: Routledge.

South Bank Centre (1994) *Salvador Dali: The Early Years*, Exhibition catalogue.

Stoller, R. (1975) *Perversion: The Erotic Form of Hatred*, London: Karnac.

—— (1979) *Sexual Excitment: The Dynamics of Erotic Life*, London: Maresfield Library.

Weir, F. (1987) 'The role of symbolic expression in its relation to art therapy: a Kleinian approach', in T. Dalley *et al.* (eds) *Images of Art Therapy*, London: Tavistock.

Whitford, F. (1993) *Egon Schiele*, Thames & Hudson.

Chapter 5

Four views of the image

Fiona Seth-Smith

In this chapter I shall present some ideas about different ways of viewing and understanding an image in art therapy. Within the context of specialist approaches developed in relation to work with patients who are psychotic, I hope to present an additional paradigm through which an image may be seen. I have selected from a multiplicity of perspectives four ways of understanding and looking at an image, which I have found pertinent to working as an art therapist with chronically psychotic patients and also useful in relation to work with psychotic processes within other patients. I shall briefly present some aspects of Lacanian and Kleinian theories of developmental levels, and explore the sense in which these levels may be encapsulated, developed and integrated through the art therapy process.

The word 'image' refers here to a multiplicity of things, from a scrap of paper to a carefully developed canvas or a piece of crudely moulded clay. In my experience of working with images in this context, I have been presented with a myriad of different phenomena; these have created a need for concepts which could enable me to assimilate and to develop different approaches to work which presents so many challenges. At best, concepts are tools which enable therapists to develop new understandings while learning to trust and to build on their own perceptions. In work with people who are 'psychotic', whatever the obvious manifestations or unforeseen consequences of this, it becomes important to hold in mind understandings, which remain hypotheses during the course of long and ambiguous therapeutic processes, without imposing premature interpretations on the patient or the therapeutic relationship.

I shall use the word 'patient' to describe those who were being treated in psychiatric hospital while I worked with them, even if the word 'client' later became more applicable when some of them subsequently attended art therapy as out-patients. I have tried in this chapter to describe, first theoretically and then using two case studies, some of the ways different understandings of the image can interact and serve to illuminate what remains – like much in human psychology and creativity – obscure and mysterious.

CONTEXT

The experience of working single handedly as an art therapist in a busy psychiatric admissions unit in London has led me to the ideas which I present in this chapter. My work was influenced by my experiences at Hill End Hospital, St Albans. Hill End had acres of gardens and an art therapy department whose doors opened onto orchards (later described by Goldsmith in Case and Dalley 1992: 40–6). In line with the model of treatment developed by Katherine Killick when she ran the department (Killick 1993: 25), patients were carefully timetabled so that they had access to their own designated space during the course of their treatment. Subsequently I worked in Australia, at Hillcrest Hospital in Adelaide where I had to carry my materials around from building to building and to set up groups in unpropitious circumstances. In this context I gained a renewed insight into the capacity the *image* has to contain and to communicate aspects of the patient, to the patient and to the therapist, *regardless* of the context in which it is made and viewed. I do not argue here against the necessity for an art therapy department, but I have subsequently found myself rethinking and re-examining the place and the life of the image, in and of itself.

The psychiatric admissions unit in which I presently work includes three wards of in-patients and a 'day hospital' where I am based. Most of the people who are admitted as in-patients are acutely disturbed; a large percentage are admitted under sections of the 1983 Mental Health Act including sections 36–42, which are applied to people who have come through, or are being assessed prior to, sentencing in a magistrates' or crown court. Many are traumatised and many are unwilling to be treated. A chronic shortage of beds means that only the most seriously and visibly 'ill' in the surrounding community are admitted. Many of the people who become patients have profound social problems. They may also be born into patterns of relationships and environments which promulgate dysfunctional relationships and behaviours. These can both contribute to the onset of major psychoses and sometimes confound their treatment. I do not wish, however, to understate the healthiness of the multicultural atmosphere in this unit, which results from the diverse ethnic composition of both the staff and patient groups. There are high proportions of Afro-Caribbean, African and Asian patients, whose numbers are, as in other psychiatric settings in Britain, over-represented in comparison to their proportions within the community. This environment has improved under the auspices of a radical manager, but the wards remain understaffed, stuffy places, where visible, and sometimes violent disturbances are still enacted in claustrophobic corridors and lino clad 'seclusion rooms'. Before I worked there, I was inspired by ideas taken from well-known anti-psychiatric theorists such as Laing (1959) and Goffman (1968). Because of my role in the places in which I had previously worked, I could divest myself of responsibility for certain issues which affected patients, such as involuntary detention and the necessity (or otherwise) for the enforced administration of psychotropic medication. In these crowded conditions, I developed more questions than answers. The ideas in this paper were inspired by this work; for despite its difficulties, and perhaps, because of them, I found that there is great scope and energy for creativity within the overt chaos; for some art therapy here has proved to be a particularly helpful and rewarding form of treatment.

There are many individual patients who have high levels of energy, particularly creative energy, who may also become extremely distressed. Some become silent. When working in a busy hospital, questions of medication, and symptom control usually override all others in the rush to empty beds. Thus patients are pushed to develop 'insight' on a fast track. This pressure means that as a therapist working with several different consultant teams at once, I need to be flexible and to keep my ears and eyes wide open, in the struggle to keep in touch with the thinking about those who become my clients. My colleagues include nursing staff, consultant psychiatrists and junior doctors, occupational therapists, social workers, managers, and occasionally physiotherapists who provide spaces for patients to 'work out' their rage. Psychologists focus their work on cognitive behavioural treatment for non-psychotic out-patients, while psychoanalysts and family therapists are based on other sites, and have, until recently, been infrequently referred to. This has placed art therapy in the odd but unfortunately not exceptional position of being virtually the only psychodynamic treatment available on site. Within this framework an art room in the day hospital is designated solely for the use of art therapy. There is, necessarily, a continuous effort on my part, and by the other therapists, to foster and present its psychological and physical boundaries within the institution as being both flexible and meaningful. This work of presentation, combined with the actuality of the space itself, creates the boundaries which lend the room its dynamic possibilities.

The art room is large, light and purpose built, with working surfaces, cupboards, a kettle, various plants, a radio which is turned on by clients with the agreement of others, and a kiln. Within separate cupboards there are folders of the artwork of out-patients and patients from particular wards. These folders are confidential, and individuals may write their names on the outside of their folders if they wish to. There are also several sets of shelves storing objects made in clay and plasticine. In other more ideal environments, as described in the *Handbook of Art Therapy* (Case and Dalley 1992), continuity of individual space can be maintained on a concrete level. This is impossible in such a setting, with large numbers of users and high rates of admission and discharge. A space for an individual is maintained only in certain groups at fixed points in the week. Therefore, much of the sense of continuity and of therapeutic process is sustained within the pictures themselves, and in the development of a particular relationship a patient has with a therapist.

THE QUESTION OF THE PICTURE

In the light of this ideal of continuity and reliability, one phenomenon which recurs both in my own department and in those of colleagues is that of a patient who asks: 'Where is my picture ... you know, the one I did last time?' In some cases 'last time' may have been 2 to 20 years before, and in another hospital. This is a commonplace occurrence, and yet it seems remarkable when people whose minds and lives have been through processes of upheaval, reversal and often radical transformation are able to invest in a picture in such a way. This phenomenon, combined with the reactions of delight, surprise or occasionally distaste that occur when clients discover their work *has* been stored, have led me to pose the question of: What it is *that is there* for the patient? In this chapter, I hope to offer some new thoughts.

Schaverien, who set out a series of important paradigms and insights in her book *The Revealing Image*, has written of the life *of* the picture subsequent to its creation.

> The effects of the picture are spatial and temporal, actual and imaginal. Its existence may continue for the duration of the therapeutic relationship and even long after termination. The picture as a physical object, can be seen and touched, it can be moved and things can be done to it. The actual and imaginal effects of the picture relate to the subject matter. The patterns, marks and figurations which are real, evoke imaginal associations in relation to them. These are all elements which contribute to the life of the picture.
>
> (Schaverien 1991: 103)

Schaverien describes five 'stages' in the life of the picture; these, as she states, are phases described in a linear form which may be far from linear in practice. They describe, however, phenomena in therapeutic work which I witness repeatedly. The first of these, which she calls 'identification', describes the beginning of movement from both conscious and unconscious undifferentiation and identification with the image, towards differentiation and the beginnings of an understanding of the 'meaning of elements' within an image. The picture may bypass the resistance aroused by verbal interpretations 'because it reveals, it shows, but it does not *fix* meaning' (Schaverien 1991: 105). This stage may often be non-verbal, but at its boundaries are words which carry the potential for separation from the undifferentiated state. She then describes the next stage of 'familiarisation', in which the picture begins to be seen from the outside and the artist/patient begins to understand the '*immanent articulation*' of the picture. This is followed by stages of 'acknowledgement', 'assimilation' and eventual 'disposal', when, in working towards discharge, the patient and therapist decide together on the fate of the images. It is on the initial stages of identification and familiarisation – in which the patient can begin to view and to think about an image and acknowledge some of the meaning it may hold – that I wish to focus here.

These processes begin, but are always encumbered by the limitations of a setting such as the one I have described. However, a more crucial difference is rendered by psychotic processes, by their effects on the patients' relationship with their images and their effects on the transference. 'Psychotic' processes, as described below, may detract from the level of conscious value a picture may have for a patient, but in other ways, may add to its therapeutic potency. This potency exists not just because of the 'immanent articulation' of a picture, but also because of its concrete properties as a real object created within the space shared between the therapist and the client. Having made an image or a series of images and begun to experience the beginnings of differentiation from and identification with the image, the patient is often ready to be discharged from the hospital. Only if a patient is able and willing to return as an out-patient to the art therapy department (which is often the case) can further working through take place. If much remains unresolved, some previous patients may request, months or even years later, that they be re-referred to the department. I seek here to elaborate on ideas about the image during these initial phases, about what it means to the patient, and how it continues to 'work' (for want of a less mechanical word) within and beyond the therapeutic relationship.

In the work of a predominantly neurotic person, a figurative or non-figurative image can be understood as a form in which conscious and unconscious memories and elements of the personality coalesce into forms which can be revealed to have some intrinsic 'sense' to the individual, to their sense of their own history, and their sense of identity. Much, although not all, of this 'meaning' may eventually be realised in the individual's conscious mind. It is arguable that all images incorporate pre-verbal elements of memory and infantile elements of the mind. For the psychotic person or in a psychotic part of the mind, we can think of there being 'elements' which have been left stranded by the failure to symbolise. The primary mode of symbolic communication within human cultures is, of course, language. A failure of the symbolic process – that is to say, a difficulty with abstracting from the concreteness of perception and thereby integrating and learning from experience – renders the parts of the personality and of experience that have not been integrated and translated into symbolic experience 'meaningless' in the sense that they cannot be expressed and conveyed to others using language. Nevertheless, these elements are present within the form and structure of an individual's images.

In my observation, art made within the context of an art therapy session, and therefore of a relationship with a therapist, can enable a patient to tolerate the expression of *several* elements, which may on one level be related to developmental layers within the mind and personality. If this is so, these elements may perhaps be manifest as *presences* within the image in its form, its content and its atmosphere. I would like to propose four views or ways of thinking about an image, which have enabled me to discern some of these different presences – and their relationships with one another. These four views relate, broadly and simplistically speaking, to two different developmental levels within the personality: those of the 'symbolic', which is necessarily related to the social realm, and those of the pre-symbolic, where experience and thinking are largely 'concrete', that is to say, they are not translated into or mediated through symbolic forms, but relate to the immediate physical environment and to a patient's body.

The purpose of looking at pictures from a variety of viewpoints is not to enable the therapist to produce sophisticated verbal interpretations, but is rather an attempt to provide conceptual tools which can enable a therapist to think more clearly about what may be taking place for the individual *and* the therapist within their relationship to an image. In this regard I often think of Winnicott, who, towards the end of his career, stressed that 'clever and apt interpretations' were of limited use, 'by and large it [psychotherapy] is a long term giving the patient back what the patient brings. It is a complex derivative of the face that reflects what there is to be seen' (Winnicott 1971: 137). He emphasised the importance of the *quality* of the therapeutic relationship and of the understandings of the patient which a therapist can hold in mind.

THE TWO LEVELS

The notion of different layers or levels of representation co-existing within language has been described by Jacques Lacan, who delineated two different levels within an utterance. I have applied his concept to the image although the enterprise is speculative, given the intrinsic differences between the image and the word. Lacan used the term 'signifier' to denote ordinary language as it is spoken and heard, and the term 'signified' to denote what lies within a linguistic utterance in the form of a 'shadow'. The 'shadow' or signified describes an imprint on the child's ego of events which the child or infant *sees but cannot understand.* For example one parent being violent to another, or a depressed mother's blank face as she fails to respond to her baby's attempts to communicate. Lacan claimed that traces of these pre-verbal experiences are present within the pattern of a patient's discourse. The shadow in this formulation is an imprint on the personality left by forgotten events, which contributes to the shape and the form as well as to the content of a person's speech. Lacan states that 'the signifier and signified are two distinct orders, separated by a line which is resistant to signification: two parallel flows connected by slender dotted lines' (Lacan quoted in Lemaire 1977: 40). Here Lacan creates a visual image of language in which two strands or parallel flows are present within the same form but are conceptually separable from one another. Insight and change are created through the formation of what is described as a 'passage' from signifier to signified (as in the original Freudian thesis); but he stresses that any passage or transformation *cannot be effected by a simple process of translation*, term by term. The two levels are not equivalent to one another in the same way that no two languages comprise words with exactly equivalent meanings.

When attempting, in a move away from linguistics, to apply a similar notion to an image, we encounter a different set of possibilities. The difficulty or resistance to translation from one level to another described by Lacan, is reminiscent of the difficulty I and a patient may have in 'making sense' of his or her images and in seeing what might or might not be there. Images may 'embody', using Schaverien's term (Schaverien 1991: 79–102), layers of condensed meaning and/or information, but these layers have their own form and structure which, like musical forms, can be spoken about but can never, by their nature, be translatable into a linguistic code.

There are an almost infinite set of ways of seeing an image, many of which involve our own projections and our own senses of aesthetic pleasure, whatever the origin of such pleasures may be. Henzell describes the epistemological divisions between images, as 'non-discursive' symbolic forms, and language, which is deciphered by means of a 'code' and is 'strung out in a definite temporal order' (Henzell 1995: 193). He describes the image as being a more 'particular' representation than a sentence, which can refer to categories and entities beyond what it immediately symbolises. Images are more opaque, having a 'determined and obdurate surface' (Henzell 1994: 194). Images are objects in and of themselves, they exemplify labels while labels (words) predicate things. Language is symbolic and therefore abstract, while artworks occupy real space: they are 'concrete' as well as having the potential within their forms to contain symbolic representations and to function in Maclagans' words as 'maps' [which] create the 'territory' (Maclagan 1995: 218). Lacan states that:

> Language is . . . the precondition for the act of becoming aware of oneself as a distinct entity. It is also the means by which the individual keeps his distance and autonomy from the world of real things which he posits 'in themselves' as being different from the concepts which convey their meaning, and different from the words or symbols which actualise concepts in the social relation of communication.
>
> (Lacan, quoted in Lemaire 1977: 54)

If we follow this line of reasoning it is clear that pictures and objects are less differentiated from the experience of 'real things' than are words. They are closer to but not the same as the 'real world' they might attempt to represent. Searles describes processes of 'desymbolisation' (Searles 1965: 580) which take place in schizophrenic breakdown, in which once-attained meanings and metaphors have been lost and the words which described them have become confusing, 'crazy' thoughts. Images are closer to desymbolised as well as to pre-symbolic modes of expression and therefore, potentially, to psychotic experiences. Images are part of the world of 'real things'; they do not present meanings and experience through an abstract linear code. They can therefore articulate and directly encompass more of the pre-symbolic realms of experience than language can. Before we are able to use words we experience both our internal and external worlds through olfactory, aural and other sensory channels and, in particular, through our vision.

The surface and content of an image is affected by physiological as well as psychological states within its maker. Simon emphasises the artist's bodily relationship with his or her images. She links the quality of the physical gesture to different psychological 'types' – which she relates to different pictorial styles using her extensive knowledge of art and art history. She states: 'I realised that an artist's spontaneous posture and gestures are as much part of his finished work as his ideas and feelings about the subject matter' (Simon 1992: 14). Physical gestures, used to make marks on an image, carry the traces of different states of mind. Some gestures contain the echoes of infantile experience and of 'primitive' or undeveloped and potentially fragmented parts of the self.

In a picture that is composed using raw physical gestures, there may also be elements or parts that seem to act as condensed forms of latent thought. Pictures and objects are 'things' that people may sooner or later tell stories about, however incongruous these narratives may seem. Images can be returned to, they can respond to different viewings by different people. As the artist discovers, they may themselves seem changed under the influence of other moods or in different lights.

Killick (1987: 43) describes the picture as a 'field' within which intra-psychic movement and action can take place: 'This field serves as a medium for the evolution of pre-symbolic structures and relationships . . . it forms an *intermediary between concrete and symbolic functioning*' (my emphasis). She develops this idea in a variety of ways, including a description of the image as part of a process of intrapersonal dialogue in which 'the client engages . . . [in] processes of embodying aspects of the self and enacting relations between them' (Killick 1987: 44).

In a later paper, Killick (1993) draws on the work of Bion, among others, to describe the evolution of the 'function' of symbolisation through the use of art therapy. The psyche can begin to transform raw experience into symbolic forms leading eventually to an increased capacity to integrate insights gleaned from experience within the realm of the symbolic. I have found Bion's (1962) conceptualisation and notation for what he described as the origin of thoughts (including unconscious thoughts) useful in helping me to picture the evolution of thoughts. The notation provides a useful tool for conceiving of psychic 'functions' (Bion 1962) which take place within pre-symbolic experience. He described two different phenomena within the deep unconscious and labelled them 'alpha' and 'beta' elements. The alpha elements are secondary to more primitive beta elements. Alpha elements resemble and may be identical to dream thoughts and dream images. They may yield latent content when interpreted; they derive from the 'processing of sensory data in relation to external reality' (Bleandonu 1994: 167). Beta elements are described as 'things-in-themselves' (Bleandonu 1994: 152). Bion used the analogy of the digestive system to describe Beta elements as undigested facts (as opposed to memories), whereas alpha elements are 'phenomena' which have been 'digested' through the 'alpha function': they have become forms which may be translated into memory. Within the beta level of functioning there is no distinction between inanimate and psychic objects; as Bleandonu (1994) states: 'this is the concrete thinking of psychosis'. The translation of one element or function to another is continuous in the process of normal or neurotic thought and dream formation, while it is impaired in psychotic breakdown or in psychotic parts of the personality. In psychotic breakdown the primitive beta elements and the pre-symbolic alpha elements may be present in some respect or other, within a picture, but not necessarily in a form or state which is translatable into thought, let alone meaning.

UNWANTED PARTS

In the mind of a person who is very psychotic, fragmented and monumental symbolic forms may recur in images and in speech: God, the crucifixion, parental figures, spaceships and, often, unusual preoccupations with aliens. The lurid and beautiful pictures of a young schizophrenic man, for example, depicted distorted representations of body parts, including heads and vaginas. He referred to these by muttering about the parts and about murders (which the therapist translated, in order to make sense of them, in terms of the murderous parts of the self, or the parts of the self that were 'murdered' or dead). But this man cannot tell either himself or others a coherent story about what these images represent. Ehrenzweig (1967: 123) describes such images as 'bizarre images' a term taken from Bion which describes the sense in which 'the psychotic' has lost the 'contact barrier' between his conscious and unconscious phantasy life. Normally this 'barrier' allows for separation between the various elements, as well as contact. Ehrenzweig argues that for both psychotic and non-psychotic personalities creative work involves an initial de-differentiation of psychic elements, but that the psychotic cannot tolerate this transformation of elements into 'more malleable material'; instead he 'compresses and telescopes' (Ehrenzweig 1968: 123) the fragments to form bizarre images which have not undergone the unconscious transformations, such as condensation and repression, necessary for the formation of dreams and of mental images as opposed to hallucinations.

Various symbols recur in my experience of this work; as an example, the recurrent crucifix. These do not always *function* as symbols but seem in themselves, as Killick (1993) has described, to be concrete manifestations of life-threatening solutions to intolerable and often highly ambivalent situations. A young girl suffering from a psychotic breakdown within the context of a deeply disturbed and ambivalent set of family relationships made a series of clay crucifixes. While the crosses embodied her own religious convictions, which flew in the face of her family's beliefs, 'Jesus' looked strikingly similar to a child in nappies. The crucifixion, which has been described as a symbol of the suffering 'at the root of all contradiction and ambivalence' (Cirlot 1962: 73), can be seen, not as a metaphor for a process within the patient's psyche, but as a description of part of the self being sacrificed or destroyed, not necessarily because of family relationships or the environment, but as an outcome of the *interaction* between the patient and his or her environment. The personal meaning of these symbols may not be accessible to the patient and are not the subject of any introspection. Something profound has happened, or continues to happen, that cannot be thought about or reflected upon using traditional psychotherapeutic methods. Psychotherapy and art therapy involve both personal relationships and the use of meaning. In psychosis, or in psychotic parts of the personality, meaning has been circumvented and personal relationships are avoided; it is all there in the images, but it 'does not make sense' to the therapist searching for a meaning. This means, for a patient and potentially for the disheartened therapist, the end of thought which might lead to progression and growth.

For the psychotic patient who creates a symbol, a certain act of bravery – of trust in the surrounding environment – is necessary. For there may be dangers in the process of looking for meaning as understandable within the social domain. As a consequence of too much of this, a patient's psychotic defences may be heightened and 'art therapy' may become, for the client, a form of intrusion, or of pseudo-therapy, in which the patient acts as if he or she is gaining 'insight' from the process but continues to hide his or her psychotic parts. The 'symbolic' artwork becomes a form of defence (and as such, incidentally, it is not without its uses). However, art therapists need to be able to formulate their own ideas about what may be there for the patient in the transference and in the image, in order to *tolerate* joining with the patient in his or her state of meaninglessness. If they are able and allowed by their clients to do so, on both conscious and unconscious symbolic and concrete levels, the image, combined with the therapeutic relationship in the context of a reliable environment, can work as a 'container'[1] for aspects of the person which exist outside the realm of language and of meaning in its linear sense as a finite collection of signs.

Images themselves incorporate shadows. They may have in their forms, or in any metaphors they suggest, some latent content (in the Freudian sense of latent content attached to dream images). But they may also include some non-figurative and undifferentiated areas. Thus different degrees of concreteness, (in which, for example, smeared paint is directly equated with faeces), of abstraction (which may, for example, relate to or evoke some affect in the viewer and/or artist) and of symbolism, may be viewed as being manifest within the same imaginal space. The most 'fragmented' images – that is to say, those with little cohesion or relationship between elements or between the different *levels* of represention (i.e. the concrete, symbolic and the unconscious) – are, in my experience, produced by patients who are in states of chronic psychosis, or by those who are very regressed. In line with this observation, the degree of genuine integration of form, content and mark making within a patient's images may increase during the process of long-term therapeutic work, as can the degree to which the patient is able to tolerate any shared meanings within the therapeutic alliance.

The image has the inherent potential to 'embody' (Schaverien 1991: 79)[2] unwanted (by the ego) parts of the mind. That is to say, it may be invested or identified with these 'parts' as Killick (1987) described, which consist of a mix-up of conscious and unconscious elements. The attempt to divest the ego and to be rid of these parts is manifested in the revulsion expressed by some patients and artists towards their pictures as they attempt to and sometimes succeed in destroying them. One reason for encouraging them to preserve their work is that a sense of overwhelming 'badness' may be mitigated by other factors within the image that emerge and are felt to be present by its maker on other viewings.

To take an example: Ms X had a marked talent for mixing paint and creating stunning colour fields, akin to those of Rothko. She was most productive when she was visibly psychotic, hearing voices which made her laugh, speaking only occasionally, and acting as if she was not only unattached to, but dismissive of external reality. When newly readmitted to hospital under section 3 of the Mental Health Act, she came straight to see me, asked to see her old art folder and searched through her large selection of previous work, telling me that: 'This one can't be mine, who put it here? How horrible. Nor this one; whose is this? . . . Ah, but this one . . . this is beautiful.' To prevent her throwing the awful and 'not mine' pictures away, I identified three folders, one for 'paintings that are not mine', another for 'paintings I want to throw away' and one for 'Ms X's paintings'. Within the ensuing weeks she made several searches through these folders and reselected *others* as being, in her words, 'mine' or 'not mine' and 'bad' or 'really very good'. The views of the image, as I present them, are part of an attempt to understand what was there for her, and is there for others when they go through similar changes in their relationships with their images. In her speech she would suddenly speak to me lucidly and unexpectedly about some fragment of her past, telling me, for example, how angry she was with her son for 'tearing her when he was born', before disappearing back into self-absorption, interrupted only by requests for me to admire her pictures. I needed to develop ways to understand how this distance from others (she was known as a difficult, inaccessible patient on the ward) was bridged mysteri-ously by abstract images, without imposing meaningful understandings on her when she was not ready to tolerate them.

The four views of the image which I use are:

1 That which I have termed 'structural relationships'; that is to say, the formal structure and internal organisation of an image.
2 That of the 'narrative' or, sometimes, story which may be attached to an image or may emerge in relation to it.
3 The view of what are broadly termed 'symbolic forms'; although, as I have suggested, they may, while appearing to be symbols, *function* symbolically to different degrees at different times.
4 'The shadow of the infant'; that is to say, the traces of infantile experience as understood and observed in infant observations and described in some psychoanalytic theories (which vary as to their usefulness within this context). This shadow may be present:

a) in the physical actions which form gestures resulting in an individual style of mark making, and,
b) condensed within the form of fragmented or 'bizarre images'.

There are, of course, a plethora of viewpoints, theoretical frameworks and languages which can be used to describe an image. What is most notably missing here, and becomes increasingly present in longer term therapy, is the view which includes the life and presence of the child the adult once was. However, these are the four which I have found to be of particular relevance to work with people who have psychotic disorders. These disorders can exist, of course, within therapists' and other so called 'normal' personalities, as well as within what are broadly termed 'borderline' patients and those who are overtly psychotic.

To summarise, I propose that within the artwork there are representations of different levels within, and facets of, the personality. These levels co-exist but do not necessarily interact with one another. Interaction between levels and between elements, when it becomes possible, may produce psychological growth and insight. Such interaction may result in, or take place through, a patient producing images which are alive and which contain the beginnings of psychic integration. However, in order for any form of working through and blending of unconscious elements to begin, the development of what is best described (using Bion's term) as a 'container' is required.

THE TALE OF BROKEN GLASS

I shall now apply these views to the first case example I would like to present. 'Charles' (a pseudonym) was a 'long stay' patient. At the age of 40 he described to me the events just preceding his first breakdown when he was 19 years old. This breakdown was the first episode of what was later described as chronic schizophrenia. His parents had split up when he was 18, the break taking place after years of violent arguments between them, but happening while the boy was at school. The break was reported to him separately, by both of them, seemingly without resistance or mourning on either of their parts. At the same time, he had begun to feel increasingly apathetic about work and about life; because of this he had come to live again with his mother. Twenty years later he began attending the art therapy department where he smoked a great deal and made himself comfortable in an easy chair, chuckling to himself and flicking ash everywhere. After all this time, he still had the air of having recently consumed a lot of red wine. When I began to see him for weekly individual sessions he told me this story: as a young man he habitually spent his holidays with his mother in the south of France. On a hot day they drove together, wending around the curving hills of the Riviera. He wore sunglasses. At a certain point on the drive he began to feel strange as if 'the safety glass was breaking'. He looked at the hills and the sea but everything in his vision became black and broken. After the 'safety glass broke' he went to hospital in France and had rarely been out of hospital since. He then added, smiling as if wryly amused: 'The safety glass started to break you know, it started to crack at first, then to shatter bit by bit. Got none of it left now. Got the bits but it doesn't work any more.' He smiled at me incongruously and in a conspiratorial way, like a boy who cannot help but be conspiratorial with women. He retained the remnants of a sexually seductive technique.

The loss of the safety glass was returned to again and again, with, at first, no movement or change. The 'safety glass' seemed to be a metaphor for a 'false self' (Winnicott 1971) unable to protect itself from the onslaught of reality or from powerful internal tensions. Both from the outside in and from the inside out, the glass began to break. Whether the windscreen of the car really broke (or he himself broke it) I shall never know. The metaphor is not so much a symbol for breakdown but a manifestation of the breakdown itself.

From the time of telling this story he began to construct plasticine penises in a variety of shapes and forms while he talked to me. He would then play with the penises moving them in sexual gestures and chuckling as he watched for my reaction. He used red yellow and green plasticine to construct erect and flaccid penises and penises with or without testicles.

I would like now, to apply the four views which I described earlier. In the first that of 'structural relationships', the penis stands alone. In a related way Charles often identified himself as Jesus Christ. The phalluses are not part of a body to which they relate. They are omniscient, penetrating space, but, partly by virtue of their numerousness, they sacrifice their relationship to a man's body (and thus to his relationship with the world). The disembodied phalluses will not join up with his body or with mine but stand in their own vortex, in a timeless 'immortal' space.

From the view of narrative, Charles frequently made verbal associations with Jesus Christ. He told the story of the crucifixion as well as the story of the safety glass. The implications of these stories within this context have been discussed above. The narrative is meaningful on one level, but it did not relate or correspond in any way on an affective level to the devastating experience of breakdown. There is no correspondence here between the form of the speech and its emotional implications.

These penises do not symbolise some unconscious phantasy (Klein 1959) or thought, rather they represent conscious and unconscious elements mixed up and compressed, functioning in fact to prevent thought (and are described by the term 'bizarre image'). The penis represents potency, masculinity and in relation to culture, claimed Lacan, power. It can be seen in these terms as representative of 'difference' (from the other). Charles was asserting that, in an important way, a core part of his 'self' survived. However, his potency – irrespective of how physically potent he may have been – was not preserved in the social sense in real space and time, but in hallucinatory space.

Within the fourth view which looks at the traces of the infant, as noted within the first view of 'structural relationships', the penises are fragments of the body and consequently of the self. These fragments have come to be, as well as to represent, the self in the context of the sessions. Some sense of this material emerges through consideration of the transference. The penis seemed to be used as a defence against a potentially castrating and engulfing relationship with me – the female therapist whose presence carries echoes of a mother. Charles enacts pseudo-sexual fantasies which imply the joining of one body with another in the sessions, but in doing so becomes even more closely merged with the mother/therapist in his mind. Charles then stopped coming to sessions, and left his penises in the individual therapy room, covering the shelves and the tables, where he would come back for the odd session and review them as they gradually fell to pieces.

Some psychoanalytic observers of very disturbed mother–child relationships have hypothesised that within the unconscious of certain mothers and their children the child does not exist as a real person but as a part of the mother, i.e. is not unconsciously differentiated from the mother. Using the terminology of Mannoni (1990) and others, the child is experienced unconsciously as the mother's 'phallus', as her active member, as part of her which is potent in the world. Did this child experience himself as part of his mother in his own unconscious? Was any process of separation between mother and child unconsciously resisted and defended against, by both of them? On the level of a very primitive aspect of the transference, the patient is acting out 'being' the penis, the paradox being that, at the same time, he is actively preventing any real psychological contact or exchange taking place between himself and someone else.

From these four viewpoints it is possible to see how the phalluses are neither 'real' nor symbolic; they are 'bizarre images', they are part of a mix up. In a deeply paradoxical sense they function as symbols of impotence, of non-existence.

THE CONTAINER

The second example I wish to use are the images of a young woman whom I shall call Maria. Maria had considerable artistic talent (which is by no means a prerequisite for using art therapy); she was also very articulate and had been studying English at university before she became too depressed to continue. She had left home several years before, although she returned there for frequent visits, and was living in a chaotic household of people of her own age who, like her, drank heavily and/or used hard and soft drugs. She had recently been hospitalised for the first time with a diagnosis of manic depression. The only daughter of parents who were still married, her mother continued to suffer intermittently from severe depression. Her father, insofar as he was described, appeared to be a withdrawn and distant man. When she first came to the art therapy department, Maria's predominant presentation was of understated but heavily depressive feelings. Beneath this reserved exterior were traces of mental pain and underlying anger. She displayed no exuberance or 'mania', which would, at least, have given her some relief from these feelings.

The first picture 'I didn't know' (Figure 5.1) was of a woman's chest being damaged by a baby's fist which contained a blade. In the group where she discussed this, she said that the picture was of a recurring nightmare which

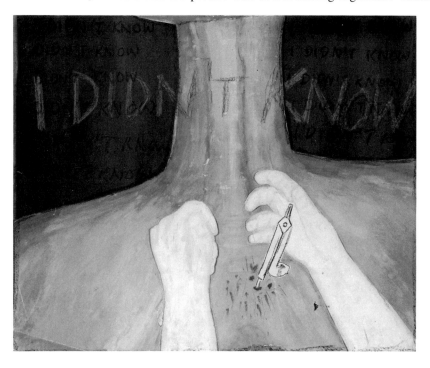

Figure 5.1 'I didn't know'

she had been having for years. The nightmare was one of several which were causing her extreme distress. She would wake up, particularly when staying at her parents' house, crying and bleeding from having banged her head against the wall repeatedly in her sleep. In the dream she was aware of a baby's fist beating continuously against a woman's chest (no breasts were visible). As the dream progressed the chest started to bleed; the baby's hand was opened by the mother, revealing something sharp like a compass. After describing these experiences she began, silently, to cry and said: 'I cry so much sometimes that it feels as if the tears are coming from another place.'

In terms of 'structural relationships' – that is to say, the way in which elements within the picture relate to one another – it is well organised, as all the pictorial space is used. There is a clearly defined composition and structure, with a central theme. This seemed to be reflective of the intactness of her ego, evident in her ability to talk about herself and about her unconscious life, and in her ability to *experience* strong emotions. Each surface was carefully worked on, showing a level of sensuousness and responsiveness to the texture of the picture. Accompanying this was also a starkness in the strong lines which described the mother's and baby's bodies. These clean lines seemed reflective of the harshness of what Freud describes as the 'superego', which, as Jackson (1994: 136)[3] has noted, is often the case in people experiencing manic depressive states. When Maria talked about herself at this time, she described a painful effort to hold onto a sense of a reality, reality being almost unbearable.

The second view of narrative includes the patient's own verbal associations with the picture, the way in which she talks, and the stories that emerge in relation to an image. Maria's account of her nightmare was delivered in a group hesitantly and quietly, her discussions of the picture tended to be curtailed. She described a difficulty in separating her dream life from her everyday life; she felt sometimes as if she was 'sleepwalking'. This was the first time she had discussed this nightmare with anyone with whom she was not closely involved, she expressed relief at being able to put the dream down on paper, and to look at it with someone else who could not be harmed by its violence (in unconscious phantasy); she felt that she had found a way to get this dream out of her mind.

The 'narrative' in this instance is inseparable from the transference: clients cannot speak in any way about themselves or their work, outside of the context of a relationship with the therapist, in which a transference will be active – as it is in all relationships. Within the transference, Maria experienced the therapist as someone who might be able to understand these disturbed parts of her; she transferred her feelings of hopefulness and may perhaps have projected the part of her that could conceive of a good parent (mother and father were interchangeable here) onto me. For my part I felt protective of her and aware of her vulnerability as an in-patient on a psychiatric ward. The picture was able to contain and articulate the aggressive and hurt parts of her which she at times felt overwhelmed by and seemed unconsciously to fear would hurt anyone who came into contact with her. After this she made a series of pictures which represented other nightmares. She did not relate these images verbally to her early life, although the relationship between her internal world and her pictures was, on an intellectual level, evident to us both. I thought and still feel that it was enough that she was able to make these images and to allow them to be seen.

From the third view, that of the symbolic, the mother and child form both a symbolic and archetypal image[4] which recurs of course in Christian and other iconography. This particular image is, however, a representation of a part of a mother's body and a baby's relationship with it. On one level the picture depicted an internal battle taking place: the assault of one part of her on another. Perhaps there had been a difficulty within the very early relationship with her mother, which she had internalised within her ego, leading to inner conflict. Perhaps this conflict created a difficulty in containing and working through unconscious material. As is consistent with this speculation, Maria's dreams were at the time barely distinguishable to her from reality, and could therefore function only minimally to contain and protect her from the elements of her internal world that had become so persecutory. At times like this the containment of a form within an image may protect the psyche from the overwhelming nature of the elements the image represents.

The infantile elements of the image relate to developmental aspects of the personality at pre-symbolic stages in which very early and infantile experiences are formative and, along with genetic predispositions and other environmental influences, form the foundations of a person's later development. In this picture these elements are present within form and the content of the image. The content – a depiction of a baby damaging its mother's chest or breast – is, perhaps, most easily understood with reference to the psychoanalytic theories of Melanie Klein, which focus principally on the infant's relationship with the mother (as represented by the breast). The theory proposes that in early life infants, in unconscious phantasy, particularly when deprived or anxious, attack the nurturing breast, aggressively robbing it of its goodness in phantasy and projecting frustration and hatred into the 'object' (breast) as it cannot contain these elements within its own mind. If the mother is emotionally unavailable at this point and so is not able to respond to the baby, or is sensed by the baby to be unable to contain this infantile rage; the infant cannot acquire the experience of containment. It experiences its own destructiveness as overwhelming and as damaging to the breast. Its world becomes persecutory, inhabited by its own damaging projections. Splitting occurs between what remains of the good breast and its 'bad' elements which are more difficult to transform (in the way that Bion described) into feelings that can become integrated within the ego.

No single theory will ultimately provide *the* correct view of someone's psychological life in relation to his or her images, in all its depth and complexity. However, psychoanalytic theory and a knowledge of art and literature may provide us with one of several working hypotheses which may or may not be confirmed in the experience of a patient, or in that of the patient and therapist together during the process of therapeutic work. While art therapists may not accept Kleinian or other theories *per se*, or may not be trained to work analytically with such material, theoretical understandings can nevertheless be borne in mind. Knowledge enables therapists, and later their patients, to make sense of damaged feelings and thus to gain insight into their origins and become less encumbered by their unconscious ramifications.

Maria's second picture was entitled 'orange squash house' (Figure 5.2).

In its structural relationships this picture is extremely well made, using a combination of paint and collage overlaid in multiple layers to get the desired, nauseous effect. The picture is full of content, but contains spaces of darkness of non-figuration which are intrinsic to the picture's overall form.

From the second view, that of 'narrative', this related to the contents of the picture. The patient related a recurring dream: that she was a little girl, locked in a house which was gradually filling with orange squash. The only

Figure 5.2 Orange squash house

room which was safe from the squash was inhabited by a seductive and wicked witch. The demonic witch would destroy the girl if she was forced into the room and she called and called 'come here little girl'. The story is composed of two strands: firstly, that of a space which is being intrusively flooded; and, secondly, that of an internal 'wicked witch' – something or someone evil which could kill or wreak terrible destruction. This would seem to relate to the anger described earlier, experienced as a poison as it was rarely expressed, and often drowned – in this case usually by alcohol. It may, at the same time, have represented an unconscious aspect of the transference, in which the therapist was experienced (unconsciously) as potentially witch-like and destructive.

The symbolic forms represented are those of the house, which is often understood as a symbol representing the psyche and everything it contains. It is also seen as being symbolic of the human body. The house contains objects: the statue of a woman's head, on top of an empty hollow body; some household objects including a light, a bedhead or cot; and a snake, ladder and arrow all pointing inexorably upwards towards the witch's room. Around the house are shadows, inside it there is also a star and a spiral; however decorative these drowned forms were, they did not mitigate the call of the wicked witch. The rigid statue represents the little girl who is drowning. The girl has an archetypal vulnerability; she represents the child part of the patient who seemed open to abuse and in need of protection, and was hidden in the form of a woman. However, a little girl contains great potential to grow and to change – a potential which, in the patient at that time, was persecuted and petrified. The witch or temptress has been described as representing something which 'drags everything down', as 'comparable with the volatile principle in alchemy, signifying all that is transitory, inconsistent, unfaithful and disassembling' (Cirlot 1962: 376). This witch can be seen as another representation of the destructive aspects of the mother figure as experienced and introjected by the child. The figurative content in this second image is more fragile and less clearly described than in the first. It depicts liquid, i.e. 'squash', almost overwhelming the forms which contain it. The image is, on one level, a metaphor for psychic structures struggling with the threat of being subsumed and overwhelmed. In another sense, the flooding may represent a fear of 'flooding' the sessions with feelings and distress.

The fourth view, which in this instance is closely bound up with the third, tries to take into account the 'shadow of the infant'. In this picture we watch a baby being overwhelmed by liquid; this was perhaps a metaphor for an excess of milk which, because there was too much of it, is transformed from being good for the baby to being poisonous (saccharin-filled orange squash). The baby may sometimes not have been allowed to experience and therefore to develop creative fantasies about its own hunger. A depressed mother, because of her inability to tolerate the expression of her baby's pain, may drown her baby's appetites, feeding the infant in an attempt to prevent her from experiencing and therefore expressing her own hunger pangs. As a result the infant may have been, metaphorically speaking, 'stuffed'; invaded, by milk which she had not been allowed to want, and which had become in the baby's mind a substance which represented unconsciously her mother's depressed feelings.

Maria was discharged and she began attending art therapy as an out-patient. She made a whole series of carefully wrought, often beautiful images, and began to be able to speak about her feelings and thoughts within individual sessions. She moved house and later began a process of longer term therapy and returned to university. In the flooding within the pictures and her dreams, the patient seemed at moments to experience a lack of internal boundaries between unthinkable thoughts and their expression. These thoughts emerged intrusively in dreams and sometimes in sadistic fantasies. Her pictures enabled her to realise the dream thoughts within a framed space within which they could begin to become symbols and objects of reflection. At the same time, the concrete nature of the pictures enabled them to mediate between the parts of her that were threatened by flooding and the parts of her that were able to use symbols. This process enabled her to reinforce and imaginatively recreate a flexible internal 'container'. That is to say, she was able to foster her capacity to grow, to play (she developed her creative life) and to experience an increasingly less persecutory internal world.

CONCLUSION

I hope that the description of levels within an image, seen through different views of the image, helps to work through and to disentangle the multiplicity of observations art therapists make in the context of their relationships with their clients. These observations are most useful to patients and to their therapists within the context of a structured art therapy treatment. Any such treatment must include access to a space within which vital processes of containment can be maintained. As Plaut (quoted in Winnicott 1971) stated: 'The capacity to form images and to use these constructively, by recombination into new patterns is – unlike dreams and fantasies – dependent on the individual's ability to trust.'

When a child's natural capacity to trust another person, and therefore to entrust that person with knowledge of his or her self, is impaired or has been broken – whatever the causes of such a breakdown – the first task for the art therapist is to provide a suitable environment in which patient's images can be made and viewed, as well as appropriate systems which relate to the setting. Within the room itself there need to be boundaries which the individual will be able to test out, to explore, and to have the opportunity to experience, a sense of containment on concrete, intellectual and psychic levels. Crucial to the maintenance of such boundaries is the presence of an art therapist who may be well informed but who is not bound by the constraints of any theory. The art therapist needs to be able to stay alive – that is, to be psychologically present for the patient and to maintain respect for the creative processes that can contribute to transformation and change. This is not always an easy task, given the forces at work within psychotic processes which serve to deny or prevent the development of viable therapeutic relationships. We need to be able to consider both the image and the art folder from as many dimensions as possible, and to avoid becoming encumbered with only one way of seeing.

ACKNOWLEDGEMENTS

I would like to express my gratitude to the patients who have given me the inspiration to write about these ideas, and in particular to 'Charles' and to 'Maria', who very generously gave me permission to use her images for the purposes of this chapter.

NOTES

1   Bion's term refers primarily to early mother–infant relationships in which the mother, through her living ability to think, feel and to provide physical holding to the baby, provides a psychic 'container' (Bion, 1962) for the baby's raw experiences and for the sense of impending 'catastrophe' generated by the infant's physical experiences of pain hunger, etc., in the context of an undeveloped sense of continuity or of meaning. This primary container is understood to be re-evoked by the presence of a therapist and a setting in which the patient can re-experience a form of psychological 'holding' on several levels, enabling him or her to begin a process of transformation and integration of experience.

2   Schaverien's term refers to an image which 'comes to combine conscious and unconscious elements' . . . a picture which 'develops from the interplay between the mental and the pictorial image' (Schaverien, 1991).

3   Jackson refers to Freud's original concept of the unconscious conscience. In melancholia, of which manic depression is seen as the extreme form, the superego possesses 'extreme harshness' resulting in self-hatred. This harshness can be understood as defence that preserves the loved object (which is felt to be too vulnerable) from aggressive feelings (which are felt unconsciously to be too dangerous). See Jackson and Williams (1994).

4   The word 'archetype' refers to Jungian theory: Jung differentiated between archetypal images and archetypes. There is a variety of definitions of archetypes, too complex to do justice to here. Broadly speaking, archetypes have been described as belonging to the inherited parts of the psyche, being linked to instinct and as a 'hypothetical entity irrepresentable in itself and evident only through its manifestations'. The archetypal image may be psychically compelling, it has the capacity to stir the beholder (Samuels *et al.* 1986: 26).

REFERENCES

Bleandonu, G. (1994) *Wilfred Bion, His Life and Works* (trans. Claire Pajaczkowska), London: Free Association Books.

Bion, W.R. (1962) 'A theory Of thinking', *International Journal Psycho-Analysis* 43 (4–5).

Case, C. and Dalley, T. (1992) *A Handbook of Art Therapy*, London: Routledge.

Cirlot, J.E. (1962) *A Dictionary of Symbols*, London: Routledge & Kegan Paul.

Ehrenzweig, A. (1967) *The Hidden Order of Art*, London: Weidenfeld & Nicolson.

Gilroy, A. and Lee, C. (1995) *Art and Music: Therapy and Research*, London: Routledge.

Goffman, E. (1968) *Asylums*, London: Penguin.

Henzell, J. (1995) 'Research and the particular', in Gilroy and Lee (1995).

Jackson, M. and Williams, P. (1994) *Unimaginable Storms*, London: Karnac.

Killick, K. (1987) 'Art therapy and schizophrenia, a new approach', unpublished M.A. thesis, University of Herts.

—— (1993) 'Working with psychotic processes in art therapy', *Psychoanalytic Psychotherapy* 7(1): 25–38.

Killick, K. and Greenwood, H. (1995) 'Research in art therapy with people who have psychotic illnesses', in Gilroy and Lee (1995).

Klein, M. (1959) 'Our adult world and its roots in infancy', *Human Relations* 12(4): 291–303.

Laing, R.D. (1959) *The Divided Self*, London: Tavistock.

Lemaire, A. (1977) *Jacques Lacan*, London: Routledge Kegan & Paul.

Maclagan, D. (1995) 'The biter bit', in Gilroy and Lee (1995).

Mannoni, M. (1990) *The Child, His Illness & The Other*, U.S.A: Bruner Mazel Inc.

Schaverien, J. (1991) *The Revealing Image: Analytical Art Psychotherapy in Theory and Practice*, London: Routledge.

Searles, H.F. (1965) *Collected Papers on Schizophrenia and Related Subjects* (reprinted 1986, London: Karnac).

Simon, R. (1992) *The Symbolism of Style*, London: Routledge.

Samuels, A., Shorter, B. and Plaut, F. (1986) *A Critical Dictionary of Jungian Analysis*, London: Routledge & Kegan Paul.

Winnicott, D. (1971) *Playing and Reality*, London: Tavistock (reprinted 1985, London: Penguin).

Chapter 6

Psychosis and the maturing ego

Helen Greenwood

INTRODUCTION

In my experience as an art therapist in adult psychiatry, I have always been inspired by patients who have emerged from serious mental illness into the realms of mental health and whose self-esteem has grown to enable them to value themselves and their place in the world. I am not referring to a medical notion of cure, as these patients may retain a potential for psychotic breakdown. Then the possible needs may include hospitalisation or continued dependence on long-term medication and various support services. The clients described in this chapter have experienced difficulties in the task of independent living. Their capacity for intimacy has been impaired so that they may have few relationships outside the therapeutic one, yet at the same time they display sophisticated levels of functioning, both mentally and socially. This seems improbable given the disabling results of long-term psychotic processes, but it has become most evident in my out-patient community work and especially so in groups rather than in individual art therapy.

An analogy with cacti comes to mind to describe my experience of working with people with psychotic illnesses. The cactus family has had to endure extreme conditions under which other plants would normally die. To survive, cacti have successfully adapted, but are often viewed as rather bizarre and almost comical in form. They grow very slowly and cannot be frequently transplanted. Yet from the node of a dull, deformed, shrivelled leaf emerge magnificent and brilliantly coloured flowers which seem to be stuck onto the stems at random. The flowers do not bloom for long and I cannot predict when they will reappear. For me, the emergence of mature defences, particularly sublimation and humour, is like the cactus when it splendidly bursts into bloom. My interest, as a therapist, with this client group is in points of growth, not in pruning or restructuring personality.

Attempting to place my work in the context of psychiatry and psychotherapy has been difficult. The ideas developed in this chapter sit perhaps most comfortably in the area of supportive psychotherapy. It is the supportive aspects of psychotherapeutic approach that are of relevance here where 'holding' (Winnicott 1971) and 'containing' (Bion 1962) are likely to be predominant features.

Supportive psychotherapy is seen as the least prestigious of the psychotherapies (Hartland 1991), and is usually practised in psychiatric services by junior staff. It has a less clearly defined theoretical framework than insight-oriented dynamic psychotherapy. Hartland (1991) usefully assesses the value of supportive psychotherapy and the high degree of skill needed by its therapists. She places dynamic and supportive therapies on opposite poles of a continuum rather than being totally separate entities. A definition is offered: 'supportive psychotherapy is a long-term psychotherapy aimed at maximising the patient's strengths, restoring his psychological equilibrium and acknowledging, but attempting to minimise, his dependence on the therapist' (Hartland 1991: 214). The goal is to help patients function independently at their optimum level with minimum input from professional carers. The key feature in this is the provision of an ongoing consistent relationship, but it is a long and complex task in preserving a balance between this and encouraging the patient to move towards a position of greater independence. In supportive psychotherapy Hartland (1991) notes how the therapist needs an inexhaustible supply of patience and optimism as rewards are not quick in contrast with patients with a stronger ego. Change, if any, will be slow.

The art therapy described in this chapter is offered on a long-term weekly basis and does not have to be disrupted by in-patient admission or discharge. Any breaks or endings can be negotiated within the therapeutic relationship. I believe supporting and maintaining elements of therapy are crucial during recovery from serious mental illness and psychotic thought processes. This approach creates the climate within which the patient can grow and possibly thrive.

I have previously described a community-based art therapy group in Birmingham (Greenwood and Layton 1987, 1988) where humour emerged as an important characteristic and an adaptive mechanism of defence at both social and mental levels. Findings of our research in Birmingham have been borne out by my subsequent experiences of the last ten years and this has prompted me to look again at the significance of humour and sublimation in art therapy for people with psychotic illnesses.

Through the study of ego mechanisms of defence, a psychoanalytical concept, I have come to understand the potential for a growth of mental health, and a maturing of the ego, even when this is against a context of psychosis.

EGO MECHANISMS OF DEFENCE

Defence mechanisms form some of the major functions of the ego, as described initially by Freud. Freud used the terms 'defence' and 'repression'

interchangeably in his early writings. In 1923 he changed from his topo-
graphic to his structural model of ego, id and superego:

> . . . the ego seeks to bring the influence of the external world to bear upon
> the id and its tendencies, and endeavours to substitute the reality principle
> for the pleasure principle which reigns unrestrictedly in the id. The ego
> represents what may be called reason and common sense, in contrast to the
> id, which contains passions.

(Freud 1923: 25)

Later in *Inhibitions, Symptoms and Anxieties* (1926) Freud, then aged 70,
introduced the concept of defences by which the ego protects against
instinctual demands and repression as a special case of this. He did not
catalogue the defences but drew the attention of those interested to the work
of his daughter, Anna. She presented him with *The Ego and Mechanisms of
Defence* on his eightieth birthday (Freud 1966). This contains definitions of
most of the defences to which we refer today.

She had added sublimation and shifted the focus of defence mechanism
derivation from instinctual drives of the id, to include the relationship of ego
to superego as well. Other developments were added by her two young
friends: in 1939 Hans Hartmann (*Ego Psychology and the Problem of
Adaptation*) expanded the concept to include an adaptive aspect in relationship to outer reality, and Eric Erikson (*Childhood and Society* 1950)
added a social reality relationship. Thus, the ego can be seen to mediate
between four sources of unconscious conflict: desire and conscience (id and
superego) but also from interpersonal relationships and reality.

In psychiatric and psychoanalytical literature there is inconsistency in
defining what defence mechanisms are, and there is a bewildering array of
proposed defences. Bond (1992) concluded that the scientific examination of
defence mechanisms has proved to be a difficult and confused exercise.
Charles Brenner (1982), on the other hand, maintained that defences were not
special mechanisms of the ego by saying that the ego can use for defence
anything that comes to hand under the heading of normal ego functioning or
development. He thought that modes of defence are as diverse as psychic life
itself. In 1977 the American Psychiatric Association invited a group of
psychoanalysts interested in both diagnosis and defences, to come to a
consensus on important defences for inclusion in the third edition of its
Diagnosis and Statistical Manual (DSM III). The result, according to Vaillant
(1993), was 'chaos' and it was not until 1987 in DSM III-R that a list of
defences was included. Here, defences were divided into psychotic, immature, neurotic and mature.

Vaillant (1994) summarises the major properties of defence mechanisms
by describing defences as an important means of managing conflict and
affect. He states that they are relatively unconscious and discrete from one
another, and are reversible and adaptive, as well as being pathological.

Defences rearrange the sources of conflict so that they become manageable. People employ several defences, not always from the same level. In the case of psychotic defences, like delusional projection, distortion or denial, he concludes, 'Psychotic defenses re-organise perceptions of a defective central nervous system (for example, sleeping, poisoned, immature, or emotionally overwhelmed). Unlike defenses at other levels, they can profoundly alter perception of external reality' (Vaillant 1993: 40).

In 'Cracked pots: art therapy and psychosis' (Greenwood 1994) I described art therapy with a woman diagnosed as schizophrenic who used to announce that she was taking a break when I gave notice of my holidays. I had arranged the timing of art therapy sessions with her mother to fit with bus times, as she had maintained that buses would arrive when she wanted one. She expressed a strong sense that she would fall to pieces if she missed a bus, and for her, time had no consistency – it stopped, and started and was blown away by the wind. Different interpretations can be made, but the significant point here is that these distortions of outer reality defended against anxiety of annihilation.

In contrast to psychotic defences, it is a feature of mature defences that components of conflict are allowed a greater sense of consciousness, so that they may begin to appear like voluntary coping strategies to the onlooker. They are more adaptive than pathological. Vaillant lists sublimation, suppression, humour, altruism and anticipation as mature defences. These represent a synthesis of sources of conflict, a reconciliation of opposites, as expressed through creativity, play and paradox. Sublimation is the process likely to be most familiar to art therapists and for some, most notably the American pioneer Edith Kramer, it is the basis from which art therapy is understood. Freud had noted the main types of sublimated activity to be artistic creation and intellectual inquiry. He put forward the process to explain how the force of sexual instincts can be directed to new, non-sexual aims, without a diminishing of intensity. Sublimated activities are generally socially valued ones, and tend to leave the users feeling good, even proud of their efforts, despite the turmoil that may have been experienced in the process of the activity.

Choice of defence can evolve throughout adult life and defences mature over time. Vaillant states idealistically that, 'As adaptive capacity matures, paranoia evolves into empathy, projection evolves into altruism, and sinner evolves into saint' (1993: 9)

Defence mechanisms can be characterised by the degree of pathology, 'But the mechanisms can vary considerably in their pathology and adaptiveness, depending upon when they are employed, against what they are directed, and the status of the various ego functions' (Bellak *et al.* 1973: 205). A defence mechanism that is adaptive or coping at one age might at a later age appear maladaptive. And, of course, adaptiveness is often in the eyes of the observer.

Defences can be arranged in a hierarchy of maturity that relates to a person's successful adaptation to the world. Research by Semrad *et al.*

(1973), Bond (1992) and Vaillant (1963) has shown that as schizophrenic patients improve, their defences become less primitive and more mature. Elvin Semrad, a psychoanalyst who studied defences in a developmental longitudinal context, investigated the recovery process in acute schizophrenia. He saw a shift in defences along a pathological continuum so that during convalescence the patient employs progressively less pathological defences, to the point of recovery of the capacity to experience relatively unmodified sadness and anxiety (Semrad *et al.* 1973). In a fifty-year follow up of patients, Vaillant (1963) found that people with schizophrenia did not necessarily deteriorate.

I have been particularly influenced by George Vaillant's book *The Wisdom of the Ego* (1993) and his positive and optimistic attitudes. Vaillant is currently an American Professor of Psychiatry who has set out to demonstrate empirically, by longitudinal research, the validity of ego mechanisms of defence. As part of the Study of Adult Development, hundreds of lives were studied for more than fifty years, each one from adolescence to adulthood. It started as a study of healthy human lives, an inquiry into people who do well. People with psychotic illnesses were not the subject of this research. He has been criticised for stretching the psychoanalytic concept too far beyond its scope (Hatcher 1994), but I am interested in matching some of his ideas to the clinical setting. What has caught my attention in this respect is how mature defences can appear in the context of psychotic illness, and also the unexpected appearance of mature defences alongside psychotic defences.

The Wisdom of the Ego explores psychosis through a psychobiography of Sylvia Plath. The ideas I wish to focus on are encapsulated in this quotation:

> The wonder is that creativity and psychosis can become, on occasion, commingled. The wonder is that instead of a laborious developmental march from psychotic defenses to immature defenses to neurotic defenses, Plath's 'hellishly funny stuff' allowed her psychosis to merge directly with mature sublimation.
>
> (Vaillant 1993: 246)

Marcus (1992), who also made observations through psychiatry and psychoanalysis, similarly writes,

> One is, therefore, working with a graduated series of defensive structures from psychotic to borderline to neurotic, even in many psychotic patients. . . . Although it is confusing, it is the very spectrum of ego defenses in most psychotic patients that makes treatment possible.
>
> (Marcus 1992: 232)

I shall now present three clinical vignettes inferring the existence of ego mechanisms of defence. Through these tableaux it is my intention to bring the theoretical discussion to life, and to highlight the value of defences and growth of ego maturity.

Clinical vignette: one

My first clinical vignette is a description of Sandra, a professional woman approaching her forties, diagnosed with a manic depressive psychosis. A growth of ego maturity will be enacted through the emergence of defences: anticipation, altruism and sublimation.

The shift from pleasure principle to reality principle depends on the function of anticipation (Bellak *et al* 1973) highly regarded by Hartmann (1939) as an ego function and adaptation process. I am not speaking of anticipation as a voluntary cognitive strategy but as an ego defence mechanism, the result of which is to spread anxiety over a period of time. During an in-patient admission Sandra requested art therapy, saying she hoped it would give her a safe space to express powerful thoughts and feelings which she feared might threaten to overwhelm her. Although I could offer this immediately, she put off engaging in therapy until a few weeks after her discharge. She had rejected offers of medication.

In the past Sandra had responded to deterioration in her mental health and increased levels of anxiety by ending relationships, moving to other parts of the country and engaging in a new profession. She was aware that the longer she stayed in one place, the more dangerous it became for her. In a sense Sandra had been resourceful and skilful enough to change her outer environment to meet her inner needs, but she felt that this was leading her further and further away from finding a sense of herself. She described the weight of responsibility of choice and contrasted this to the whims of adolescence. Her last career choice had left her feeling 'on stage without a script'.

Art therapy provided a dependable, reliable environment with regular sessions at the same time each week. Sandra's time keeping was notably erratic but she was rarely absent altogether. Her need to run away was contained. This was the first time she had lived in a council flat and not rented accommodation. Sandra had tentatively decided to take six months off work to sort herself out and rebuild her confidence. I assisted this process by referring her to an occupational psychologist.

Sandra had coped with minimal support from psychiatric services. Although she had a psychotic illness and employed psychotic defence mechanisms, it seemed as if, over the years, she had increasingly made mature defences available to herself. Also important in this was her use of anticipation. She found the diagnosis of manic depressive psychosis useful to understand her symptoms and experiences. She described to me how shrewd she had to be to 'survive' her illness. Once, she drew herself asleep in a maze beneath a romantic castle – she was trapped and felt pressure on her to be ingenious to find a way out. Sandra invented a process of altering the temperature of her morning shower as a control on her mood level. Each room of her flat was painted a different colour to accommodate her mood swings.

These were not simply voluntary coping mechanisms; Sandra strove to establish an internalised balanced structure, wanting this to be intuitive, aware that when her efforts were too conscious and concrete she lacked spontaneity.

Sandra employed a process she called 'embellishment', by which she ended up getting further from herself while at the same time in search of herself. In rebuilding her confidence and preparing herself to return to work, Sandra started attending typing classes. She could not face the effort of walking to the class so she started driving lessons. She described how her typing could lead to typing recipes which she would catalogue on different coloured card, and then she would have to cook them all, therefore needing a microwave.

To contain her need for expansive activities, she once barricaded herself into her flat for several days and studied the sky, knowing it was too dangerous to wander the streets of her estate at night. Following this experience, she decided to consider taking medication, as all her energies were going into maintaining her mental health. According to Marcus (1992), medication can strengthen secondary process ego function, characterised by conscious mental activity and verbal thinking. This is in contrast to primary process thinking which Freud saw as governed by the pleasure principle, and exemplified in dreams.

Sandra feared the depressive, negative side of herself. Emptiness, morbid thoughts, isolation and doing nothing, were all threats to her. In manic depressive psychosis patients have described to me how the comfort of mania can be hard to give up. Sandra once said to me that at nearly 40, it was too late in life to find her real self, and that this would mean looking very deeply within herself. The following week, and prior to a two-week break, she arrived with an enormous *papier maché* deep-sea-diving helmet and asked if I minded if she painted it in the session as it was needed that evening as a stage prop in a play.

When Sandra created an appropriate background or structure where she was able to play and experiment, conflict was reconciled, rather like a quest for adventure within a safe structure. This was clearly illustrated in art therapy where most pictures were worked on for several weeks. In her first picture (Figure 6.1), Sandra set the scene with sky, sea, a big wave and a series of islands, some volcanic. In subsequent weeks she added a multitude of images: a boat perched on top of the wave was beginning to lose its precious load of jewels in the sea. Elsewhere coral was beginning to grow. In the sky there were two people in a hot air balloon with an anchor thrown over the side. There was a black bird and a white bird. Paradoxical juxtapositions were contained within the context of the scene, holding a balance of destruction and creative potential in a rather joyful game. Six months later, a picture produced in the same way seemed to illustrate a taming of images (Figure 6.2). The volcanoes had gone, a man takes a dog for a walk in front of a swimming pool, holding the string of a flying fish helium balloon.

Figure 6.1 Volcanic exotica

Figure 6.2 Walking the dog

There was a miniature golf course, tennis court and other images of leisure. This was a man-made landscape where a jellyfish lurked in the swimming pool.

Generally, Sandra did not work spontaneously in her art until she had planned the background. In another picture (Figure 6.3) she started to draw the sea and saw this as her illness out of control. Some uncomfortable thoughts were hidden in black at the bottom of the sea. The sun shone brightly. Sandra described the scene as attractive but dangerous. At the time she was fearful of making a choice of job and getting in a worse mess. By the following week, she had contacted a manic depressives' self-help group and was relieved to hear that other professional women had taken a drop in their career prospects. In the picture the sea became a wave and she added a surfer being brought back to the beach away from the sun. She was left feeling positive and pleased that the dangerous feelings had been transformed.

Sandra's involvement in art illustrates processes of sublimation, whereby conflicts were re-experienced, resolved and integrated. She was aware that this level of expression was not available to her in any other form of communication, hence her initial request for art therapy. Like humour and displacement, sublimation is an ingredient of play.

After reducing her activities to art therapy and a drama group, Sandra started doing more but with a much greater sense of tranquillity. She took up voluntary work with MIND and successfully ran a group for a few months,

Figure 6.3 Surf rider

almost using therapy as supervision. Working towards an ending in therapy, she started art classes but became frustrated by the discipline required – it was not exciting enough for her and did not provide a space for sublimation. Prior to discharge she became a member of an art therapy group for people with psychotic disturbances.

Clinical vignette: two

My second clinical vignette describes Lorraine, a 52-year-old woman who 'feared losing her mind'. I shall depict the employment and eventual surrender of psychotic defences in someone not diagnosed with a psychotic illness. These defences seemed to appear as protection against unbearable depression when significant losses were experienced all at once. During therapy, processes of sublimation emerged alongside psychotic defences. I shall begin by telling Lorraine's story from her viewpoint, using some of her words and phrases, and then introduce my understanding of what was happening. When I met Lorraine she believed there was a plot to destroy her by forcing her to have a lodger and lover she did not want. Several years ago, she had an affair with a work colleague. While asleep, she believed she had been hypnotised to respond to the colour yellow and a bugging device had been inserted up her 'arse' so that the police would always know where she was. Her lover had brought in the police and other uniformed professionals to protect Lorraine with a behaviour modification programme, as she was so lonely and vulnerable. The police were always there for her in stressful situations, such as driving on the motorway and in crowded places. Uniformed men were sexually attractive and exciting, they were there for her protection, but they were also experienced as persecutory. The police were pawns in a game, whose object was to force her to take a lover and lodger she did not want.

Lorraine described to me how she was persecuted and attacked by her neighbours, and lost a series of jobs when she thought the police had intervened. Her world was peopled by persecutors, and held in check by the police force who were, to varying degrees, both entertaining and destructive. An inevitability was maintained that she would go to court, as 'the game' would end in rape or murder; the law could defend her and her abusers would be punished; she would go to court to prove her sanity.

Lorraine's perceptions of me as her art therapist fluctuated. For two years I was the only professional she would agree to see, except occasional visits to her GP. At times she acknowledged therapy as a useful check on reality, but on the other hand she said she felt better for not seeing me as I was the only person she shared her mad thoughts with and she was feeling more insane each week. I had to be part of the game to explain my presence in her life, and at worst I was seen as orchestrating the whole scenario.

Therapy sessions sometimes started at the same time the police helicopter actually flew overhead, and Lorraine believed the police could listen in to what was said in our sessions. When I responded to Lorraine's request to end therapy, she immediately contacted me again, regretting her decision; I then negotiated establishing therapy in the neutrally safe environment of her GP's surgery. This was a tiny clinical room with no windows, and for many months she experienced no intrusion from the police. They were not visible from the room and were not in the forefront of her mind. The police force and the other players of the game still existed, but were bothering her less.

When we worked in the GP's surgery, sublimation was illustrated in Lorraine's use of art. Previously her art had reinforced her feelings of hopelessness and humiliation. In the surgery she made a spontaneous shift from watercolour to acrylics, and her imagery became symbolic. She would get stuck and frightened in the process of painting, especially when her images moved beyond what she was familiar with. She realised she was becoming emotional about her art. Destruction, new life and potency were all given form (Figures 6.4 and 6.5). New shoots grew from fallen decaying autumn leaves, 'shitty' messes transformed into marble, chopped down stunted trees became animated with branches. Lorraine expressed wonder at nature and history. She felt connected to culture and civilisation, and longed to leave her mark in the world.

Lorraine's defences then became more pathological, especially when she became fearful of her dependence on me. Messages were left on my answer phone as a way of recording evidence. She was enraged that she came to see me simply because there was no one else in her life. Lorraine was very

Figure 6.4 Growth from decay

Figure 6.5 Renaissance

threatening and abusive but dreaded breaks in therapy. She claimed that things had not changed 'one iota' since we first met and pointed to the scar on her leg, yellow paint on her car, and a broken window at home. Anyone who stepped over her boundary was threatened with murder. Therapy was agreed to only if I believed everything she said. She would slam down the phone or storm out of sessions saying anything that happened would be my responsibility. Lorraine feared I might change sides if it all ended in court.

During the process of therapy, Lorraine's story unfolded and became clearer. The police had been brought into her mind when she had experienced considerable losses in a short space of time. Her marriage ended in divorce, her adoptive father died, she had tests for cancer and then, following her affair, she lost her job and moved to a different part of the country. She was a very intelligent woman who developed a successful professional career but had felt dreadfully humiliated by her loss of face at work, when her dyslexia had become public and she was under pressure of assessment of her work performance. Lorraine described herself being too busy responding to her thoughts of the police force to mourn her adoptive-father's death. She recounted a disturbed childhood and marriage, but this was not the focus of therapy. She had received some psychiatric help in the past but had not been treated for, or diagnosed, as psychotic.

It was the feeling that her employers wanted to get rid of her that Lorraine could not bear, and over a short period of time her world crumbled. Her mind could not tolerate the loss of self-esteem and loss of relationships that occurred all at once. Defence mechanisms can be useful in acute situations of stress, which we have not rehearsed for. Biological vulnerability and personal crisis occurred together for Lorraine thereby promoting the use of psychotic defences. I think the image of the police force being called in to protect her symbolised the employment of new defence mechanisms. These were not visual hallucinations – the police existed, but it is as if reality experience was changed to correspond more closely to Lorraine's unconscious view of the object world. Her inner conflicts were externalised and given tangible reality.

Lorraine did actually end up in court accused of a catalogue of offences, mostly drink related. I had previously introduced her to a psychiatrist colleague but it was only at this time she agreed to take neuroleptic medication to prevent her shouting at the neighbours and getting into more trouble. Initially, she thought the consequences of the court would be to force her to take a lodger. However, she began to see that the game had ended when the police put her in a cell overnight and she realised that their reaction to her was the same as to any drunk person and she was not special. She felt alone and devastated when the police had all gone, and the wonder and excitement of the game had ended. She considered the police had lost their significance and she had not noticed this. Her story began to piece together but she was worried that she could not salvage anything. Lorraine deduced that she had been 'off her rocker'.

When her psychotic defences were finally surrendered and the police started to go away, an alternative mode of coping was required. Medication and her relationship with me helped provide the necessary support. Mature defences were not available to her. After another night in a police cell, she was lifted by the excitement of going to watch a cooling tower being blown up. It occurred to her then that the only other space where she experienced these senses of wonder was in art therapy, referring back to the pictures produced in the GP's surgery. She set about recreating the explosion in a picture, but instead of an ego-enriching experience of sublimation she became distressed by the illustration of the destruction of her world, as if her artistic skills and creativity had also deserted her.

The law seemed to provide some sort of ultimate boundary she could keep within, and prolonged actual court appearances over twelve months symbolically kept her in order. Her dependence on me at this time was at its most intense. Lorraine continued to paint each week but she said nothing happened (Figure 6.6). She looked to me to find meaning in her pictures and feared her creativity would not return. Her pictures were spoken about, but only in terms of 'pattern'. Symbolism and processes of sublimation were absent. It felt to me as if I had to be a partial replacement before new defences emerged and her own ego functioning engaged. Supportive psychotherapy can involve the therapist taking over some of the functions of the patient's ego on her behalf.

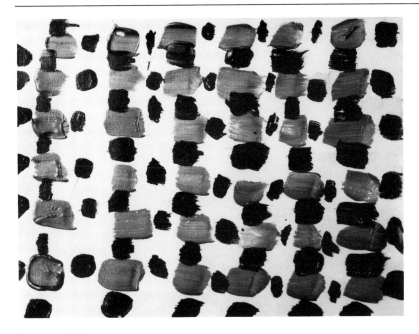

Figure 6.6 Pattern

Working with Lorraine demanded greater flexibility in my role and a need for me to be more of a real person in contrast to therapy where clients have higher ego strength. There was a warm humour in Lorraine's relationship with me. Her threatening attitude was balanced by a caring concern for my health and survival, alongside a tremendous gratitude for remaining through disturbing experiences with her.

Guntrip notes how strong ego development is not possible without object relations. He follows Winnicott in stressing the importance of the quality of the therapeutic relationship in patients with deep schizoid, borderline and psychotic problems. He writes,

> If the therapist persists in being, in reality, a merely objective scientific intelligence with no personal feeling for the patient, he will repeat on the patient the original trauma suffered at the hands of parents, which laid the foundations of the illness.

(Guntrip 1992: 335)

Clinical vignette: three

My final clinical vignette portrays the struggle of the ego to mediate between instinctual drives of the id and the superego (between desire and conscience) and also intrapsychic conflict caused by stress of interpersonal relationships. Abandonment of defences exposes these sources of conflict.

Patrick was a young man in his twenties with a manic depressive psychosis. He was referred by his social worker to art therapy following hospitalisation for an acute, manic episode. Having experienced the breakdown of a relationship, loss of employment, and incurred serious debts Patrick had moved back to his family home. In his life, he had struggled hard to lift himself above his tattered background, striving to attain an educated middle-class and professional existence. When I first met Patrick he was feeling dependent on parental figures he despised and he felt he was back where he had started. I shall offer Patrick's description of himself, as expressed in therapy.

Patrick explained how his defences did not work for him. In bed, he felt raw and exposed – then a suit of armour clicked into place when he got up. This felt at a distance to his skin, as if he had been given a shield but could not relate to it; he did not know if it was working or not. Spots and blemishes on his skin exposed his inner imperfections to the world. All situations of communication were like an examination where his badness was exposed. Patrick tried to scrub himself clean, inside and out.

Patrick was afraid of what he would express in the art process and most weeks did not want to attend therapy. He tried to blank out his mind before he arrived and then talked continuously. He thought 'sex' was the issue but wanted to put this to one side and bring in other problems. He described himself as a walking sex bomb and feared his art would be pornographic. To describe how repulsively he saw himself, Patrick explained to me that you

Figure 6.7 Sinful pleasure

would not want to share a meal you had just eaten. By this I understood that Patrick was seeing the process of therapy involving my consumption of his regurgitated or defecated food. In his art, scenes of sexual behaviour and violence were hidden and covered over by multiple layers of drawing, painting and collage (Figure 6.7).

His inner journey was defended against by planning a world tour. His life was filled with activity and people, but then he felt trapped by the things he had set up and wanted to pull the plug on them. The intimacy of relationships always eluded him. He described an image of himself scrambling on a climbing net, negotiating all the twists and turns but not noticing that the net was hanging in the air and there was a big drop. Interactions with people were hazardous. Sources of warmth and love were given to him at whim, when it suited others, and also withheld at whim; at the end of the day Patrick saw that others go back to their own stable relationships.

Outwardly, Patrick presented himself as a smart young man, always spotlessly clean and polite. Verbally he was articulate and eloquent; inside he saw his feelings as like 'shit' and 'sludge' and a 'swirling pit of hot oil'. He described his inner world as a deep well with craggy sides. Thick black liquid threatened to drown him, so Patrick tried to climb up the well and cling on to its sides. Contact with the outside world gave him a hand to hold onto; but while he was relating to other people, ghouls leapt to life in the thick liquid and stirred things up (Figure 6.8), so that when Patrick went back into himself the situation was worse. When people related to him, he felt they said one thing but at the same time fed the hell inside him. Clinging onto the edge of the well gave no quality of life. The ghouls were like a virus that strengthened as his immune system weakened, until there was a point of breakdown when he had to 'leave' and find a way of taking time out. It was probably at this point that his defences reorganised and came to his rescue. When Patrick or those around him deemed his defences too pathological, his medication was increased or he was admitted to hospital.

Working with Patrick was at times like being with someone whose defences had deserted him. He was tortured by inner conflict, by conflict in his relationships, by trying to establish a place in the world, and especially by his conscience. He was not only drawn to badness but also absolutely repulsed by it. Outwardly he conserved his 'Mr Nice Guy image'. Despite his terror, Patrick valued the space of using art materials as the only 'hole' in the week for himself, without the impingement of the outside world. He made his session day a break in the week, and a rest from negotiating the rapids.

There was an attractiveness in Patrick's personality and he was able to make friends. When he was not overwhelmed by depression and anxiety, he held a good sense of humour and altruistic attitude to others. He started running a support group for young people with mental health problems, and also helped out at youth clubs, football training and conservation groups.

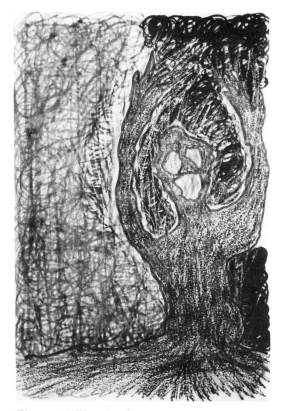

Figure 6.8 The ghoul

Anna Freud (1966) describes altruism as a combination of projection and identification for purposes of defence where one's own wishes are fulfilled vicariously by their surrender to another person.

Verbally Patrick was able to play with ideas and images, but initially this was more difficult in art form where his conflict was exposed too directly. When Patrick moved out of his parental home into a new flat, he first decided to use clay. He was convinced that nothing would emerge from it if he did not force it into something. Although apprehensive, he became delighted with the process of using clay, as if the capacity for sublimation was liberated. His first sculpture filled the natural shape of his hand (Figure 6.9(a)). It was a piece of furniture, a chaise longue, but one that would be uncomfortable – inviting and attractive, but not functional, like an art exhibit! Patrick enjoyed the irony of the image and went on to paint it the following week. The chair was turned over to create a cave where he had become trapped by the tide, in his childhood.

Figure 6.9 Chaise longue (a) and old woman (b)

Associations with his sculptures were explored within the therapy process, but, unlike his pictures, Patrick was left feeling good about them and did not hide them away. His favourite piece (Figure 6.9(b)) had started off as a long sausage, which he found crudely phallic by reminding him of the tabloid press and smutty jokes. It was transformed into a rock pinnacle that would stand off the coast for rock climbers to ascend. The proudness of the form was offset by its leaning attitude – a challenge for rock climbers but a danger to small people standing under it. The image finally evolved into an old lady with her head and back bent from working. She was facing death with the experience of being fulfilled in her life, having numerous children and being well respected in the community; she did not need a stick.

Patrick became aware of a process he called 'side-stepping' by which he had a sense of avoiding conflict, holding it in mind but not engaging in head-to-head confrontation. This sounds like the defence of suppression where disturbing thoughts are postponed but not ignored. Mature defences rearrange sources of conflict so that they become manageable. When Patrick was able to use humour, sublimation and altruism, he could gain a sense of value and self-worth, taking some pleasure in life.

EGO MATURATION

I have been intrigued by the emergence of mature ego mechanisms of defence alongside psychotic defences and also in the context of psychotic illness, as narrated in the three vignettes. Investigation of the theoretical concept of ego mechanisms of defence introduced the divisions of psychotic, immature, neurotic and mature defences, and also the idea that several defences could be employed at once, but not always from the same level. In this final section I want to consider how maturation can be facilitated through art therapy, and also to shed more light onto some of the complexities I am presenting.

There has only been reference here to the polarities of psychotic and mature defences, which oversimplify the continuum of defences from psychotic to immature to neurotic to mature. Insight-oriented, dynamic psychotherapy is generally offered to people employing neurotic defences who are able to form sustaining relationships; interpretation is then a useful tool of therapy. Examples of neurotic defences are displacement, isolation/intellectualisation, repression, reaction formation (Vaillant 1993). Supportive psychotherapy, on the other hand, is useful to address immature defences such as splitting, projection, hypochondriasis (Vaillant 1993) where these can be understood and managed rather than interpreted.

The works of Winnicott (1972) and Kohut (1966) are useful in understanding the value of empathy and management, instead of confrontation and interpretation where immature defences predominate. In an environment of empathy, understanding and mirroring, defences can become less pathological. The social milieu needs to be more predictable and supportive. The therapist alone cannot provide the necessary holding environment for growth of ego to resume, and in my experience recovered peers become a valuable source of constancy. Self-help groups can become a useful adjunct to psychotherapy, and vice versa; Sandra and Patrick both found such groups. Part of the value of group therapy can be the way members form lasting support networks from relationships built up in the group (Greenwood and Layton 1987).

Admiration of patients' attempts to change and grow means that mature defences require no response from the clinician other than applause. Vaillant states, 'it is important that clinicians retain as much respect for mature defenses as they do for the immune system and white blood cells' (1992: 89).

In applying Vaillant's ideas to psychotic states, I have been interested in how expressions of ego maturity, in the form of ego mechanisms of defence such as sublimation, altruism, anticipation and humour, can appear as non-psychotic areas of ego function. Valuing these defences has given me a hopefulness and excitement in my work with people experiencing psychotic illness. It seems that sophisticated levels of functioning are within the reach of those with serious mental illness although it has been difficult for researchers to validate and explain this paradox.

Art therapists are concerned with creativity, art and play, and it is through these experiences that sublimation and humour become more available in the range of defences. However, we cannot make defences mature; they are involuntary and unconscious processes. I do not believe that all activity in art therapy takes the form of sublimation. Murderous, sexual impulses cannot be converted to inspirational poetry at will. Lorraine could not force processes of sublimation, creativity and symbolism to occur although she longed to re-experience a sense of meaning and value through her art.

I acknowledge some cautionary thoughts. Marcus (1992) warns that many schizophrenic patients may seem 'creative'. He maintains,

> The observer may admire them but the schizophrenic patient cannot use them and their own experience of them may be bizarre, real and frightening. Nonetheless, artistic schizophrenics may experience an esthetic from their creative productions, even if that esthetic experience is bizarre and frightening.
>
> (Marcus 1992: 146)

He notes that in acute schizophrenia there is little or no intermediate creative play area left, but some patients maintain a sense of humour even if bizarre and concretely experienced. Similarly, Baker warns about the use of humour with people with psychotic disorders, stating that,

> these patients have access to humour of a most moving and relevant type. However, the underlying persecutory nature of their inner world is often such that the humour is not of the same order as that which is observed in healthier characters.
>
> (Baker 1993: 958)

Patrick was aware that he felt very creative when he was manic, but sensed his work lacked quality as he did not have the necessary concentration at these times. To utilise his mania, he related himself to a car that needed a driver.

When the patient is able to engage in a therapeutic relationship, shifting allegiance from the pleasure principle to the reality principle, I believe that mature defences can grow from this capacity for creativity. Freud thought that secondary processes developed alongside the ego's adaptation to the external world. Arieti (1976) proposed the expression 'tertiary process' to designate a special combination of primary and secondary process mechanisms: 'Primary process mechanisms reappear in the creative process also, in strange, intricate combinations with secondary process mechanisms in syntheses that, although unpredictable, are nevertheless susceptible of psychological interpretation' (Arieti 1976: 12). And again, 'Instead of rejecting the primitive (or whatever is archaic, obsolete, or off the beaten path), the creative mind integrates it with normal logical processes in what seems a "magic" synthesis from which the new, the unexpected, and the desirable emerge' (Arieti 1976: 13).

Arieti notes how schizophrenic patients have special access to the primary process but that, generally, they cannot combine this with secondary processes for creative purposes. This is more likely to occur in stages of recovery, though Arieti notes that reports of such cases are rare. Marcus (1992) also makes mention of the paradox that tertiary processes may seem more intact than either primary or secondary processes in schizophrenia.

In the process of art, id impulses are allowed more than usual freedom and this can enrich the ego. Sublimation in art is more than a discharging of affect. The capacity to sustain paradox, and bring order and meaning out of chaos, are indicators of ego maturity. Sublimation and humour are the defences most closely related to these features. I think that art therapists should grasp the uniqueness of their skills as both artists and psychotherapists in working with people with serious mental illness, to provide the opportunity for ego development and to value mature ego mechanisms of defence.

I have applied to clinical work Vaillant's idea of psychosis merging directly with mature mechanisms of defence. In *The Wisdom of the Ego* he sought the association between art and psychosis, proclaiming that the

> threat of madness can sometimes drive one to art. Great art can stave off insanity. Art is not dangerous; it is the circumstances that bring it forth that are perilous; and it is failure to harness the passions with mature defenses that may be fatal.
>
> (Vaillant 1993: 246)

REFERENCES

American Psychiatric Association (1980), Diagnostic and Statistical Manual of Mental Disorders, 3rd edn (DSM III). Third edition revised (DSM III-R) (1987), Washington, DC, pp. 393–5.
Arieti, S. (1976) *Creativity. The Magic Synthesis*, New York: Basic Books.
Baker, R. (1993) 'Some reflections on humour in psychoanalysis', *International Journal of Psycho-Analysis* 74(5): 951–60.
Bellak, L., Hurvich, M. and Gediman, H. (1973) *Ego Functions in Schizophrenics, Neurotics and Normals*, New York: Wiley-Interscience.
Bion, W. (1962) *Learning from Experience*, London: Heinemann.
Bond, M. (1992) 'An empirical study of defensive styles. The defense style questionnaire', in Vaillant (1992).
Brenner, C. (1982) *The Mind in Conflict*, New York: International Universities Press.
Erikson, E.H. (1950) *Childhood and Society*, London, Hogarth, 2nd edn, 1963, New York: Norton.
Freud, A. (1966) *The Ego and Mechanisms of Defense*, New York: International Universities Press.
Freud, S. (1923) 'The ego and the id', in *Standard Edition of Complete Psychological Works of Sigmund Freud*, (ed. and trans. J. Strachey) 19: 17, London: Hogarth Press and Institute of Psychoanalysis.
Freud, S. (1926) 'Inhibitions, symptoms and anxieties', in *Standard Edition of Complete Psychological Works of Sigmund Freud*, 20.
Greenwood, H. (1994) 'Cracked pots: art therapy and psychosis', London: *Inscape* 1: 11–14
Greenwood, H. and Layton, G. (1987) 'An out patient art therapy group', London: *Inscape* 10(1).

—— (1988) 'Taking the piss' *British Journal of Clinical and Social Psychiatry* 6: 3.

—— (1991) 'Taking the piss', London: *Inscape* (Winter): 7–14.

Guntrip, H. (1992) *Schizoid Phenomena, Object Relations and the Self*, London: Karnac.

Hartland, S. (1991) 'Supportive psychotherapy', in J. Holmes (ed.) *Textbook of Psychotherapy in Psychiatric Practice*, Edinburgh: Churchhill Livingstone.

Hartmann, H. (1939) *Ego Psychology and the Problem of Adaptation* (trans. D. Rappoport), New York: International Universities Press.

Hatcher, L. (1994) 'Review: *Ego Mechanisms of Defense: A Guide for Clinicians and Researchers*, by Vaillant,G. 1992, American Psychiatric Press, Washington', *International Journal of Psycho-Analysis* 75(1).

Kohut,H. (1966) 'Forms and transformations of narcissism', *Journal of American Psychoanalytic Association* 14: 243–72.

Marcus, E. (1992) *Psychosis and Near Psychosis. Ego Function, Symbol Structure, Treatment*, New York: Springer-Verlag.

Semrad, E.V., Grinspoon,L. and Feinberg, S.E. (1973) 'Development of an ego profile scale', *Archives of General Psychiatry* 28: 70–7.

Vaillant, G. (1963) 'Natural history of the remitting schizophrenics', *American Journal of Psychiatry* 120: 367–75.

—— (1971) 'The theoretical hierarchy of adaptive ego mechanisms', in *Archives General Psychiatry* 24: 107–18.

—— (1992) *Ego Mechanisms of Defense. A Guide for Clinicians and Researchers*, Washington DC: American Psychiatric Press.

—— (1993) *The Wisdom of the Ego*, Cambridge, Mass.: Harvard University Press.

—— (1994) 'Ego mechanisms of defense and personality psychopathology' *Journal of Abnormal Psychology* 103(1): 44–50.

Winnicott, D.W. (1971) *Playing and Reality*, London: Tavistock.

—— (1972) *The Maturational Processes and the Facilitating Environment*, London: Hogarth Press.

Part II

Context and history

Chapter 7

Has 'psychotic art' become extinct?

David Maclagan

For you I would invent a whole new
universe, but you obviously find it
cheaper to rent one.

(Jack Spicer, *Language* 1963)

We still lack a proper history of the crucial shifts whereby psychosis acquired its modern identity: a history, not just of psychiatric techniques or diagnostic categories, but of the tacit assumptions and cultural motives at work beneath their surface. In the early years of this century, when 'dementia praecox', with its connotation of irreversible degeneration, was being replaced by 'schizophrenia', the artworks created by a relatively small number of psychotic patients surely played a role in this redefinition. With their striking peculiarities of form and their strange, often impenetrable symbolism, they came to represent, first for psychiatrists and later for the general public, an image of deranged creativity that was at once fascinating and threatening.

This is the image of psychotic art evoked by the classic creators such as Adolf Wölfli (1862–1930) (Figure 7.1) or Aloise Corbaz (1886–1964), and that is exemplified in a large proportion of the exceptional works housed in the Collection de l'Art Brut in Lausanne. It is an image that still colours the wider category of 'Outsider Art' (art produced by untrained individuals, whose originality owes nothing to convention or tradition). It seems a paradox that work stemming from such a confined situation should display such baffling extravagance (Wölfli only left the asylum for a one-day trip in thirty-five years); yet the asylum may, in such cases, have acted as a kind of 'greenhouse', concentrating and intensifying, as well as 'deforming', the need to create.

Like psychosis itself, 'psychotic art' is not a fixed and changeless phenomenon; it has a history, a beginning, a climax and perhaps an end. It originated in the collections of patient artworks made by a number of psychiatrists around the turn of the century.[1] Psychiatric interest in the drawings and paintings made by the insane followed in the wake of attempts to use their writings to measure and document the full extent and nature of their mental

Figure 7.1 Waldorf-Astooria: Hotel Windsor in New York, 1905, Adolf Wölfli

disturbance. It served, therefore, diagnostic rather than therapeutic purposes. Nevertheless, a conflict is apparent, even in the early published literature, between a predominantly medical perspective (e.g. Lombroso) and a more 'artistic' one (e.g. Réja). We shall see that this conflict reflects the difference between a view of the artwork as *symptomatic* of psychosis, and one that is more concerned with its *expressive* or even creative aspects.

This difference overlaps with that between what might be called a 'circumstantial' definition of psychotic art, i.e. any work made by a designated psychotic, and a 'stylistic' one, where any work with certain traits – for example, crowded composition, the 'nesting' of figures one within another, a tendency to treat figures in an abstract or diagrammatic way, a complex liaison between text and texture – could be called 'psychotic' in much the same way as art historians use the term 'baroque'. This led some psychiatrists to jump to the rash conclusion that any modern artist whose work presented unusual difficulty (eg Cézanne or Kandinsky) could be tarred with the brush of mental disorder.

The perspective from which psychiatric diagnoses are made is as much subject to historical influence as are judgements in the history of art. In the case of psychotic art, the two overlap. The original criteria by which artworks were judged to exhibit a 'disorder' that might have psychopathological implications, whether or not the artist was a designated mental patient, were

Figure 7.2 Le Pays des Meteores, 1902, Le Voyageur Français

based on the artistic assumptions of a pre-Modernist culture. Yet the revolutionary developments of Modernism were soon to question most of the representational, symbolic and even expressive conventions upon which such psychiatric judgements were based. It is clearly significant that both the 'Golden Age' for the creation of 'psychotic art' (approximately 1880–1930) and the publication of most of the major psychiatric studies of it coincide with these cultural upheavals. This brings into question not only the basis for psychiatric diagnoses of psychotic art (Figure 7.2), but also the assumption that the patients who produced it played a largely passive role.[2]

Psychotic art in its original form was created in conditions of extreme isolation. The advent of art therapy, itself a practice situated uncomfortably between the psychiatric and the artistic,[3] brought with it the possibility of trying not only to understand, but to work with, the patients who produced such work. Yet by this time (the years following the Second World War) it is arguable that 'psychotic art' in its original form was already an increasingly rare phenomenon. Also, the stylistic characteristics that used to be its peculiar hallmark were now to be found in a much wider range of artworks that were no longer confined to a psychiatric provenance. In part this was attributable to the long-standing interest of avant-garde artists in the art of the insane, reflected in the establishment in 1948 of Dubuffet's Collection de l'Art Brut; but it may also be a result of other, more general, cultural shifts that have thrown the original identity of psychotic art into doubt.

All of these factors raise questions about the relation of current art therapy with psychotic patients to 'psychotic art', about the reliability of psychiatric diagnoses based on the formal features of artworks, and about the very nature of the connection between works of art and mental states in general. These issues have historical roots.

Psychiatry's early interest in the paintings or drawings of psychotic patients stemmed from two overlapping needs: the desire to gain access to the mental world of the psychotic, and the wish to give as specific an account as possible of the various ways in which it departed from the normal. By definition, psychosis involves severe distortion or even erosion of the normal capacities of communication, and of the normal functions of perception, thinking and feeling on which they depend. This 'deficit' is still a characteristic of diagnosed psychotic states today (see, for example, Sass 1992: 71–2).

Yet this impoverishment was not always global. It was sometimes accompanied by a strange extravagance: speech and, to a lesser extent, writing or drawing, seemed to exude in a relentless, surplus flow. And these expressions were, at one and the same time, passionate and obsessive in character and yet strangely indifferent to their immediate audience. Some of these features are probably a consequence of the institutional confinement of psychosis: this confinement has multiple aspects, physical and mental, and can result, in some cases, in an intensified concentration on one's own thought and the forms of its expression.[4] At the same time, many of these features are also characteristic of artistic creation, so that in several ways (as I shall show later) the phenomenon of 'psychotic art' can be seen as an extreme or exaggerated version of it.

At first written texts by psychotics seemed to offer the most detailed point of comparison with normal modes of communication or expression (see Will-Levaillant 1980). The elaborate rules of language, its grammar and syntax, and its close association, if not identification, with thought, made it an obvious choice. But art, too, with its conventions governing representation, symbolisation and ornament, seemed to have a corresponding 'language', the improper or disordered use of which could, in theory, be calibrated in a similar way. Furthermore, the supposedly visual nature of much hallucinatory experience seemed to fit the notion of a picture as a sort of window into the artist's mind.[5] Alternatively, the failure to represent, or the conspicuous distortion of recognisable forms, could be taken as evidence for a corresponding disturbance of perception or thinking.

Nevertheless, certain fundamental problems are immediately apparent. For a start, only a small fraction of psychotic patients actually engaged in any artistic activity: Prinzhorn estimated that fewer than 2 per cent of the patients in his Heidelberg clinic engaged spontaneously in creative activity (Prinzhorn 1922/1972: 267). One has then to ask in what sense this fraction of psychotic patients is 'typical': the idea that they represent or speak for other, inarticulate patients entails a number of dubious assumptions. One is that, because a psychotic has made an artwork, the work itself must be 'psychotic'. This is not necessarily so: MacGregor (1989), for instance, repeatedly cites instances where psychotic patients were able to produce perfectly 'professional' work that was seemingly uninfluenced by their illness.

Another is the idea that such artworks provide a direct 'window' into the patient's mind – witness such cases as the use of an undated sequence of Louis Wain's cat paintings (Figure 7.3) to illustrate the progressive 'disintegration' of psychosis (eg Bader and Navratil 1976),[6] or the presentation of one of Wölfli's pictures as 'a glimpse into the world of a schizophrenic' by the manufacturers of a well-known anti-psychotic medication.

Then, it soon becomes clear that, historically, different writers in the psychiatric field differ widely in the lengths to which they are prepared to go in order to find meaning in this kind of work. For some the work is presumed automatically to be psychopathological; for others the artist's intentions (where they have been recorded) play a crucial role in any attempt to understand their work (e.g. Morgenthaler); while for others the work itself may be considered as 'art', regardless of its context. Sometimes the same writer adopts all these positions at various times (e.g. Prinzhorn).

Even when psychotic art is allowed some aesthetic quality, there is still a question as to how far the patient can be held responsible for this. Answers to this question actually bring up even more fundamental issues, which are already beginning to be rehearsed in Modernism, about the differences between conscious and deliberate composition and spontaneous or 'primitive' creativity, and the extent to which works that are the result of automatism belong to their authors or can be seen as personal expressions rather than products of some kind of 'unconscious' creativity.[7]   Nevertheless, leaving aside those cases where patients already had some artistic or graphic training, there is evidently a phenomenon to be accounted for: that patients with no previous history of involvement with art-making begin to create at some point in their confinement. This might be either a brief surge or a prolonged career; but in either case it occasionally resulted in works of astonishing power and quality. The catalogue of the Prinzhorn collection shows that some of these works were poignant in the directness of their expression, while others were almost wilfully enigmatic or perverse. Where does such a variety of creative output come from?

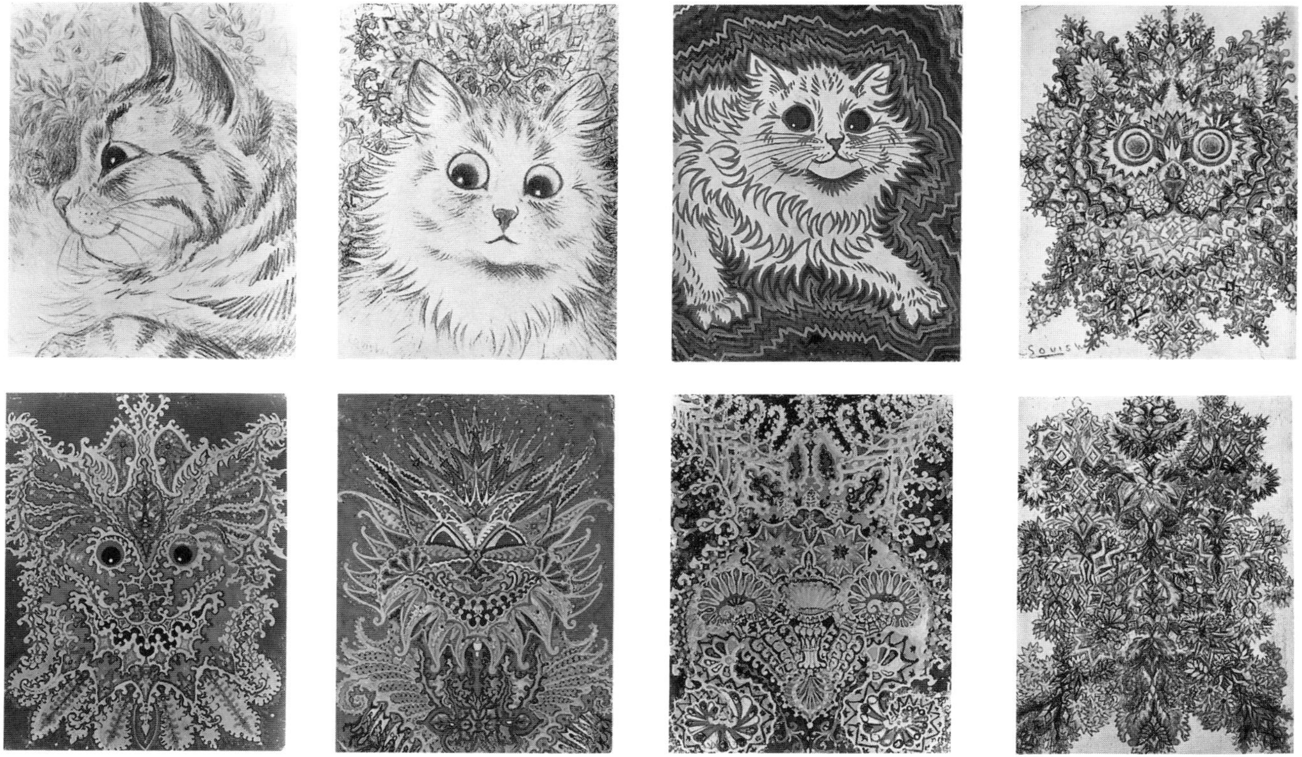

Figure 7.3 A series of cats by Louis Wain, undated, untitled

One way of explaining this is to suppose that such patients had an underlying artistic potential that was exposed by psychosis (as Morgenthaler suggested was the case with Wölfli). A second is to suggest that the disturbance of psychosis itself was in some way responsible (as Prinzhorn did with 'schizophrenic art'). In practice, these two types of account are convergent: distortions or exaggerations that appear 'creative' are often ascribed to the operation of 'configurative urges' (Prinzhorn 1922/1972) or 'fundamental form constants' (Bader and Navratil 1976) that have been cut loose from conscious control. But in either case the background presence both of a medical model of illness and its characteristic processes, and of a psychological model of instinctual or 'unconscious' function, leads to descriptions and analyses in terms of rules and laws of which the patients themselves are presumed to be unaware. However, this discovery of an order that is, in one sense or another, 'unconscious' can be applied to much modern art as well, where it is given a higher value than the purely instinctual.

Prinzhorn's view was that psychotic illness exposed a fundamental layer of creativity that was latent in all men, but that this had a quite impersonal character. Speaking of 'schizophrenic configuration', he wrote:

> The persons who produced our pictures are distinguished by having worked more or less autonomously, without being nourished by the tradition and schooling to which we attributed the more customary works of art. . . . The configurative process, *instinctive and free of purpose*, breaks through in these people without any demonstrable external impulse or direction – they know not what they do . . . it is certain that nowhere else do we find the components of the configurative process, which are subconsciously present in every man, in such an unadulterated state.
>
> (Prinzhorn 1922/1972: 269, my emphasis)

Starting from these assumptions, Prinzhorn embarked on a series of lengthy formal analyses in which he tried to demonstrate that the distortions of the configurative urge to be found in psychotic art amounted, in effect, to definitive characteristics. The stylistics of psychotic art were parallel to, and hence an equivalent of, the symptomatology of psychosis.

What are the features of psychotic art that Prinzhorn and other pioneer writers in the field singled out as typical, if not symptomatic? Some are matters of content: religious, political or sexual or emotional expressions that are judged excessive, primitive or offensive. Others are more purely formal: repetition and cramming; the elision of boundaries between word and image, or between representation and ornament; and distortion, confusion or illegibility, whether on a representational or a symbolic level. These distinctions between form and content are, however, difficult to sustain: is the deformation of a human figure, for example, to be seen as a simple failure to represent properly, or might it have some expressive or symbolic significance? How is one to decide whether pressure of content has led to distortion of form, or vice versa?

Prinzhorn, who had an art-historical training that stressed stylistic analysis, eliminated from his book those works whose content was most obviously expressive, which in fact constituted a considerable part of the five thousand works he collected (see *Die Prinzhornsammlung* 1980), in order to concentrate his attention on the formal characteristics of 'schizophrenic configuration'. Yet this choice actually predetermines his findings: such works are characterised, he says, by an opacity, an 'aimless logic', an absence of discernible intention.

But is this an absence or a refusal? In his sophisticated model of the three main avenues open to the 'configurative urge' – representational, ornamental or symbolic – and of the various ways in which each of them can become exaggerated when not subordinated to proper conventions and tethered to some recognisable intention, Prinzhorn is actually mapping out the conventions governing traditional pictorial discourse. He acknowledges that, at the same time that psychotic art subjects these to disintegration or explosion (or perhaps we should say implosion), modern artists are engaged in remarkably parallel forms of expression. Furthermore, this formal similarity stems from an experience common to both the psychotic and the modern artist: a sense of alienation from external reality and the attempt to represent 'pure psychic qualities', which Prinzhorn takes a rather sceptical view of.[8] The only difference between the two is that the schizophrenic is compelled by a 'gruesome, inescapable fate', whereas the modern artist exercises a degree of rational and conscious decision (Prinzhorn 1922/1972: 271–2).

Even at the time it was made, there was some doubt about this convenient distinction between compulsion and choice: just as an element of craft (in either sense) could be detected in psychotic art, so the inventions of avant-garde art, particularly those under the aegis of automatism, were not necessarily deliberate. To go a step further, is it just a coincidence that these artistic conventions were being distorted in work produced within the asylum at the same time (and sometimes before) the avant-garde outside was challenging them? The appearance of unintentional or 'unconscious' modes of artistic production (most conspicuous in Dadaism and later in Surrealism) is surely not attributable solely to the influence of psychoanalysis. Indeed psychoanalysis itself, with its attempt to find an explicable order in the apparent chaos of dream imagery, can be seen as a product of the same cultural shift. These efforts to document and elaborate unconscious imagery, from both clinical and artistic points of view, belong to a parallel and simultaneous cultural process, one that we are only now beginning to see clearly.

I am not saying that all psychotic art, or even its most outstanding examples, is a kind of misunderstood, excommunicated version of Modernism; but I do want to suggest that there is a pervasive crisis of representation at work in the first few decades of this century, whose effects can be detected in a wide psychoanalysis), and that it also had an effect on psychotic art. The original production of psychotic art may or may not have been influenced by this crisis, but its interpretation or understanding certainly was. One of its symptoms is the attempt to reinforce or insist on the notion of representation at the very moment it is under threat; for example, in the psychoanalytic theory of the psychic representation of drives, in the linguistic relation between signifier and signified, or in theories of artistic expression based on the artist's intentions.

Psychotic art, as I mentioned earlier, is not an absolute or constant category: it is a cultural construct, marked by specific agendas. Whatever it may have meant to its creators, it has cultural, as well as clinical, functions. Like its first cousin Outsider Art, psychotic art functions as an extreme image of creativity: instinctually driven, totally possessional, strikingly original yet strangely impersonal; it acts like a magnified and exaggerated reflection of the post-Renaissance myth of the heroic artist. The triumph of the artistic power of invention over cultural restraints, the inherent power of the image to exceed rational explanation, and the anti-social inclination of indi-vidualistic expression, are all features that find an echo in the profile of psychotic art.

These aspects are also what would have made it impossible for psychotic art, in its classic form, to be the focus of any active form of art therapy, even

Figure 7.4 Train (detail), Aloise Corbaz, undated

had it been available at the time. There seems to be an inherent contradiction between the solitary, compulsive or obstinate character of much psychotic art, its persistence in its folly, and the willingness to enter into the kind of dialogue or negotiation that might be a part of therapy. This contradiction is expressed belligerently in a recent book on psychotic art:

> The exercise of art in the form of a hygenic practice [art therapy] discourages the potential creator from any initiative by pre-empting it and by prejudging its meaning; more precisely, by giving a sense of adjustment to an expression that is antisocial in its momentum.
>
> (Thévoz 1990:81; my translation)

Perhaps the most that could be achieved in the way of 'therapy' in this context is the kind of witnessing or *laissez-faire* exemplified by Jacqueline Porret-Forel's twenty-year-long relationship with the psychotic artist Aloise Corbaz (Figure 7.4). The special respect shown to Aloise, not only by Porret-Forel but by the nursing staff, allowed her to reach a compromise between institutional routine and her creative needs. As her need to draw (at first in secret) was tolerated, so Aloise gradually became more able to take a part in mundane tasks:

> She ironed a basket of washing every morning, and spent the rest of her time drawing, quite openly. The job of ironing balanced that of drawing which seemed to involve no effort on her part.
>
> (Porret-Forel 1994: 9)

All one can say, is that there was obviously some relation between the gradual abatement of Aloise's more violent psychotic symptoms and the evolution of her art, signalled by it becoming larger-scale and being more openly carried out. As one of Porret-Forel's friends commented, after Aloise's death:

> She had cured herself by the method that consists of no longer fighting the illness and of undertaking, in a quite contrary fashion, to cultivate it, to make use of it, to be astonished by it, to make it into an absorbing reason for living.
>
> (Porret-Forel 1966: 95)

Or, to put it another way: if the art itself is a kind of therapy, in the sense that it gives a material shape and structure to psychotic *délire*, then it is one that elaborates and reinforces madness, rather than one that seeks to make sense of it in other terms. If this can be described as 'therapeutic', then it is in a very different sense from either the use of art as occupational therapy or in its various connections to psychotherapy (including art therapy).

However, this is only one side of the coin. Works of art are not just vehicles into which the artist decants his or her feelings; they also prompt us with an important part of what we subsequently identify as our feeling or thinking. The creation of psychotic art in an institutional context, while it is often associated with a quietening of the patient, can also have more negative side-effects, which may amount to a form of auto-intoxication; sometimes soothing or entrancing, but at other times overwhelming or terrifying. It may be that anti-psychotic medication reduces this hypnotic intensity: certainly the only such cases I have witnessed were of unmedicated patients.

The period when art therapy begins to emerge, i.e. after the Second World War, is also the one in which the 'Golden Age' of psychotic art begins to recede. The administration of more sophisticated anti-psychotic medication may be partly responsible, along with changes in patient management. The introduction of art therapy itself is sometimes blamed for the 'normalisation' of psychotic art[9]; but this has more to do with the traditionally suspicious relation between art and therapy than with the actual practice of art therapists, most of whom were extremely respectful and protective towards psychotic artists.[10] Several monographs have been published dealing with therapy with schizophrenic patients that involved artwork during this period (for example, Naumburg 1950; Meares 1977), but here the art seems to be addressed to the therapeutic situation and is treated as a symbolic message to be eventually understood.

'Psychotic art' is a domain with circumstantial boundaries and, like certain kinds of solitary creation in Outsider Art, it may have reached a point of effective closure.[11] But the cultural (as opposed to the strictly psychiatric) needs that constructed a mythology around it have not disappeared. The traditional alliance between art and madness (Wittkower and Wittkower 1963) has been given a new and specific twist through the fact that, once reproductions of psychotic art began to be published and collections exhibited, many artists adopted its stylistic mannerisms.[12] Although it is tempting for some to see this as merely a purloining of certain kinds of extreme or 'original' imagery, it does also raise, implicitly, questions about the relation between 'madness' in its broadest sense and art, and the extent to which a purely psychopathological account of psychotic art is adequate.

In any case, I think we may now have reached a point where the imaginative or creative dimension of madness has largely evaporated, or gone 'off screen'. The idea that certain forms of creation that might be diagnosed 'psychotic' actually exceed any clinical understanding, not just in their elaboration and complexity, but in some more fundamental way, no longer seems to be able to marshall contemporary evidence to support it.

Art therapy's relation to psychotic art has always been ambivalent: the artist is thrilled by its compacted invention, the subversive delights in its irony or perversion; the therapist tries to make sense of it, but is often baffled or uncomfortably aware of fitting an artistic quart into a clinical pint pot. The strictly clinical use of art therapy with people experiencing psychotic states, whose artwork may have few if any of the hallmarks of 'psychotic art', has an obvious value, but there is something about the original forms of psychotic art that does not fit into either psychological or therapeutic pigeonholes. Perhaps it is an indication of the limits to therapy's understanding, or maybe it represents a strange, pyrrhic victory of the creative imagination?

NOTES

1 Lombroso, Tardieu, Simon, Hrdlicka, Hyslop, Marie, to name a few, all established collections well before the First World War (MacGregor 1989).
2 The problem is compounded by the possibility that an ironic stance on the patient's part may make it impossible to know whether we are dealing with parody or unconscious distortion (Maclagan 1983; Thévoz 1990).
3 For example, the pioneer art therapist Edward Adamson has said that he initially saw his job as being to encourage the creation of artworks; their clinical interpretation was left to the psychiatrists (personal communication, 1991). Many other pioneers (E.M. Lyddiatt, Rita Simon, John Henzell) felt that the inherent therapeutic effects of art-making were more important than those factors specifically associated with a psychotherapeutic relationship.
4 An extreme example is that of Antonin Artaud, who continued to write throughout his nine years of psychiatric internment; a work that in its vehement and obsessive rhetoric reflects Artaud's social and cultural solitude.
5 There is a whole complex issue here, about the ways in which visionary or imaginary experience is cast into the mould of external sense perception (e.g. Hillman 1979; Maclagan, 1989).
6 Patricia Allderidge has pointed out that these drawings were bought in the 1930s from a Camden junk shop and bear no date or anything that might enable them to be reliably put in a sequence. In any case, Wain suffered from dementia rather than psychosis.
7 See, for example, the no-man's-land of automatic writing and the different readings of it from spiritualist, clinical and Surrealist perspectives (Shamdasani 1994).
8 He describes it as an 'extravagant, grandiose, often compulsively distorted attutude' (Prinzhorn 1922/1972: 272).
9 Both Dubuffet and Victor Musgrave were hostile to art therapy, as is Michel Thévoz. Leo Navratil, on the other hand, claims that the 'Artist's House' at Gugging, where long-stay patients were given high-quality materials and encouraged to exhibit their artwork, was a form of art therapy.
10 In many instances art therapists not only provided a sanctuary for these patients in the art department, but often preserved their work from destruction. Edward Adamson's collection at the Netherne is a famous example; but here, too, there was an eventual conflict between its artistic and its clinical status (see Rona Rumney, unpublished dissertation, Goldsmiths College, 1980).
11 John MacGregor has recently argued that the massive publicity and commercial interest surrounding Outsider Art have made it less and less likely that a solitary creator like Henry Darger will ever be discovered again.
12 The list of influence is long, and similar to those who borrowed from 'primitive art': it includes Klee, Dali, Ernst, Dubuffet and Arnulf Rainer.

REFERENCES

Allderidge, P. (1995) 'Pictures by Louis Wain in the Guttmann–Maclay collection' (leaflet for Bethlem Royal Hospital Archives).

Bader, A. and Navratil, L. (1976) *Zwischen Wahn und Wirklichkeit*, Frankfurt: Bucher Verlag.

Die Prinszhornsammlung (Catalogue) (1980), Konigsberg: Athenaum Verlag.

Hillman, J. (1979) *Image-sense* Dallas: Spring.

MacGregor, J. (1989) *The Discovery of the Art of the Insane*, Princeton.

Maclagan, D. (1983) *'Methodical madness'*, Dallas: Spring.

——— (1989) 'Fantasy and the figurative' in A. Gilroy and T. Dalley (eds) *Pictures at an Exhibition*, London: Routledge/Tavistock.

Meares, A. (1977) *The Door of Serenity*, Melbourne: Hill of Content.

Morgenthaler, W. (1921) *Madness and Art*, (trans. A.H. Essman), Lincoln: University of Nebraska Press.

Naumburg, M. (1950) *Schizophrenic Art*, London: Heinemann.

Porret-Forel, J. (1966) 'Aloise et son Théatre', in *Cahiers de l'Art Brut* No. 7 (Paris).

——— 1994 'Aloise', in *L'Oeuf Sauvage* No. 9: 2–14 (Paris).

Prinzhorn, H. (1922/1972) *Artistry of the Mentally Ill*, (trans. E. von Brockdorff), New York: Springer-Verlag.

Sass, L.A. (1992) *Madness* and *Modernism*, Cambridge, Mass.: Harvard University Press.

Shamdasani, S. (1994) Introduction to *From India to the Planet Mars*, Princeton.

Thévoz, M. (1990) *Art Brut, Psychose et Médiumnité*, Paris: Editions La Différence.

Will-Levaillant, F. (1980) 'L'analyse des dessins d'aliénés et de médiums en France avant le Surréalisme', *Revue de l'Art* No. 50 (Paris).

Wittkower, R. and Wittkower, M. (1963) *Born Under Saturn*, London: Weidenfeld & Nicolson.

Chapter 8

The history of art therapy and psychosis (1938–95)

Chris Wood

Since the end of the Second World War, art therapists have had a consistent history of offering therapy to people who experience psychotic episodes. They have been unusual among those professionals offering psychotherapy in attempting to create the circumstances for this work within public sector services. The history of art therapy and psychosis is not well documented, but it is possible to see what has been recorded in order to think about and plan for development in the future. This chapter will describe some of the techniques developed by art therapists for this particular client group during three periods of the profession's history. It will also begin to consider possibilities for the future against a background of community care legislation in Britain and other countries.

That art therapists have sustained and developed ways of working with people with serious mental disorders is inspiring, but the continual change of circumstances in which many public sector art therapists currently find themselves working is often seriously undermining them and the clients they are endeavouring to help. The title and subject of Claire Baron's book *Asylum to Anarchy* (1987) sometimes seems to be fitting for the move towards community settings. Baron is at pains to point out the dangers of abandoning a clear frame of reference – even an institutional frame. However Berke *et al.* (1995) discuss how the history of therapeutic communities has developed out of the wide-eyed enthusiasm of people wanting to be helpers, 'This is a point the importance of which we did not quite appreciate at the time. Really, the Arbours was established for helpers seeking a new framework, a new home, just as much as for everyone else' (Berke *et al.* 1995: 173).

It is difficult for people who work in the public sector and want to be helpers in the mid-1990s, as they feel that they and their patients have been thrown out of the old asylums or big houses. They are trying to work with people in the midst of deep distress, without having a reliable setting or a sense of containment for themselves and their work. There are not enough services for this client group and this is distressing for clients and workers alike. The courage required to maintain good work practices in the face of all the changes and the deprivations is not always recognised.

MIND and various campaigning bodies point to the absurdity of trying to replace services with supervision orders. One client asked a government minister at a national MIND conference, 'Why do you imagine that, for me, someone diagnosed as paranoid, a supervision order will make me feel better?' The substitution of supervision orders will not really touch what has become a major crisis of mental health provision in many large inner cities. What MIND proposes is a combination of services – crisis intervention, continuing care, day care, work and occupation, accommodation and a place in the community. Mental health strategies for people with enduring mental health problems, even those coming from central government, are often impressive – but the funding is not.

The user movement is flourishing despite this grim backdrop. The demands of this movement are that professionals and government alike really consider the rights of users. This has implications for therapeutic approaches in general, as do the social economic circumstances in which people live and work. The development of the Voices Movement (an organisation originating in the early 1990s in the Netherlands intended both to challenge explanations of the phenomena of 'hearing voices' and to support voice hearers through self-help groups) is a force for change. Their demands are clear. They are not 'anti-psychiatry' but they do ask for more judicious prescription of medication, psychological intervention and professional support in establishing self-help groups. The user movement is beginning to make it much more difficult to forget the millions throughout the world who succumb to psychosis. The art therapy profession could certainly have a part to play in developing and providing future services.

AN OVERVIEW OF THE 1938–95 PERIOD

I view the recent history of art therapy in Britain as having three main periods of development. I consider these periods to be, firstly, the time between the late 1930s and the end of the 1950s when the first ideas about using art as a therapy in hospital settings began to emerge. Secondly, the period between the early 1960s and the late 1970s when, in the wake of the creation of the British Association of Art Therapists, many art therapists found themselves allied to the anti-psychiatry movement and to humanistic schools of therapeutic thought. Finally, the third period which had its beginnings in the early 1980s and continues through the mid-1990s, is a period when art therapists have lived through many changes in public sector legislation, the increasing professionalisation of their work and a more obvious linking of it to models from psychoanalysis, psychotherapy and group process. My understanding of the profession's history has been greatly helped by the historical analysis made by Diane Waller (1991). Although there are many areas of overlap, essentially the clinical practice of the three historical periods can be seen, in the first, as upholding the power of expression; as taking an anti-psychiatric stance in the second; and as strengthening a psychotherapeutic base in the third. Surprisingly it is not always clear what the impact of these different periods have meant for practice. Where clients have a history of psychosis it is sometimes particularly difficult to find evidence of just how the therapist behaves. This is true of a good deal of clinical literature about therapy with this client group, the omission is by no means confined to the writings of art therapists. It is possible that the omission suggests something about the difficulty in describing this particular work.

It is interesting to consider that the development of psychotherapeutic work in public sector services in Britain coincided with the more modest developments of art therapy from the early stages of the Second World War. Both psychotherapy and art therapy were employed in the movements to rehabilitate people (mainly armed service personnel) traumatised by war.

A number of historical accounts of the modern history of psychiatry describe the decade after the Second World War as being a crucible for the production of many powerful new ideas for psychiatric practice. Equally powerful impulses in the world of art were felt at this time, in the push towards expressionism. The trauma and stress of war had a wide-reaching impact for most people and psychiatrists in post-war Britain and Europe were necessarily affected. Two world wars had provided the economic need to find more immediate understanding of the nature and treatment of mental distress. A number of rehabilitative initiatives that had prophetic power were developed as a result of this wartime experience, not least of which were the initiatives 'to site psychiatric care in the community, at least in general hospitals, providing outpatient facilities' (Newton 1988: 11).

The actual process of de-institutionalisation and its origins are extremely interesting. The 'Open Door' policies in mental hospitals and community care strategies followed the advent and use of neuroleptic medication for the treatment of psychotic disorders. However, a number of historical accounts of psychiatry do intimate that numbers of patients in the large mental hospitals began declining before the advent and use of neuroleptics. Richard Warner (1985) makes a very coherent analysis (with adequate statistical support) of the cluster of factors which may have influenced this decline in the asylum population. In doing so he convincingly demonstrates the need for much more careful consideration of community care strategies.

Warner points to the difference between studies of mental hospital population decline made in northern Europe and those made in America. He points to work in Norway by Örnulv Ödegard who studied the figures for patients first admitted to all Norwegian psychiatric hospitals before and after the introduction of the anti-psychotics. Ödegard found a small increase in discharge rates during 1955–59 compared with those admitted during 1948–52, prior to the use of drugs. But he found a much bigger increase in the discharge rate when he compared the 1948–52 group with patients admitted in the late 1930s. Warner also points to similar patterns observed in Britain at Bexley Hospital in Kent; and to findings by Michael Shepherd and colleagues after studying discharge rates at St John's Hospital, Buckinghamshire. There was no significant change as a result of the introduction of the drugs. Warner also records that similar findings were recorded at Mapperly Hospital in Nottingham.

The evidence in the United States, however, suggests that the steady decline in the psychiatric hospital population did coincide with the introduction of neuroleptics. However, even in America the famous study made by Henry Brill and Robert Patton could not lay claim to conclusive evidence. They concluded that 'the abrupt population fall was in nature and degree due to the introduction of the new drugs' because 'no other explanation could be found' (Brill and Patton 1959: 116, 495–509).

The differences between psychiatric provision in America and in Britain were quite marked. In 1958 when the new drug treatments were firmly established, St Lawrence Hospital in New York became fully 'open door'. However, as early as 1946 in Britain a small but influential number of psychiatrists were involved in trying to develop different patterns of institutional life through the establishment of therapeutic communities and the use of psychotherapeutic groups. A small number of art therapists were involved with these early therapeutic communities. Initially the ideas of the therapeutic community were not applied to work with people with a history of psychosis, the elderly or to people with long-term problems, but the new ways of working did have an influence on institutional practice and the general climate of treatment. Warner (1985) suggests that the different standards of care and attention in Britain and America directly influenced the way community provision is viewed:

> Antipsychotic drugs then appear to be more effective for the psychotic patient who is living in an inadequate setting and to be less valuable where the environment is designed for his or her well-being.
>
> (Warner 1985: 86)

This is a claim worth considering very seriously because of the implication that the elements of care and respect in this particular work are centrally important. This is something I have written about elsewhere (Wood 1992). The elements of care and respect are important in humanitarian terms and also in terms of the outcome of the therapy. I am thinking about the outcome as a cluster of effects which includes the rehabilitative influence on the client's life, staff morale and the effects of both of these on the general level of therapeutic hopefulness.

I have already suggested that art therapists are unusual among those professionals offering psychotherapy to people with a history of psychosis in attempting to create the circumstances for this work within public sector services. There is evidence to show that the attempt by art therapists to maintain this work in the public sector is not exclusive, though it is long lived.

The gradual introduction and development of therapeutic community ideas did not at first encompass work with people with a history of psychosis. Similarly, the psychotherapeutic group work developed by Wilfred Bion at Northfield Hospital in 1942 was not aimed at people in the midst of psychosis. In general his methods were not appreciated by the army. However, his influential work has enabled strands of psychotherapeutic understanding to be woven into public sector services. Foulkes succeeded Bion at Northfield and he worked there with Harold Bridger, Joshua Bierer and Tom Main. They have all become very well known in the history of innovative psychiatry and the use of group psychotherapy. Diane Waller's (1993) comment about their work is telling, 'They too make use of group psychotherapy but took care to integrate their approach into the overall treatment philosophy and hence were able to stay on with much success' (Waller 1993: 5).

The question of how to integrate a therapeutic approach into the overall treatment philosophy must necessarily tax the mind of anyone working in public sector services. This is particularly complex when working with a group of clients whose needs are potentially so widespread as those with a history of psychosis. For art therapists this has been a thorny question throughout the history of the profession. During the period between 1991 and 1995, art therapists, in common with others working in the public sector, found themselves facing an extraordinary lengthy bout of service reorganisation. It is particularly important for art therapists to consider the nature of their work and its relationship to these many changes which have the aim of taking the main point of contact with clients into the community.

In the period shortly after the Second World War, the development of therapeutic communities and their particular philosophy of care anticipated the later development of some aspects of community care. Within the framework of the therapeutic community, staff and patients worked together to establish a community environment in which the traditional methods of the institution and its power relations were challenged. Patients were encouraged to take and share responsibility for the therapeutic work of the community. Staff and patient roles were blurred, and open honest communication was encouraged. As already stated, this form of community was not, in the first decade, directed towards work with people with a history of psychosis. Initially, Maxwell Jones and Tom Main worked with people described as having personality disorders. At the Henderson, a therapeutic community in south London, Jones worked with many people who had experienced long-term unemployment. Peter Cole, an art therapist based at the Henderson, described in an early edition of *Inscape* (1976) the gradual inclusion and acceptance of art therapy within the therapeutic community. Cole's account confirms quite clearly that ideas about the range of clients amenable to psychotherapeutic work was widening within certain sectors of the public services. Throughout the 1960s and 1970s these ideas were introduced into many psychiatric wards in the NHS and were used in the attempt to help a whole range of patients hitherto not involved in psycho-therapeutic approaches. This included people with a history of psychosis and even those in the midst of a psychosis.

In Britain the ideas were introduced in some hospitals with much more conviction than in others. A number of hospitals gained a reputation for their innovatory work in the use of the therapeutic community – for example, Littlemore in Oxford, Fulbourne in Cambridge, Dingleton in Scotland. Dr Ben Pomryn, who had worked with Maxwell Jones at the Henderson, set up therapeutic community wards for the elderly, for brain-damaged patients and for adult psychiatric patients at Littlemore Hospital during the 1960s. I include mention of his work to show how wide the net of the criteria of suitability for psychotherapeutic work had become in some sectors of the NHS. I agree with Warner (1985) that the explanation for the sharp twists and turns in the treatment philosophy of the public sector are fundamentally influenced by the political and economic circumstances of the day: 'Both the concept and management of psychosis appear to have been influenced by political and economic factors. Ideology and practice in psychiatry, to a significant extent, are at the mercy of material conditions' (Warner 1985: 127).

It does seem that the period of post-war economic recovery and the boom times of the late 1960s and early 1970s coincided with real strides forward in psychiatric practice. The difficult economic climate of the late 1980s and early 1990s has coincided with what have been reactionary backward moves in psychiatric practice. The tenets of community care, which include vision-ary aspects and could lead to inspired development, have not in this economic climate been able to achieve much that resembles either community or care. The mid-1990s was a difficult period in which to work in psychiatry. Nevertheless, many psychiatric workers in all disciplines struggled bravely to generate ways of working that have meaning and value. Peter Barham (1992) writes (first quoting S. Shah and later the Seebohm Report):

> Community Care in Britain at the present time, it has been recently said, is 'an unknown quantity with an unknown distribution around the country'. Depending on the good or bad fortune of his location, 'a young man with severely disabling schizophrenia might block an acute psychiatric bed for a year, enter a slow-stream rehabilitation ward, move to a hostel in the centre of town, return to his parents' home, stay in bed and breakfast accommodation or sleep in a cardboard box'. As has been widely remarked, the hopes that have been entertained for resettling the disadvantaged into integrated communities in which they will benefit from a 'network of reciprocal social relationships' have paid scant regard to the realities of late twentieth century Britain.
>
> (Barham 1992: 104)

I find it interesting that the range of interest described by Barham's first two publications *Schizophrenia and Human Value* (1984) and *Closing the*

Asylums (1992) moves from the careful consideration of the details of therapeutic work in his first book to a shrewd analysis of the political realities of mental health legislation in the second. In public sector settings, people working therapeutically now need to give attention to the intimacies of their therapeutic relationships and at the same time have an understanding of the political and economic circumstances of the work. Many art therapists have had to develop this kind of oscillating consciousness.

It is interesting to follow the development of the different forms into which art therapy has crystallised for work with people with a history of psychosis. It is perhaps in this particular work that the tension between the inner process and the outer political world is most radical. I think this is the case because people in the midst of psychosis, or with a history of psychosis, find it difficult to defend themselves in the face of difficult social and economic circumstances and a great deal of institutional change. Similarly, it is becoming increasingly difficult for therapists and people in other disciplines to offer work which provides a container for the most disturbed clients, because in the midst of so much organisational change few staff themselves feel contained by their respective institutions. Consequently, it has been a combination of pragmatic survival tactics and desperate need which has led psychiatric staff to take an increasing interest in the political circumstances of their work.

The White Paper, *Care for People* in *Community Care: The Next Decade and Beyond* (1989) and *Working for Patients* (1989) both built on the Griffiths Report (1988) and prefigured The National Health Service and Community Care Act (1990). This Act asserts that the promotion of choice and independence are underneath all the government's proposals and that their key components should be the responsive nature of the service. These should allow a range of choices for consumers and provide services that intervene no more than is necessary to foster independence. The particularities of how this legislation and its recommendations have affected mental health policies and practice is complex.

Scull (1977), along with Warner (1985) and others, might reject explanations which propose that the effectiveness of psychotropic drugs is central to the shift towards the community. To Scull the motives for change are more negative – he uses the phrase 'decarceration' as a shorthand to describe a state-sponsored policy of closing down the institutions which had enabled the earlier policies of segregation and control. He sees the state as moving towards a more *laissez-faire* position as a direct result of the increased costs of segregation and the fiscal crisis of the state. He warns of the dangers of hiding a lack of provision for the mentally ill under the apparently humane mask of community care. Joan Busfield (1986) (citing Sedgwick as support) suggests that the analysis by Scull actually misses a very significant shift in mental health care practice which requires more than an economic explanation. She asserts that the move towards community care has been associated with a significant reorientation of the attention of the mental health services. This reorientation has seen resources being allocated to services for acute less serious mental disorders and not into services for chronic long-term mental illness. Community services for the former group of clients have been enlarged during the post-war period, whereas services for the people with long-term mental illnesses have not. Resources for these latter services have always been meagre. It now seems highly probable that some attempt to influence this distribution of resources will be made during the 1990s. Therapeutic work may be reserved for people with enduring mental health problems. This may have the effect that the largest group of potential clients (those who do not have a history of psychosis) are increasingly to be encouraged towards 'independent' living. Joan Woddis (1992) has suggested that White Papers like *The Griffiths Report* have done little to clarify the situation in practice:

> The notion of day units, possibly conducted on therapeutic community lines for the use of both acute and long-stay patients, remains largely a matter of precept not practice ... and the issue of the difference in approaches between practice in the community and hospital settings remains a crucial factor.
>
> (Woddis 1992: 32)

These are powerful issues for all disciplines working in the field of mental health, but what follows is a result of my looking specifically through the literature written by previous generations of art therapists. Although this literature is well worth exploring it is generally not very specific about the techniques of work being used, consequently I have tried to form or conjure an image (by the implication of what they write) of how they worked with people with a history of psychosis.

The first period

Possibly the impulse for much psychotherapeutic work with people with a history of psychosis comes from the wish to understand more in order to be helpful. Tracing the origins for this particular work in the world of art therapy is not straightforward. It is very clear that Adrian Hill, a much heralded pioneer in Britain, did not encounter people with a history of psychosis. His work developed from an art education approach, to one which gradually became more psychologically minded. The same might also be said of Arthur Segal, in his wish to forge links between medics and artists, something for which Waller (1991) records that he was commended by Freud. In the art world since the end of the nineteenth century there had been steadily more concern with the outreaches of human experience. Klinger's etching *The Plague* (1903) graphically portrays the frightening dreamlike preoccupations of the turn of the century (see Figure 8.1). The two world wars compound what seems to have been a general sense that an innocent understanding of the surface of

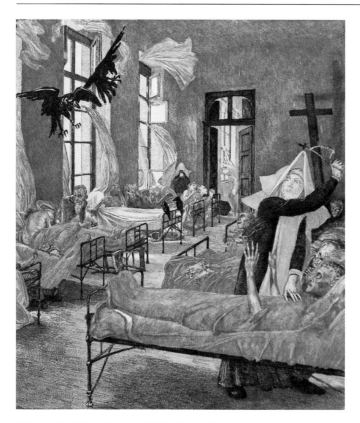

Figure 8.1 The Plague, 1903, Max Klinger

human experience is not enough. It was into this reeling world that what has become known as 'art therapy' emerged in Europe. Gradually it became apparent that the artwork made by people in the midst of psychosis often resonated with a more general need to understand those matters which lie below the surface. Art therapists working during the first period, between the late 1930s and the end of the 1950s, clearly did work with people in the midst of psychosis. Although it is clear that the pioneers, Adrian Hill and Arthur Segal, did not work with this client group, there is evidence in their writings that both Edward Adamson (1984) and E.M. Lyddiatt (1972) did do such work.

I personally began work as an art therapist at Netherne Hospital in Surrey in the late 1970s. Netherne Hospital had been the psychiatric hospital in which one of the pioneer art therapists, Edward Adamson, had worked for many years after the Second World War. I was very interested to meet at Netherne some of the long-term patients who remembered 'Mr Adamson'. The studio and the gallery he had established were still in existence. The studio was a long, white wooden building with windows on three sides. The equipment for each person included an easel, a white wooden chair and a white wooden frame with two shelves for art materials; each person was able to have a small self-contained area in which to work. It was probably possible, given the size of the room, to work in a way which did not feel overlooked. I was interested to discover from Waller's book (1991) that Edward Adamson was involved in work when he was first at Netherne in 1946, which was part of a controlled study by the two psychiatrists Dax and Reitman. The study was concerned with the effects of leucotomy. Adamson was given a clear brief by the medical staff: 'He was not to attempt to "interpret" pictures, nor to show any interest in the patient's life history or psychological problems in case he may have influenced the work produced' (Waller 1991: 54).

In my conversations with some of the people who remembered working with Adamson, all of them mentioned the quietness of the studio and Edward Adamson's equally quiet presence. They also remembered the respect with which they felt themselves to be treated by him. It may be that, partly as a result of the medical brief and partly as a result of his personality, Adamson provided a very powerfully receptive container for many of the patients who worked with him. His way of inviting people to do some painting was very simple: he would sit down next to them and ask them if they would like to do some painting. One artist was still living as a patient at Netherne when I was working there between 1978 and 1981. By her account she had been very disturbed when she first met Adamson. She spoke to me quite movingly of him having really understood her needs. Of her he writes:

> During this time she worked intermittently in the studio. When she was very ill, she was unable to produce anything, but as her spirit slowly gathered strength, her creative ability was renewed and she succeeded in composing some exceptional works. Her work transcends natural self-pity, to portray elements of universal suffering.
>
> (Adamson 1984: 53)

Whereas this artist (who had achieved a degree of public recognition) was unable to produce artwork while she was very disturbed, Adamson encountered other people who apparently had the impulse to make artwork throughout even very difficult periods. One man presented him with a picture entitled *Graffiti on Lavatory Paper*:

> These drawings were presented to me by a very ill man who had been on a locked ward in the hospital for years. He was incontinent and unable to speak clearly. He had drawn vigorously on the only paper he could find. The top strip is filled with strange shapes and words which had a special meaning for him. The second strip depicts a lion and its mate, which he loved to draw repeatedly when he later came to the studio. . . .
>
> (Adamson 1984: 9)

Of the work in general Adamson writes:

> The hospital residents who came to the studio were accorded the dignity of helping to cure themselves. The very fact that they came to the studio each day placed a responsibility on their shoulders, rather than allowing them to become the passive recipients of authoritarian care. We were all working very much in the dark in those early days. I must confess that within a few weeks of starting my new job, I was in two minds whether I would have sufficient courage to continue. On looking back I realise that I stayed mainly in response to the overwhelming need of those who queued up everyday outside the studio, eager to begin.
>
> (Adamson 1984: 2)

The comments about working in the dark and having the courage to continue must be recognised by all therapists when they are trying to contend with the sorts of feelings evoked by working with psychotic processes. However, it does seem that Adamson's methods were broadly similar with all of his clients. There seems to be very little mention of special or different work with people with psychotic disorders:

> When a person comes to the studio, I never suggest what he should draw; it is essential that the idea should be entirely his own. This particular approach demands a considerable amount of patience, sometimes it is often weeks, months, or even years, that we are both obliged to wait for someone's creativity. All I can do is try and create a permissive atmosphere and have the necessary paint and paper on hand. If the person is prepared to come and spend the time with me, then I must be prepared to join in the vigil.
>
> (Adamson 1984: 7)

Occasionally there is an indication of how disturbed some of his patients must have been, but little to distinguish what he did with them from what he did with less disturbed people. I glimpse something of his steady work of containment in occasional sentences here and there, for example, 'Rich veins of surrealism are discovered in the studio. When, sometimes they are fearful and persecuting, painting ventilates them within the safety of the studio' (Adamson 1984: 6).

It would have been very interesting to know whether or not the people involved in the group murals, which Adamson describes, had a history of psychosis. From what he says of them it suggests they might have had: 'Many of them had regressed and would not communicate, or if they did, it was in a private language, unintelligible to me' (Adamson 1984: 44). He goes on to describe how, over a period of eight hours, this same group of twelve people went on to paint an 'unusually integrated picture of a fishing scene'. I myself have seen groups of very disturbed people get involved with group pictures; the ways in which they are able to co-operate and plan the work is impressive.

He also established small individual studios for particular patients (some famous, some not) in the round summerhouses dotted around the grounds of Netherne or in small cupboard-like rooms off its large main corridors. The physical effort involved in helping the female sculptor to cast her large claymade sculptures in Plaster of Paris suggests that the quality of Adamson's involvement was not as passive as some of his writing might imply. He was no mere pawn in the outcome of controlled experiments. He was very much engaged with people who had serious disorders.

Martina Thomson (1989) gives a very moving account of her apprenticeship to the art therapist E.M. Lyddiatt. The account made me seek out Lyddiatt's book *Spontaneous Painting and Modelling* (1972), and I was impressed to find in her introduction the following assertion:

Diagnosis and other medical procedures are not the concern of an art department. A person may be suffering from a disease that is labelled schizophrenia, but he remains a human being – his mind still works as do other minds, although certain notions may have become exaggerated. In essence he is unaltered and frequently he can be restored to health.

(Lyddiatt 1972: 5–6)

Repeatedly I find evidence in the early writings of art therapists of the insistence on being with people, no matter how disturbed, in as ordinary a way as possible. Respectfulness seems implicit in much of what is written, and given the damage which people feel as a result of stigma, respectfulness can be a real balm and a very good place to begin for a therapist. I have come across many people working in the psychiatric services who understand this. The understanding often seems to have less to do with their professional training than with what comes from themselves. John MacGregor (1989) suggests that there is something about the artwork and the writings of real men and women offered partly in the attempt to explain their condition, which does invoke respect.

In the introduction to Lyddiatt's book the Jungian E.A. Bennett writes:

Although the range of Miss Lyddiatt's experience has been wide, her methods remain much the same with all who use the art room. That they are patients is forgotten; they work in an informal group, yet by the nature of the treatment they must do so as individuals. Some prefer to paint unobserved, and there is nothing against this.

(Bennett in Lyddiatt 1972: xiv)

Thomson (1989) describes the chaotic, rich muddle found in Lyddiatt's art rooms. This is in sharp contrast to the cool order of Adamson's rooms. References which Lyddiatt makes to the studios in which she worked throughout her book suggest a very homely rambling collection of small rooms full of artwork in progress. Thomson remembers Lyddiatt saying with a smile, 'my house is a mess but my dreams are in order', and suggests that this was somehow expressive of her approach to art therapy. Lyddiatt writes:

> Even if it is an over-simplification it may sometimes be a useful plan to describe spontaneous painting in three stages: firstly, imaginative material is given form; secondly, it 'works back' on the maker and is experienced; and thirdly, one feels more alive. Often these stages blend.
>
> (Lyddiatt 1972: 6)

Later in the book she describes how she considers that understanding the content of pictures which are made is a problem which is 'exceedingly complex'. She does not see intellectual understanding as being the key; she quotes Jung: 'the important thing is not to interpret and understand fantasies but primarily to experience them' (Jung quoted in Lyddiatt 1972). This does resonate with my own experience when I have been presented by clients with images and ideas I have found difficult to understand. Lyddiatt's book gives the impression of clear beliefs and a certain confidence about her work. However, in some of the examples of work with particular individuals it seems that her confidence is not altogether sustained in the face of some of her more disturbed clients. What is refreshing is her honesty and humour about her doubts:

> He was deeply involved in the idea of the journey from hell to heaven. I believe he wanted me to take the part of the Holy Virgin Mary and to act with him, but, afraid, I pleaded that I was busy. Then, quiet and meditative, he asked to work in the side room which was full of odds and ends, wooden boxes, rope, a table and chairs – and these he deliberately rearranged about the room.
>
> After a period of silence he declared, 'Now I am ready for you', and then insisted on a further silence before he led me round the room, climbing, jumping, scrambling on the pilgrimage from hell to heaven. The Communion was half-way; subsequently he fell to the floor from a 'hill' back to the first corner, where he said, 'Now we do it again and that will be on a higher level'. At each change of direction he genuflected, and at the climax walked backwards. Seeing the reflection of sunlight on lavatory windows of the distant hospital building, this was shown to me as 'holiness', and I was told, 'You must start and assimilate the lowest'.
>
> At one point he gripped my shoulders fiercely and declared that I was the victim, and I stupidly produced orange juice to drink in the hope of providing a diversion. This, however, became part of the play – and holding up the glass to see the light through it, he told me,
>
> 'When you see the spirit you must hold it fast – then it swings and moves'.
>
> Later that same morning he painted his 'holy' picture; it was of the pilgrimage. In it, dragons and animals, as well as men, make this journey

which is finally accomplished when man is carried to Christ by an animal from a mountain-top high on the right side. The figure of Christ, 'He Himself', is portrayed in pencil in a dull yellow circle in the top left corner.

Incidents of the moment were made one with this picture – a fly flying out of the window was going to Christ, and dust, and paint happening to drip – all were incorporated in the experience and all were real.

The picture has a strange quality which bewilders and fascinates me. At first sight it appears confused and messy – yet this man knew exactly what each fragment was intended to be. Looking at the picture one finds more and more. The colour is mainly Indian red and dark grey. A dull green hill is at the bottom left and a grey-blue building with tiny people higher up. To achieve this, I imagine paint was put on and then the pictures he saw in the accidentals were established by drawing in pencil on top of the paint. There is much detail that cannot be understood without explanation and I have often regretted that I did not spend more time with the painter that day.

A member of the staff from whom I asked advice, wondering what the afternoon would bring, shocked me by declaring that the patient was 'playing up'; but I have since reproached myself that I let him down through my fear and lack of understanding.

(Lyddiatt 1972: 63–4)

A number of the people with whom she worked had had leucotomies, and Lyddiatt writes of how the sensitivity of their image-making deteriorates after these operations. In reading these descriptions, it becomes clear how hard it must have been at that time, in such a context, to maintain some sense of clarity and confidence about work with people with a history of psychosis. Yet it does seem that her basic approach of treating people with respect and of trying not to evade the 'ever-present phenomenon' of the unconscious in everyone, are the cornerstones of a method of work which, if it can be adhered to, has much relevance for practice today.

Some of the underlying Jungian inspiration for Lyddiatt's work does resonate with what was developed at Withymead. This was a therapeutic community in Devon, which made the use of art a fundamental part of its therapeutic work. It was established by Gilbert and Irene Champernowne towards the end of the Second World War. Irene Champernowne had been analysed by both C.G. Jung and Toni Wolff in Zurich, and perhaps it is fair to say it was her vision and energy which provided the original inspiration for the community. Anthony Stevens (1986) gives an account of Withymead which might have been written in the 1940s. The community does appear to have been a remarkable place in its attempts to run along democratic lines. There was a prodigious amount of contact between the clients and the staff (particularly the Champernownes). It provided many studios and access to different forms of art and music. People with a history of psychosis certainly did stay at Withymead although the majority of the community members did not have such a history. However Champernowne did herself acknowledge that the community did not work easily in the service of some of its more disturbed members. Stevens writes: 'Irene's rather condescending attitude to the use of drugs may seem naive, . . . unlike many Jungians, Irene was not against the use of drugs on principle', and 'Schizophrenics were clearly better off taking their Largactil at Withymead than in a conventional mental hospital ward' (Stevens 1986: 49–50).

When she was giving a lecture in 1970 (published in 1971) Champernowne gave a more substantial glimpse of how she thought about the question of psychosis:

> It is true that in therapeutic practice many of the creative forms arise from the depths of the psyche – a place where the universal experience of all mankind also originates. This is true particularly of the psychotic patient whose ego has already been flooded with images and experiences; over-whelmed quite often by archetypal patterns, and thus deprived of the simple human ways of living and loving. Creative expression which is recognised and called Art is often the result. A psychotic patient may sometimes paint out a very great deal of his archetypal involvement through his paintings or even crystallise out and freeze some of the unacceptable elements in his psyche in aggression or perversions in art form. But my experience of many series of paintings of this archetypal nature often displayed in exhibitions is that they have had little effect upon the individual painter's total way of living. The creator is often unable to observe and learn from what the unconscious has expressed. The ego is already too drowned in the unconscious experiences itself to be illumined by that which has been created. In any case it is such a highly skilled job deciphering the mysterious messages of these statements that it is rare for the painter already swallowed up by the flood of images to come through to a conscious grasp of his own creation, though people like C.G. Jung and Godwin Baynes and others have struggled and in many cases wonderfully succeeded in effecting healing through their understanding of them.
>
> (Champernowne 1971)

It is worth noting that both Michael Edwards and Patsy Nowell Hall were among those art therapists who developed the work of art therapy during the following second period. They were both prominent among the number of art therapists who lived and worked at Withymead during this early first period.

The second period

The second period, between the early 1960s and the late 1970s, was perhaps not surprisingly, given the historical context, a time of many rich influences in the development of art therapy. The emerging humanistic schools of therapy were prevalent at the time, as were existential ideas and the anti-psychiatry movement. The influence of psychoanalysis was becoming more publicly and popularly acknowledged. All of these developments informed ways in which art therapists felt able to work. During the first period between the late 1930s and the late 1950s, it has been suggested (Jones1987, Waller 1991) that the class origins of most pioneer art therapists were such that they could easily appeal to the sympathies, and thereby gain the patronage of, psychiatrists and medical superintendents. In the 1960s the social origins of many art therapists were equally middle class but the tenor of the times was different. The first period had been characterised by a 'wholesome' approach to the plight of the mentally ill; with the 1960s came challenges to accepted ideas about what constituted madness.

Although the influences acting upon art therapists in this second period were rich ones it is still difficult to find substantial descriptions from that time, of what art therapists actually did when working with people in the midst of a psychosis. Again, I feel the need to add that I think actual accounts of this work have not commonly been made by any profession in any period. However, it is possible to identify a cluster of attitudes to the work from the implications of the writings of art therapists during this time. Also, I trained at the end of the 1970s and so I think elements of my training embodied the main preoccupations of the period.

MacGregor (1989) suggests that a new sensibility towards the art of the insane developed during the first quarter of the twentieth century. He considers that the origins of this new sensibility, largely among a few cultured psychiatrists, are to be found in the development of philosophical, literary and aesthetic Romanticism. It is possible to trace aspects of this earlier Romanticism among some of the art therapists writing during the 1960s and 1970s and this is in keeping with more general characteristics of that time. Art therapy literature at that time regularly refers to the notion of a creative illness. Michael Edwards wrote: 'There were some uncomfortable paradoxes – one person's work was drawn with extraordinary refinement and conviction at times when he was most ill, turning to pleasant but very ordinary little flower paintings in recovery' (Edwards 1978: 12).

An idea related to creative illness is that of the mad genius; it recurs at different points in the history of western culture and it provided a cultural image, which in part suited the ethos of the 1960s. This image might view the idea of a cure as something barbaric; or the idea of treatment as being beside the point. Concerns which seemed connected to these are seen in the discussion in the art therapy world at that time about whether or not the products of the insane were to be considered as art or not. Philosophically, in settings adjacent to art therapy practice the questions are of interest, but there does seem to have been a defensive element in the way they were posed. This is perhaps not surprising given that the mainstream art world was at that time regularly dismissive of the concerns of art therapy. Possibly this is comparable to defensiveness during the early days of the psychology profession when it was anxious to be considered as a serious science in relation to medicine.

MacGregor(1989), although publishing nearly a decade later, was almost certainly writing during this time. He would have us resolve the issue by defining the 'art of the insane' as only consisting of those rare works worked on during lifetimes of incarceration by artists such as Wölfli, Aloise and Emile Nolde. MacGregor would no longer include all works by 'madmen' in the category 'the art of the insane'; he describes the ultimate conclusion of his position as being a moral obligation upon physicians to anticipate the rare emergence of a 'schizophrenic master'. These physicians should then, 'attempt to create an environment in which creativity and independent growth exists, whatever form it may take' (MacGregor 1989: 103).

MacGregor clearly considers that the production of art by severely mentally ill will soon cease almost entirely. He saw the conditions for the creation of such art as prolonged hospitalisation, prolonged psychosis (i.e. before the use of medication) and the absence of therapy. Although MacGregor's writing is replete and scholarly, his focus of attention and actual conclusions do seem perversely romantic. It is the myopic tenets of such romanticism which led to the tragic and cruel incarceration of the poet John Clare between 1837 and the end of his life in 1864 (see Roy Porter 1987: 76–81).

In *The Inner Eye*, the catalogue of art made in psychiatric hospitals and clinics, and shown at the exhibition held in Oxford in 1978 (Elliott 1978), the art therapists Peter Byrne, Michael Edwards, Diana Halliday and John Henzell wrote about some of the concerns of the art therapy world. Byrne, Edwards and Henzell do address the issue of whether or not the work resulting from psychiatric patients is art or not. Edwards quotes Jung:

> Although from time to time my patients produce artistically beautiful creations which might very well be shown in modern art exhibitions, I nevertheless treat them as wholly worthless according to the tests of serious art. It is essential that no such value be allowed them, for otherwise my patients might imagine themselves to be artists, and this would spoil the effects of the exercise. It is not a question of art – or rather it should not be a question of art – but of something more, something other than mere art, namely the living effect upon the patient himself.
>
> (Jung 1933)

Edwards writes about how his assumptions about art itself were severely shaken by his first visit to an art department in a psychiatric hospital in the 1950s. Byrne too grapples with how, when aestheticians refuse 'the art of the insane', they provoke questions about the function of art in society and a potential critique of the art world and its values. The excitement which all four art therapists who wrote articles in the catalogue felt in relation to the artworks on view in the exhibition and the aesthetic questions they provoked is evident and is entirely characteristic of the period. I would like to suggest that it is this excitement about the art that enabled the art therapists of the period to respond to their 'schizophrenic' patients with such sustained respect and interest. Once again I find myself writing that the influence of such genuine interest must for many patients have been a real relief from the effects of stigma.

The main indication of Byrne's approach to his work with his more disturbed clients seems implicit when he writes, 'These are not images of illogical worlds, but their logic is obscure. In unravelling the meaning of these pictures, some of which seem only too obvious, others of which seem to defy analysis, we will certainly gain new insights into man's creative capacities' (Byrne 1978: 11). The idea of unravelling the meaning of pictures made by people in the midst of psychosis in order to achieve some form of universal understanding, does seem on some level to be the quest of most periods. It is a quest which grew large during this period as a result of the work of R.D. Laing. His central proposal is that the communications of people in the midst of psychosis are meaningful, even though they might initially seem to be a nonsensical 'word salad'. He wrote prolifically throughout his life about the question of psychosis in a manner which provoked a strong, lasting and wide-ranging response (Wood 1991).

Edwards writes about the private quality of much of the work on view in *The Inner Eye* exhibition (1978). He suggests that it was made as part of a process of private contemplation with possibly only one person other than the artist originally being able to see the work. He names such art 'inner' art and describes three sets of circumstances in which such art might emerge. Firstly, he suggests such work may be a spontaneous occurrence; secondly, that it may arise as a result of being invited to paint dreams and fantasies by a psychotherapist; and, thirdly, he suggests that inner work may develop out of: 'a planned therapeutic environment where art materials are freely available and an art therapist is providing encouragement, support or sympathetic non-interference' (Edwards 1978: 14). It is interesting to compare this idea of an 'inner' art with the earlier description made of Lyddiatt's 'spontaneous' art. Edwards' early training had come as a result of his living with his family at Withymead. Although his thoughts about the process of art therapy might be generally applied, they are not intended as particular precepts for work with people in the midst of psychosis.

The influence of Irene Champernowne must have been in the roots of his work, just as Jung was in the roots of hers. Edwards is at pains to point to an aspect of Champernowne's belief which might be central to work with any client but would be particularly sensitive in therapeutic work with someone in the midst of psychosis:

Central to her thinking was the belief that 'illness' was not to be projected onto the 'patient', creating a 'them' and 'us' situation between patients and staff, but that any individual engaged in therapeutic work must be prepared to face up to and be conscious of his or her own 'ill' or less integrated aspects – throughout life.

(Edwards 1978: 18)

Perhaps Edwards comes closest to writing something about work with people in the midst of psychosis, when he describes the work of Adamson with this client group as being dependent on 'intuition and sensitivity, rather than on preconceived theoretical considerations' (Edwards 1978: 17).

Halliday (1978), in her paper in *The Inner Eye* catalogue, rather tantalisingly makes reference to some work with a 12-year-old boy who had been deemed autistic. She describes his work as 'typical of many autistic children' in its repetitiveness. She says very little about the process involved, other than indicating that she felt the relationship was fundamentally reparative of early relationships, in the mirroring work she felt she was able to provide. This way of gliding over the process and technique of the work is characteristic of much art therapy writing of the period.

Henzell's paper (1978) in the same catalogue is a brief but interesting account of the ways in which he views the very human history of various attempts to understand the expressions of insanity. In trying to glean an impression of what this might have meant for his practice as an art therapist at the time, I am struck by a number of comments which imply a strong valuing of the actual process of image-making. Of the Romanian refugee Arthur Segal, Henzell writes:

Segal was a painter who, through his association with the Blaue Reiter group, had known Prinzhorn. He left Germany in 1936 and set up his school of painting in London where he taught artists as well as psychiatrists and their patients. He believed art possessed therapeutic properties; the laws of psychological functioning and art were linked and therefore a valid art experience, that is one in conformity with the laws of art, was highly integrative.

(Henzell 1978: 32)

Waller (1991) records that framed on the wall of Segal's studio was a letter to him from Freud which warmly applauded the way in which Segal aimed to bring together doctors, patients and artists in the one studio. The practical focus of the work of some art therapists during this period are seen in Henzell's comments about the distance between the focus of art therapy and those of the artists involved in Dubuffet's *Compagnie de l'art brut*:

Leo Navratil has drawn attention to the creativity of schizophrenia while Arnulf Rainer and Ernst Fuchs have argued that, far from treating madness, we should consider it an ultimate form of sanity and set up institutes of insane culture where forms of psychotic expression could be encouraged.

(Henzell 1978: 32)

Henzell also, almost prophetically, describes what he sees as an emerging 'transformation of psychoanalytic approaches to art and to aesthetics' through the work of Anna Freud and Melanie Klein. He highlights Anna Freud's ideas about creative activity providing a form of ego defence against potential psychotic upheaval.

Finally, he was perhaps able to summarise a particular tension with which the decade of the 1970s had begun, a tension that had been first expressed by Irene Champernowne (1971):

> Hence the first art therapists were caught in the same dilemma that had faced analysts and psychotherapists in attempting to reach a *modus vivendi* with institutional psychiatry. As a result they tended to adopt one of two courses of action: they stressed the clinical side of their work, adapting current theory to this end, and here there is a connection between pragmatism and a certain theoretical conservatism; or they minimised their therapeutic responsibility and concentrated on the art ingredient of their practice so as not to conflict with their psychiatric patrons.
>
> (Henzell 1978: 33–4)

This can, of course, still be felt in the 1990s; however, it does depend on how this tension is expressed as to whether it is experienced as enlivening or deadening within the art therapy world. Certainly work with people in psychotic states does require the therapist to have made some very urgent, if only temporary, synthesis of these polarities.

Towards the end of *The Inner Eye* catalogue, some twenty-one art therapists who were practising (mainly in psychiatric hospitals) at that time give brief accounts of their approaches. It is interesting to find that none of the accounts makes any specific reference to work with people in the midst of psychosis. However, it is again possible to find written comments which seem to imply such work. Included in these twenty-one, Robin Holtom, the art therapist then at Springfield Hospital in London, writes:

> The art therapy department in a psychiatric hospital is often an asylum within an asylum. That is to say it is a refuge from the depersonalising manoeuvres of a large institution and its agents. It also provides people with space to express inconvenient or unspeakable feelings. The relationship between an art therapist and the hospital that employs him is often abrasive. It can scarcely be otherwise since it often happens that people paint their best pictures when they are most 'ill' and the pictures often get worse as a person gets 'better'. This paradox is central to art therapy.
>
> (Holtom 1978: 40)

My own training as an art therapist ended in 1978 and I do think this account by Robin Holtom epitomises much that was prevalent in the ethos of my training course. I think art therapists (together with other workers in psychiatry) need access to ideas which help them understand and work within the prevailing climate of established psychiatry. During this second period, the works of Erving Goffman and those of R.D. Laing were centrally important in this respect. Goffman's work reversed the focus of attention from the concerns of staff in institutions to those of the patients or, as he put it, other 'inmates'. This reversal was in keeping with the ethos of the 1960s. In his book *Asylums* (1961) he considers the assault on the person's sense of self upon admission to a mental hospital. He discusses what he sees as the institution's mortification processes acting upon patients and the possible responses they might make. This includes a sort of underlife which can develop in large hospitals. In one sense Laing's project was also concerned with how the structures of self are influenced by the social network of relationships in which a person lives. Laing himself did not confine his attention to the family, although the focus of his attention was concerned with intimate familial relationships and their influence upon a person's sense of security in the world. Goffman's project was more widely sociological.

The effects of what both Laing and Goffman propose are still relevant. At the end of the 1970s when I was training, the effects of what they were proposing in their writing were still evident. It often seemed that the response to their writing was as powerful as the content. Indeed, sometimes the response bore little relation to the content. My response, when I first began working in a psychiatric hospital, was to adopt a mental set which caricatured and stereotyped all those people who had not been diagnosed as mad. It would have been easy to caricature my position as a pompous exaggeration of Laing's dictum to treat patients as people and not as things. I related to many staff as inanimate objects and reserved the status of people for patients. I discovered the craziness of my stance in relation to staff quickly and painfully, greatly helped by the good-natured banter of staff with whom I worked.

The art therapy literature of the period is sometimes attributed to being part of the profession's adolescence (Waller 1987). There was a powerful sense at that time of the need for change. In psychiatry many were receptive to what Laing was writing about the plight of the 'schizophrenic' left alone on a back hospital ward in a world no one would share. Many art therapists (along with many in other professions) read Laing's work – particularly *The Divided Self* (1959) and *Self and Others* (1961). It is remarkable, therefore, that although many art therapists did use these ideas in practice I can discover none who at that time wrote in any detail about how the ideas influenced their practice.

Laing wrote in his introduction to *The Divided Self*:

No attempt is made to present a comprehensive theory of schizophrenia. No attempt is made to explore constitutional and organic aspects. No attempt is made to describe my own relationship with these patients or my own method of therapy.

(Laing 1959: 9)

He did nevertheless describe his ideas about psychotic experiences which offer valuable insights. For example, his description of the forms which can be assumed by psychotic despair – 'engulfment', 'implosion' and 'petrification' – have helped me move a little closer towards some of the people I have been working with.

The psychiatric establishment behaved as though Laing was proposing the non-existence of madness. I think this has been a very persistent misconception, which goes some way to explain the force of the reaction against him. I believe Laing himself made only the modest claim that it is 'far more possible than is generally supposed to understand people diagnosed as psychotic' (Laing 1959: 11).

The account given by Mary Barnes and Joseph Berke (1973) shows the very human lengths to which Laing, his followers and the clients were prepared to go in order to achieve this understanding. Of course the way in which Barnes became a painter and her use of her art is interesting for art therapists. Berke, her main therapist, made few attempts to unravel the details of her artwork, although he was clearly involved in encouraging Barnes to paint and in providing a continuing response to the work. It seems as though she did use her artwork, particularly her wallpaper picture stories, to explore her own life story. Of painting she says: 'Paint I did. Gradually it seemed to me perfectly right again to paint. Painting when I wasn't too "bad" to do it, got me together, in my body and soul. All my insides came out through my hands and my eyes and all the colour' (Barnes and Berke 1973: 145). Later when her engulfment of Kingsley Hall with her paintings created real conflict in the community, one angry resident took all of them down from the walls. Barnes writes: 'Soon after the paintings had come down, I had a period of intense loneliness' (Barnes and Berke,1973: 176).

The art therapy world at the end of the 1970s, myself included, took much sustenance from all of this, it seemed to confirm and deepen what art therapists had been proposing in the twenty years immediately after the Second World War. We may not have understood all that was brought to us, but we could respect the people who shared their artwork with us and we could really pay attention to it and to them. The effects of this care and respect enabled many of the clients deemed psychotic to develop helpful relationships with art therapists, in the context of mainly public sector settings.

The third period

During the second period of the profession's history, the effects of paying such careful attention to the patients themselves and to the nature of their artwork began to lead to a plethora of quite difficult questions. The emergence of another phase of development often contains much of what has gone before. This is true of the early stages of what I have called the third period, which begins in the early 1980s and continues to the present, the second half of the 1990s. Art therapists have now begun to give a much clearer account of psychosis and of the particular styles of therapy which have developed out of work with clients experiencing it. The first two periods have left art therapists with a legacy of using the same careful approach to therapeutic work, an approach which does not single out any particular client group. Clients in the midst of psychosis are regularly offered art therapy. There is now a quest for a greater clarity of understanding for this particular client work. It was in 1960 that Enoch Powell made his famous water-tower speech sounding the death knell for the large Victorian asylums: 'brooded over by the gigantic water-tower and chimneys combined, rising unmistakable and dauntingly out of the country side – the asylums which our forefathers built with such immense solidity' (Powell 1961). Yet at the beginning of the 1980s not a single hospital had yet closed and it was not until the beginning of the 1990s that the commitment to closing the old asylums had been embraced by government policy. Nevertheless throughout the 1980s art therapists were aware of the impending shift into the community (Wood 1985). It seems that this awareness coupled with the effects of many years of work with clients with a history of psychosis has resulted in a shift in the approach of art therapists.

The series of questions asked by Terry Molloy in his article (1984) about the role of art therapy in psychiatric rehabilitation, were pertinent to the experiences of many art therapists at the time. He discusses the difficulties of establishing basic conditions and boundaries for psychotherapeutic work within many psychiatric rehabilitation services in the health service. He wryly suggests the need for art therapists to be able to perform George Orwell's 'Doublethink' if they are to make the attempt. He refers to a survey made by the Salford Project in 1975, which was a research project considering the possibilities for establishing a 'Continuous Care Register' for those discharged into the community yet deemed to be in need of continuous care. Molloy refers to many accounts given in the Salford Project publication by people who had received some form of psychiatric treatment. He highlights areas which seem to have been of particular concern, such as a sense of not belonging, of being different, feelings of emptiness, inability to prevent feelings overwhelming aspects of everyday life, difficulties in rehabilitation, difficulties with medication with some people wanting to get off all medication and others being grateful for it. Molloy carefully explores the ways in which an art therapist might respond to and work with these feelings. His account is impressive in the way that he demonstrates the range of psychotherapeutic work which is possible with clients who are rarely offered it. He is very clearly arguing for art therapists to challenge standard approaches to work with this client population and to try to use their work as a balance to other rehabilitation programmes. He sees this balancing of the work as being most effectively achieved through close team work, when this is possible. He writes of:

inner emptiness ... a psychic paralysis resulting from the terrifying confrontation of two worlds, inner and outer. In such cases no amount of practical training in coping with work and the realities of life is likely to be of much use. Art therapy can help break through the emptiness and as rehabilitation progresses, can support a patient's return to reality.

(Molloy 1984: 4)

Molloy does not underestimate the terrifying nature of some feelings with which clients have to contend, but he did not at that time identify any particular approach to art therapy as appropriate for this client group.

In my own review of work with long-term psychiatric patients, written in 1992, I stressed the possibility of using art therapy as a form of psychotherapy with this particular client population – which, by the time I was writing at the beginning of the 1990s, was largely to be found in the community. Like Molloy, I understand very clearly (together with many other art therapists) the need continually to propose a case for this way of working, with this client group, in the public sector. Many of the services have been preoccupied with what has seemed interminable change over the last few years, so that it has not always been easy to maintain the basic conditions needed for therapy. It is understandable that what some art therapists have spent their energy upon is the repeated need to discuss and argue for very basic work. Ideas about the specific techniques for art therapy with this client group have not yet been widely elaborated.

The climate of the period has meant that focus has been upon individual survival, deregulation in all areas of public life and constant change in the public sector as it struggles to express itself as a marketable commodity. Reaction to this climate has, when not confused, been varied. David Smail's work (1987) powerfully and usefully challenges the position and function of therapy in society. Other less-considered challenges to the role of therapy and, in particular, psychoanalysis have tended to focus on therapy and not on the wider political context as the source of difficulty (e.g. Malcolm 1982; Masson 1989).

Nevertheless, the experience of working increasingly in the community with very disturbed clients has driven the need for more clarity about the work. I think this need is reflected in the literature of many of the helping professions – the work of Bentall (1992), Barham (1984, 1992, 1995), Boyle (1992) and Lefevre (1994) is exciting and encouraging. All of these have made persistent and dogged attempts to establish the basis for therapeutic work within the public sector with those most in need. Similarly, many art therapists have persisted, although from a less powerful position, to continue such work. Increasingly with the developing maturity of the profession they are not shy of making allegiances with whomever will support the work.

Some of the most innovative ideas about art therapy and psychosis to date have been proposed by Helen Greenwood and Geoff Layton (1987, 1988) and

Katherine Killick (1991, 1993), and recently in a jointly written chapter by Killick and Greenwood (1995). Between the end of the 1980s and the present time Greenwood, Layton and Killick have been putting forward the idea that very particular approaches are needed in art therapy with people who experience psychosis. These approaches depend upon whether or not the client is in the midst of psychosis or comes to the therapist with a history of psychosis. In many ways in their writing, Killick addresses the former scenario and Greenwood the latter, but much of what both write lends a helpful clarity to practice and holds the promise of further development. The clarity comes from a careful application of psychoanalytic ideas in the Kleinian tradition, particularly those of Bion (1967) and Hanna Segal(1986), and also from the object relations and independent school of psychoanalysis. Historically there have been and there remain deep philosophical conflicts between the way in which the Kleinians characterise psychosis and the approaches of other psychoanalytical schools (Jackson 1995: 12).

What is clear is that these conflicts will be reflected in the differing approaches to the work of different art therapists. However, it is not yet apparent where the conflict in philosophy will emerge in practice. What is different in this third period, compared with the first two, is the clarity about aspects of technique. Both Killick and Greenwood insist that in the early stages of the work there is a need to suspend questions about the content of the artwork which clients make. Killick argues: 'Images produced by psychotic patients do not serve a symbolic purpose until a containing relationship is formed' (Killick 1991: 6).

Also, it is no accident that Killick, Greenwood and another art therapist, Anna Goldsmith, refer in detail to the nature of the rooms in which they meet with clients who are either in the midst of, or have a history of, psychosis (Killick 1991; Goldsmith 1992; Greenwood and Layton 1987). The very details of the rooms and the manner in which they are used all contribute to the work of containment. Goldsmith's account of the room previously used by Killick describes the therapist's sensitive attention to the use of the room when working with an in-patient in the midst of psychosis:

> The programme for this kind of functioning state may be designed so that the table is kept entirely for that person's use and the work and other objects put on or near the table are left totally undisturbed. The table and its environs (including any images) may be experienced as an extension of the psychotic person's self structure. To interfere with, or make unsafe, that safe area of experiencing is to risk gross intrusion into fragile 'self' defining structures. . . . To support it can enable the psychotic person to relax some of the defensive strategies and experiment with others that later may be more viable in the world of relationships and symbolic structures.
>
> (Goldsmith 1992: 45)

It is interesting to note both the similarities and the differences between this last description and that of Greenwood and Layton when describing work with people (no longer in the midst of psychosis) in a community setting:

> When we came to develop a psychological model we started by considering how in psychotic states the boundary, space or structure between inner and outer reality, or between conscious and unconscious aspects of the self, are frail or flawed. It is useful to understand that reconstruction and strengthening of psychological boundaries can be facilitated by the social and physical setting of the group. Both staff and patients need to feel secure about the setting. A regular time and place for the session is important. The therapists reserve a time in the timetable and a space in the building which corresponds to a time and place in their minds. Therapists have to take responsibility for this setting and ensure that the session is not interrupted, or threatened by others who might want the room for other purposes.
>
> . . . At the outset the group was offered the following facilities: a large room with an area of comfortable chairs, tables that need to be erected, art materials and time of 1.5 hours and two therapists.
>
> (Greenwood and Layton 1987)

The differences between in-patient and out-patient settings (even to the tables that need to be erected) are quite markedly connected with the relative transience of the setting and the 'container' it is possible to offer, and the extent to which the therapists themselves feel contained by their work setting.

Both Killick and Greenwood (1995) are clearly inspired by the client group and are involved in the process of thoroughly exploring those psychoanalytic concepts which might lend clarity and understanding to the process of art therapy. A jointly written chapter produced a series of specific recommendations. These five recommendations (1995: 114) include methods which enable the therapists to foster ways of mediating between concrete and symbolic thinking. They propose that therapists pay very careful attention to 'dynamically structured and maintained boundaries' in ways which enable projected material to be contained within the relationship. This requires a time scale which enables clients to develop sufficient ego strength 'to assimilate what has been projected'. They describe different places upon the possible continuum of the range of therapeutic work it might be possible to offer people with serious mental disorders. Their joint chapter contains much that is helpful, but I personally would be interested to see what would have emerged in terms of the theoretical differences and the nuance of practice, had they written individual chapters. Possibly the editors of the book missed an opportunity when they commissioned only one chapter. The needs of practice in this third period demand elaboration.

Killick (1993) describes the way in which her thinking has developed during many years of working with people with serious disorders in a psychiatric setting. She, along with many other art therapists during the 1980s, found herself in a position where she was able to offer long-term therapeutic relationships in a sufficiently containing psychiatric setting. Killick's ability to offer well-contained long-term work in the NHS was not uncommon in the 1980s, but it would now be rare. During the second half of the 1990s, with the advent of community care and the relentless pace of change in public sector settings, it is no longer clear that work of such length and depth could take place.

The community ethos within which Greenwood finds herself employed does not make work at the depth which Killick describes feasible. Greenwood's work is usefully informed by knowledge of the psychoanalytic theory. The situation in which knowledge of theory is useful to the work, although it will not always be appropriate to apply it in public sector settings, is one which repeatedly affects contemporary art therapy practice. Many art therapists like Greenwood are currently engaged with other colleagues in trying to make an appropriate transition from more contained institutional settings to the community services. In the community, the therapeutic frame is not always well supported and some quite complicated questions arise about where it is appropriate to conduct therapy. For example, there may be quite strong expectations (generally problematic) within community teams that some client work is done in the client's home. Woddis is correct in suggesting that the technical questions provoked by the move into community settings have still to be addressed. Questions of technique are ever present during this period.

There has been a gradual theoretical shift which has seen the profession become much more influenced by psychotherapeutic practice – indeed there is now a debate within the profession about its title. No one model of psychotherapy has been adopted by art therapists during this period (although strong influences have come from different psychoanalytic traditions). The increasing claim by art therapists to the psychotherapeutic nature of their work has been reflected in the content of the recognised training courses. It seems to me that what characterises art therapy in the current period, as distinct from art therapy in the two earlier periods, are questions of technique and a general quest for more clarity of practice. Some art therapists who became established during earlier periods warn of dangers of too uncritical an adoption of psychotherapeutic methods. In the present period David Maclagan continues in his writing – most recently in an article in *Inscape* during 1994 – to highlight these issues and the understandable concerns they give rise to.

However, the quest for clarity of technique seems to me to have been driven by the very wide range of client need which art therapists have encountered in their work. Perhaps the need is nowhere more apparent than in work with clients who have a history of psychosis. By technique I intend to indicate something about the full range of skills which contribute to what I would like to name 'the philosophical craft'. It appears that what characterises the contemporary period in the development of art therapy is the greater exposition of its technique and philosophical craft. It is not until this third period that significant numbers of art therapists have written or edited books about the nature of art therapy practice. These art therapists include Dalley (1984), Dalley *et al.* (1987), Case and Dalley (1990, 1992), Dalley *et al.* (1993), Gilroy and Dalley (1989), Gilroy and Lee (1995), Liebmann (1986, 1990, 1995), Schaverien (1991, 1995), Simon (1992), Thomson (1989), Waller (1991, 1993), Waller and Gilroy (1992). The subject matter in these books indicates something of the wide range of practices. In their pages it is possible to find evidence of art therapists using widely differing models of practice; art as healing (Hill 1945; Adamson 1984; McNiff 1992), person-centred art therapy (Silverstone 1993), brief art therapy (McClelland 1992; Skailes 1990). There are also more examples of supportive art psychotherapy (Greenwood and Layton 1987, 1988; Greenwood 1994). Much art therapy writing during this period might be described variously as art psychotherapy (Killick 1993; Case 1994; Dalley *et al.* 1993), group analytic art therapy (McNeilly 1984); group interactive art therapy (Waller 1993); and analytical art psychotherapy (Schaverien 1991, 1994, 1995). The clarity of explanation beginning to be available in such books and in journal articles (particularly in *Inscape*, the journal of the British Association of Art Therapists) will undoubtedly contribute to the development of increasingly substantial accounts of the techniques of art therapy.

Much that has been written so far by art therapists about this client group has taken the form of occasional papers or chapters in books. An increasing number of people in the art therapy world are writing about their work with people with serious mental disorders (e.g. Thornton, 1990; Mann 1991, 1995). Their work is varied in its technique but it does share a broadly supportive art psychotherapy approach. A great deal of work has not yet been subject to much scrutiny; for example, many art therapists have worked in groups with people who have a history of psychosis but so far only one paper exists about such group work (Greenwood and Layton 1987). The theoretical conflict within the world of art and that of psychoanalysis in relation to psychosis has not yet found exposition within the writings of art therapy. The demands of the work will increasingly involve art therapists in taking different positions in relation to conflicts about the nature of psychosis and responses to it. It will be very helpful and interesting to see what they have to say in the future about the ways in which art therapy with these most disturbed clients continues to develop.

CONCLUSION

I hope that this chapter has demonstrated how the methods of work employed by art therapists with people who experience psychotic processes, have gradually become much more explicit. During the first period, art therapists focused on the powerful means of expression which they might offer to people with serious disorders and also on the provision of respectful containment. During the second period art therapists tried to counter some of the alienating effects of psychiatric institutions by providing an asylum within an asylum. In the third, contemporary, period the work of art therapists has become more influenced by psychotherapeutic practice and by the problematic transition from asylum to an unknown community; during this time questions of technique have become paramount. Each of the three periods has had its own drive and development. They have all contributed in powerful ways to a belief in the possibility of such work. The single thread which has run throughout the three periods is the fundamental need for care and respect, which is heightened when working with very disturbed people.

REFERENCES

Adamson, E. (1984) *Art as Healing*, London: Coventure.

Barham, P. (1984) *Schizophrenia and Human Value*, Oxford: Blackwell (reprinted Oxford: Blackwell, 1986).

Barham, P. (1992) *Closing the Asylum*, Harmondsworth: Penguin.

Barnes, M. and Berke, J.(1973) *Mary Barnes: Two Accounts of a Journey through Madness*, Harmondsworth: Penguin.

Baron, C. (1987) *Asylum to Anarchy*, London: Free Association Books.

Bentall, R.P. (1992) *Reconstructing Schizophrenia*, London: Routledge.

Berke, J., Masoliver, C. and Ryan,T.J. (1995) *Sanctuary*, London: Process Press.

Bion, W. (1967) *Second Thoughts*, London: Heinemann (repinted by London: Karnac, 1984).

Bornat, J. Pereira, C. Pilgrim, D. and Williams, F.(1993) *Community Care: A Reader*, Hampshire and London: Open University Press.

Boyle, M. (1992) 'The non-discovery of schizophrenia?', in Bentall (1992).

Brill, H. and Patton, R. E.(1959) 'Analysis of population reduction in New York State mental hospitals during the first four years of large scale therapy with psychotopic drugs', *American Journal of Psychiatry* 116: 495–509.

Bryne, P.(1978) 'Art and madness', in Elliott (1978), pp. 9–11.

Busfield, J.(1986) 'Managing madness: changing ideas and practice', Chapter 10, *Community Care*, London: Unwin Hyman.

Case, C.(1994) 'Art therapy in analysis: advance/retreat in the belly of a spider', London: *Inscape* 2.

Case, C. (1995) 'Silence in progress', London: *Inscape* 1.

Case, C.(1987) 'Images of art therapy', in Dalley *et al.* (1987).

Case,C. and Dalley, T. (eds) (1990) *Working with Children in Art Therapy*, London: Routledge.

—— (1992)*The Handbook of Art Therapy*, London: Routledge.

Charlton, S. (1984) 'Art therapy with long stay residents of psychiatric hospitals' in Dalley (1984).

Cohen, D.(1988) *Forgotten Millions*, London: Paladin.

Cole, P.(1976) 'Art therapy at the Henderson', London: *Inscape* 12.

Champernowne, I. (1971) 'Art and therapy: an uneasy partnership', London: *Inscape* 3.

Dalley, T. (1984) *Art as Therapy*, London: Tavistock.

Dalley *et al.* (1987) *Images of Art Therapy*, London: Tavistock.

Dalley, T., Rifkind, G. and Terry, K. (1993) *Three Voices of Art Therapy: Image, Client, Therapist*, London: Routledge.

Edwards, M. (1978) 'Art therapy in Great Britain', in (1978).

Elliott, D. (ed.) (1978) *The Inner Eye*, Oxford: Museum of Modern Art Catalogue.

Ellwood, J.(1995) *Psychosis, Understanding and Treatment*, London: Jessica Kingsley.

Gilroy, A. (1995) in Gilroy and Lee (1995). *Art and Music: Therapy and Research.*

Gilroy, A. and Dalley, T. (eds) (1989) *Pictures at an Exhibition*, London: Tavistock/ Routledge.

Gilroy, A. and Lee, C. (eds) (1995) *Art and Music: Therapy and Research*, London: Routledge.

Goffman, I.(1961) *Asylums*, London: Penguin.

Goldsmith, A. (1992) in Case and Dalley (1992).

Greenwood, H. and Layton, G.(1987) 'An out-patient art therapy group', London: *Inscape* (Summer): 12–19.

Greenwood, H. and Layton, G. (1988) 'Taking the piss', *British Journal of Clinical and Social Psychiatry*, 6: 74–84.

Greenwood, H. (1994) 'Cracked pots' London: *Inscape* 1: 11–14.

Halliday, D. (1978) 'The use of therapeutic art in child guidance' in Elliot (1978).

Henzell, J. (1978) 'Art and pschopathology', in Elliot (1978).

Hill, A. (1945) *Art versus Illness*, London: George Allen & Unwin.

Holtom, R. (1978) in Elliot (1978).

Jackson, M. (1995)'Learning to think about schizoid thinking', in Ellwood (1995).

Jones, K. (1987) 'A little bit of what you fancy does you good. Art Therapy and the National Health Service 1939–81', unpublished Goldsmiths College Special Study.

Jung, C.G. (1933) *Modern Man in Search of a Soul*, UK: Redwood Burn Ltd. (1953); *Two Essays on Analytical Psychology, in Collected Works*, Part II.

Killick, K. (1991) 'The practice of art therapy with patients in acute psychotic states', London: *Inscape* (Winter).

Killick, K. (1993) 'Working with psychotic processes in art therapy', *Psychoanalytic Psychotherapy* 7(1): 25–36 (reprinted in Ellwood (1995)).

Killick, K. and Greenwood, H.(1995) 'Research in art therapy with people who have psychotic illnesses' Chapter 6 in *Art and Music: Therapy and Research*, London: Routledge

Laing, R.D. (1959) *The Divided Self*, Harmondsworth: Penguin.

Laing, R.D. (1961) *Self and Others*, Harmondsworth: Penguin.

Lefevre, D. (1994), 'Countertransference power in groups with long term psychotic inpatients', unpublished lecture given at Essex University Conference 'Psychosis'

Lewis, S. (1990) 'A place to be: art therapy and community-based rehabilitation', in Liebmann (1990).

Liebmann, M. (1986) *Art Therapy for Groups*, London: Croom Helm.

—— (1990) *Art Therapy in Practice*, London: Jessica Kingsley.

—— (1995) *Art Therapy with Offenders* London: Jessica Kingsley.

Lyddiatt, E.M. (1972) *Spontaneous Painting and Modelling*, New York: St Martin's Press.

MacGregor, J.M. (1989) *The Discovery of the Art of the Insane*, Princeton: University Press.

Maclagan, D. (1994)'Between the aesthetic and the psychological', London: *Inscape* 2.

Malcolm, J. (1982) *Psychoanalysis: The Impossible Profession*, London: Picador.

Mann, D. (1991) 'Some schizoid processes in art psychotherapy', London: *Inscape* (Summer).
—— (1995) Review of 'Psychoanalytic studies of the personality by W.R.D. Fairbairn', London: *Inscape* 1.
Masson,J. (1989) *Against Therapy*, London: Fontana.
McNeilly, G. (1984) 'Directive and non-directive approaches in art therapy', Sheffield: *Inscape* (Winter).
Mcniff, S. (1992) *Art as Medicine*, Boston and London: Shambala.
McClelland, S. (1992) 'Brief art therapy in acute states: a process orientated approach', in Waller and Gilroy (1992).
Molloy, T. (1984) 'Art therapy and psychiatric rehabilitation, harmonious partnership or philosophical collision', Sheffield: *Inscape* (Summer).
Murphy, E. (1991) *After the Asylum*, London: Faber & Faber.
Newton, J. (1988) *Preventing Mental Illness*, London: Routledge.
Porter, R. (1987) *A Social History of Madness, Stories of the Insane*, London: Weidenfeld & Nicolson.
Powell, E. (1961) 'Address to the National Association for Mental Health', in *Emerging Patterns for the Mental Health Services and the Public*, London: NAMH.
Radnor Commision (1908) 'Report of the Royal Commission of the Care and Control of the Feebleminded' London: HMSO.
Romme, M. and Escher, S. (1994) *Accepting Voices*, London: Mind Publications.
Schaverien, J. (1991) *The Revealing Image: Analytical Art Psychotherapy in Theory and Practice*, London: Routledge.
—— (1995) *Desire and the Female Therapist: Engendered Gazes in Psychotherapy and Art Therapy*, London: Routledge.
—— (1994) 'Analytical art psychotherapy: further reflections on theory and practice', London: *Inscape* 2.
Scull, A. (1977) *Decarceration*, Englewood Cliffs: Prentice Hall.
Sedgwick, P. (1982)*Psychopolitics*, London: Pluto Press.
Segal, H. (1986) *Delusion and Artistic Creativity & Other Psychoanaytic Essays*, London: Free Association Books and Maresfield Library.
Seebohm Report (1968) 'Report of the Committee on Local Authority and Allied Personal Social Services' London HMSO.
Shah, S. (1989) 'Mental disorder and criminal justice system: some overarching issues', *International Journal of Law and Psychiatry* 12: 231–44.
Silverstone, S. (1993) *Art Therapy – the Person Centered Way*, London: Booksprint.
Skailes, C. (1990) 'The revolving door: the day hospital and beyond' in Liebmann (1990).
Simon, R. (1992) *The Symbolism of Style*, London: Routledge.
Smail, D. (1987) *Taking Care*, London: Dent.
Stevens, A. (1986) *Withymead: a Jungian Community for the Healing Arts*, London: Coventure.
Thomson, M. (1989) *On Art and Therapy*, London: Virago Press.
Thornton, R. (1990) 'Valuing the middle ground: art therapy and manic depression' in Liebmann (1990).
Waller, D. (1987) 'Art therapy in adolescence: a metaphorical view of a profession in progress' in Dalley *et al.* (1987).
—— (1991)*Becoming a Profession, The History of Art Therapy in Britain 1940–1982*, London: Routledge.
—— (1993) *Group Interactive Art Therapy: Its Use in Training and Treatment*, London: Routledge.
Waller, D. and Gilroy A. (eds) (1992) *Art Therapy: A Handbook*, Buckingham: Open University Press.

Warner, R. (1985) *Recovery from Schizophrenia*, London: Routledge.

Widgery, D.(1991) *Some Lives*, London: Sinclair Stevenson.

Woddis, J. (1992), 'Art therapy; new problems, new solutions?' in Waller and Gilroy (1992), p. 32.

Wood, C. (1985) '*Psychiatrica Democratica* and the problems of translation', Sheffield: *Inscape* 1.

Wood, C. (1991) 'A personal view of Laing and his influence on art therapy', London: *Inscape* (Winter).

Wood, C. (1992) 'Using art therapy with "chronic" long-term psychiatric patients', in Waller and Gilroy (1992).

Chapter 9

Art, madness and anti-psychiatry: a memoir

John Henzell

INTRODUCTION

This chapter recalls a period in the history of art, psychiatry and madness. It will focus on a radical form of psychiatry which, through its understanding of the social contexts within which individuals live their lives, stood in opposition to the orthodox view of medical psychiatry. Hence its originators called it anti-psychiatry. A number of artists worked with these 'anti-psychiatrists' and with other, particularly Jungian, psychotherapists. They were all interested in the problem of madness which had a certain avant-garde edge at the time. In the middle years of the 1960s these artists created the profession of art therapy. A number of philosophers and writers, some of them psychoanalysts, were also interested in the connection between psycho-analysis and art, while other writers were intent on exploring the unusual artistic creations of those working outside the confines of the world of art, and these included works by artists who were psychotic. An exploration of fresh and unorthodox experience was a characteristic of the period as a whole, which is best understood by looking at actual instances. At a very local and microcosmic level I shall describe events in a particular psychiatric hospital between 1960 and 1968. This was an important period of my own life, and, as such, what follows can hardly be impartial. If the reader feels I am at times being polemical, expressing a loyalty for certain points of view, or that my narrative is over detailed or personal, then bear in mind it might be hard to avoid this while recollecting events in which one was involved. I consider that these have a considerable bearing on our present day concerns.

ARTIST TO THERAPIST

In 1957, after I left art school in Western Australia, I became an art therapist at a repatriation hospital for ex-servicemen. This was at the suggestion of Guy Grey-Smith, an Australian artist who had developed tuberculosis while serving in the Air Force during the Second World War and had, as a consequence, been a patient at King Edward VIII Hospital in Godalming,

Surrey. While there he had experienced working with Adrian Hill who coined the term 'art therapy' for the relaxing and morale-boosting effects of artistic activity on seriously ill TB patients at the hospital (Hill 1945). Grey-Smith took this technique back with him to Western Australia after the war and practised as an art therapist with TB patients in Perth. My father, Linley Henzell, was Commissioner for Public Health in the state of Western Australia. He was a doctor specialising in chest illnesses, particularly TB which, until the 1950s, was still a disease of epidemic proportions. Grey-Smith became a friend of my parents who bought some of his work and I got to know him through this connection. He wished to devote more of his time to painting and offered me some of his art therapy sessions at Hollywood Repatriation Hospital in Perth. Initially I was concerned with men suffering from tuberculosis, later on also with others who had severe drinking problems. Some of these men were Korean War veterans. I found that many of them used my art sessions as a pretext to reveal some of their distress, problematic feelings, questions, and memories to me – although they were much older than I. The underlying meaning of the pictures concerned their feelings rather than the ostensible subject matter depicted. I was both moved by the nature of these communications and by the fact that I had been trusted as a witness to others' personal and interior lives.

Two years later I came to England and through Grey-Smith's and my father's good offices met James Braithwaite who was Secretary of the South West Metropolitan Hospital Board. He was a passionate art lover who had helped develop art therapy in a number of hospitals in his region. He arranged for me to work for several months at Warlingham Park Hospital, a large psychiatric hospital in Surrey. The art therapist at Warlingham Park was Jan Glass, one of the few who pioneered this work in England. In effect I became her apprentice and she taught me the fundamentals of my work. From her I learnt how to accept the patient's form of expression as something to be valued and enjoyed in its own right, that this was the importance of what the patients painted, drew and modelled, as well as the conversations that grew from them, rather than as a form of psychiatric assessment or diagnosis. I was also hugely impressed by the striking power and beauty of many of the patients' images – they had a fascination often lacking from images of the official art world. Yet, most of the patients I met in the art studio were severely psychotic, in orthodox medical terms supposed to be suffering from a psychological deficit. In a nearby room patients attending occupational therapy spent the day making woollen rugs to preformed patterns which the staff unpicked at the end of the day to enable the wool to be used again the next morning!

Indeed, like most big mental hospitals at the time, treatment methods and philosophies at Warlingham Park were largely conservative with a few members of staff exploring more progressive therapeutic ideas related to art, psychoanalysis, group psychotherapy and existential philosophy. Among these were the psychiatrists Aaron Esterson and Brian Lake, the hospital chaplain Derek Blow and, of course, Jan Glass. Esterson, Lake and Blow all became well-known psychotherapists, Esterson becoming associated with the work and ideas of R.D. Laing. All were interested in the human meaning and philosophical nature of ideas underlying psychiatric practice and seeing how these connected to wider contexts and practices in society. That such adventurous souls could gain a foothold in a large and isolated institution was in part due to the liberal administration of Stephen MacKeith, the hospital's medical superintendent. It was he who told me of a vacancy for a more permanent appointment as an art therapist at another large mental hospital near London, Napsbury Hospital, where I started working in 1960.

NAPSBURY HOSPITAL AND RADICAL PSYCHIATRY

Napsbury was a typical late-nineteenth century mental asylum building designed to accommodate many hundreds of inmates and attendant staff. When I worked there it retained numerous features and 'customs' which had been present for many decades. These included not only forms of treatment and administration, but annual rituals in which there were parts to play for patients and staff alike; for example, dances, dinners, church services, plays and games – each year there was a football match between the male patients and staff (in one of my first years working there the staff were heavily defeated by a patients' team which included a professional player). It was a considerable distance from any major conurbation, although its patients came from densely populated north London suburbs. It possessed many acres of farmland for crops and livestock, providing much of the food eaten by inmates and staff each day. A large body of patients still worked on this farmland and in the substantial and carefully tended grounds, which were laid out in a formal garden style. Viewed externally, the building itself was designed in a Victorian 'Dutch' manner. It was divided into two large complexes of building, East and West Hospitals, housing well over two thousand patients. Several hundred staff – doctors, nurses, psychologists, therapists, social workers, ancillary staff, engineers, clerical workers and administrators – either commuted from London or St Albans each day, or lived in the small town of London Colney which had developed around the hospital. In the centre of West Hospital was the tall chimney and water tower, surmounted by a slate-tiled pointed roof, which visually dominated the surrounding countryside. Some miles to the south could be seen the equivalent tower, chimney and plume of smoke of Shenley Hospital, another large mental institution. A short distance southwards down the road one drove past yet another large late-Victorian institution for the mentally handicapped, Harperbury Hospital.

Within the 'East' and 'West' buildings were a succession of male and female wards arranged symmetrically either side of imposing entrances and connected by interminable corridors, the one in West Hospital being over half a mile long. Patients entered this structure, which had architectural as well as social, physical and spiritual meanings, in the admission wards at the back of East Hospital, all named rather hopefully after flowers or trees. If their condition worsened, the patients slipped westwards, as it were. The furthest one could go in this fall from outside social life were the chronic wards at the male or female ends of the long corridor in West Hospital. The ward's label would no longer be graced with a floral or arboreal touch, but would now be simply, say, F23 or M17. In all, West Hospital comprised forty wards and East Hospital seven wards, including a 'Deep Insulin Ward',[1] and as well an 'ECT Suite' and an operating theatre originally intended for brain surgery (whose electrical supply was protected in the event of a power cut by an ancient collection of wet cell batteries, glass jars of acid connected by wires kept in a mouldering cellar). By 1960 the use of these latter facilities had been largely discontinued and the deep insulin ward now housed a therapeutic community. The hospital also possessed an isolation ward for patients who, in addition to their psychiatric condition, might suffer from an infectious illness or require ordinary medical care.

In fact this apparently antiquated Victorian set up concealed a fascinating array of advanced methods of psychiatric and psychotherapeutic care. In the late 1950s and during the early 1960s Napsbury employed staff carrying out radical treatment and research in psychiatry, therapy and community care. The philosophical and social implications of some of this work were to spread far beyond the clinical field – and indeed beyond Britain.

The staff involved in this radical enterprise included R.D. Laing and Aaron Esterson – whose research into schizophrenia led to the publication of their *Sanity, Madness and the Family* in 1964 (second edition in 1970), Dennis Scott and Tom Fairwell who were devising methods of crisis intervention which were to become clinical paradigms, Rosemary Gordon who in years to come was to write seminal works about depth psychology and artistic creativity, Alan Edwards, Louis Zinkin, Jim Patterson (the medical superintendent)[2] and many others. Gordon, Edwards and Zinkin all became influential members of the Society for Analytical Psychology. Several of the more junior staff were in psychotherapy training at the Tavistock Clinic, and Laing's and Esterson's research was being conducted through the Tavistock Institute of Human Relations. The patients the author worked with were also the patients of these staff members, and their problems, the forms of their psychological disturbances as well as their images were the subjects of many discussions. I also took part in the research being undertaken by Laing and Esterson.

Several important preoccupations combined together in this fertile environment; what they shared was an investment in exploring madness, at times as if it were a critique of the sanity from which it was excommunicated by an orthodox and respectable consciousness. Laing and Esterson were concerned with a radically alternative account of 'crazy' experience, and also with a critical examination of the often oppressive social norms embedded in the family, medical practice and our 'official consciousness'. Scott and Fairwell were developing methods of intervening in family crises so as to reveal the dramatic interplay of human problems involved, thereby helping any of the protagonists to avoid chronic hospitalisation or dependence on health care professionals. Edwards and Gordon, in their different ways, approached the experience of psychotic patients from a Jungian perspective. Those members of staff immersed in 'object relations' theory were naturally interested in the states of mind that had occasioned Melanie Klein to redescribe infantile experience in the language of madness and pathology – those 'positions' she called 'schizoid', 'paranoid' and 'depressive'. The psychoanalysts were also concerned to apply their psychotherapeutic under-standing to the radical problems of madness as well as to the issues represented by their more traditional work.[3]

ART, THERAPY AND MADNESS

Following on from my earlier work I was interested in the images produced by psychotic patients and the imaginative world they exemplified, this connected with my artistic preoccupations and interest in 'outsider art'. Through getting to know these patients and being concerned for them, as well as understanding something of their plight, it also seemed to me that my work might be a way in which art could be rescued from the exclusive world of formalism or decorative artifice, and applied instead to the real and pressing problems of people – including their wild or 'unauthorised' forms of consciousness. At this time there were no institutionalised forms of training for art therapists; with hindsight I think there were some advantages to set against the disadvantages of this. While I was having to learn from scratch, and therefore doubtless made mistakes viewed from the point of view of orthodox practice nowadays – for example, my knowledge of working with transference was more intuitive than organised in any systematic way – it permitted me to rely more on imagining myself into the states of mind of those I worked with unrestricted by codified rules of professional practice. I tried to reach behind the extraordinary behaviour, expressions and utterances I encountered towards the experiences from which these might derive without my sense of this being blunted by overly clinical preconceptions. And in any case, I had available to me the opinions of most talented and experienced colleagues.

Furthermore, my perceptions of being 'mad' relied as much on poetic or aesthetic realisations as it did on psychodynamics or clinical theories. I realised that insanity might be shaped as much by the perverse aesthetics of what might appall one, or by the force of a terrible poetry, as by the disorder of a system or the cause and effect of neurology. I came upon this as an artist who had attempted to 'see' into other human beings via myself, while many of my colleagues at Napsbury had reached similar conclusions from different starting points in medicine or the social sciences. Many years later I came to see that some of the very best images and descriptions of madness or other troubling psychological states have been made by artists and writers – Munch's images of adolescence, terror and melancholy for example, or Musil's remarkable descriptions of madness in the Moosbrugger sections of his *The Man Without Qualities* (1930–42). I also think that the therapists and psychiatrists who best describe the psychology of their patients are also good writers. Laing at his best is an example, as is, many years later, Murray Cox whose striking reflections on the words of his offender patients is a kind of poetic realisation in its own right (Cox and Theilgaard 1987).

When I started at Napsbury I inherited a small art room that had been used by the previous art therapist, Mary Webb. In 1961 one of the visiting areas in the female side of East Hospital was converted into a large and well-equipped art studio. It was an unusual and interesting space, 80 by 10 feet with windows and several doors down the south side of its length which opened onto a garden and courtyard. It was possible to work inside and outside with different media, ranging from painting, drawing, print-making, modelling, carving, casting and working with metal. On average, between six and twelve patients attended the studio each day, varying from those coming for just one session a week and others spending the entire week with me. In the centre of the studio was an area that could be partitioned off; this was both an office and a space where private conversation could take place.

Using this situation I applied what I had learnt from Jan Glass to my work with patients at Napsbury. To contrast this with much current practice in art therapy, I would say its distinguishing feature was to base an attempt to understand the psychological life of others on their pictorial work, which, as far as possible, arose from the patients' responses to the image-making situation, rather than the image-making being in many essentials shaped by psychodynamic precepts. Like E.M. Lyddiatt, who I met at this time, I did not allow the language or habits of orthodox psychotherapeutic practice to distract patients from the play of imagination made possible by the materials.[4] Because of this, patients were able to enter a reflective contact with unexpected elements of their psychic life, and with the native forms in which this existed, undistracted by the therapist's professional need to translate this imagining into Freudian, Jungian, Kleinian or other such schema. I am not suggesting that the concepts of psychoanalysis and analytical psychology have no part to play in such work, indeed at the time I was coming to see how important they were as theories of meaning. They can only function usefully, however, when meeting the image as a phenomenon in its own right.

For example, a young woman who had behaved with violence towards others, including staff and their property, came to my studio two or three and sometimes five days a week for two years. When she came she would make at least one, and often two, paintings. Sometimes she would talk to me about these, and our conversation grew out of their style and content. She was seldom disruptive in the art studio save on one or two occasions when she tested out the limits of my tolerance in ways that, though very annoying at the time, now seem ironically amusing. Mostly, though, she just painted. The vast number of images she created over these two years came to possess remarkable expressive power. When I thought of her images, and recollect them now, it was more in terms of art than those of psychodynamics or psychiatry; in particular they reminded me of the heroic and disturbing force of Max Beckmann's painting. Eventually she became pregnant by her Indian boyfriend who had been the subject of many of her paintings, and she left Napsbury for a refuge for young single mothers run by the Church. Keeping her baby, she obtained employment and eventually married, not, as it happens, to the father of her child. She corresponded with me for several years after leaving the hospital, eventually revisiting to take the hundreds of pictures she had done away with her, leaving a few of them with me.

By all ordinary standards this young woman's life had been transformed from one of isolated pain and strife to one in which she was sustained by love and contact with others. While at Napsbury she attended my department for a substantial part of each week and had a weekly session of Jungian psychotherapy. She had no other form of therapy, and as far as I knew had little or no medication. It is always difficult to know what helped someone achieve a metamorphosis of this kind. Was it the images she made with me? Was it her psychotherapy? Was it her Indian lover, or their child? Was it the refuge who helped her with her baby? Her job? The man who became her husband? Or some capability of her own? All I think we can say is that psychotherapeutic change involves numerous factors, many of which are apparent to our general understanding of human action. Thus, while I cannot prove in any final sense that the hundreds of images she made, and the conversations these led to with me, were 'x per cent' responsible for her change (even if one could quantify this!), it would be quite implausible to claim they had no part to play in the outcome of her life.

A wide range of patients of both sexes and varying age attended the art studio. This included acute admission patients suffering from neurosis, depression, organic disorders, and from the onset of psychosis, as well as longer stay patients who had become chronic mental hospital inmates. Most of this latter group were classified as psychotic or schizophrenic. I also worked with a variety of out-patients some miles away at a day hospital in Watford. In many ways it was the psychotic patients, the mad men and women, who presented the greatest challenge to my understanding. Among them were people whose actual perceptions of the world and of the place they occupied in it was radically at odds with the consensus most of us agree to about such things. There were those who believed they possessed additional limbs and bodily parts (these could actually cause sensations) and made drawings, paintings and models of their arrangement; those who heard voices – including their own though they had not spoken, who thought the images they made might literally harm others or exact retribution on whoever had the temerity to make them; and those who had constructed elaborate hypotheses to account for the mysterious and, by ordinary standards, unaccountable influences and sensations which affected their lives. Of course such states of mind are systematically classified by psychiatric nosology. But by becoming friendly with these patients, and through talking about their images and experience in the terms they elected to use themselves, I began to understand something of the phenomenology of madness. As I have suggested, other therapists, etc., at Napsbury were also interested in this phenomenology and how it might have come about. Many of the patients I worked with were also their patients.

Views were exchanged about these matters at weekly case conferences, in the experimental work of Laing, Esterson, Scott and Fairwell, in consultations between staff and daily at morning coffee where there were informal meetings between doctors, psychologists, therapists, social workers and senior nurses. As well as the radical opinions often expressed in our discussions I was introduced to writing that questioned psychiatric and psychoanalytic orthodoxy, for example Goffman (1961) and Szasz (1961).

Not only was Napsbury enlighteningly democratic as between its different staff groups, but I had the advantage of being Australian and therefore outside England's class system (I remember the curious embarrassment I felt when I heard an experienced charge nurse address a much younger doctor as 'Sir').[5] Because of this I ignored differences in authority, training and age among colleagues and took the fullest advantage of the expertise and friendship they offered me. While I gained an enormous amount from these discussions, and I was made very welcome from the start, others were interested in my opinions. I think this was partly because of my background in art, as I was the only member of staff to have a training that was not in one way or another based in medicine or science. Consequently I had a certain 'take' on things which others found refreshing; I had been trained to enjoy and value sense impressions for themselves rather than subject them too soon to a conceptual framework, and because of this I was often able to make 'aesthetic' sense of crazy experience. My colleagues were also impressed by the results of the atmosphere created in my studio. Many remarked on the absorption in imaginative work that was so tangible inside this space, and how patients who were isolated, deluded and hallucinating, became engrossed in artwork. As much as the atmosphere that pertained in the studio, the images that were made there were often of striking expressive force and testified to extraordinary richness of psychological experience rather than the paucity of mental life so often supposed to be characteristic of schizophrenia. Several of their images figured in exhibitions, including shows at the Institute of Contemporary Arts in 1964, Gallery 48 in 1967, The House of Commons in

1968 and 1969, and later at the Museum of Modern Art, Oxford, in 1978.[6] Given the poor prognosis for those suffering from the major psychoses, whether the onset of their symptoms was recent or they had been chronically institutionalised over many years, it became evident that many of those who attended my studio showed a relative but marked improvement in their condition. By orthodox clinical measures one might consider this form of therapy to have shown some success, but how appropriate these criteria are to this kind of work is another and complicated matter.

I ceased working at Napsbury in 1968 and continued to work with psychiatric patients at a number of public sector hospitals and clinics near London during the late 1960s and through the 1970s. None of these later settings, however, matched this initial working environment, which contained a mixture of good and not so good practices to be sure, but which was so richly imbued with human perception, experimentation and instructive support.

ART AND ANTI-PSYCHIATRY: CULTURAL
CONTEXTS IN THE 1960s AND 1970s

The concepts and practices that underlie radical therapy and anti-psychiatry arose in the 1960s and early 1970s. They were part and parcel of the whole range of 'alternatives' that came into being during this period as objections to the state, orthodox professional practices, and the imprisoned frames of mind that were felt by many to compose it. Broadly speaking these revolutionary attitudes tended towards the political left, though not in any consistent sense because politics of whatever traditional persuasion were often felt to be yet another establishment institution. Its adherents were for the most part young, though some of their heroes were relatively advanced in years to occupy the position of *enfant terrible* to which their youthful supporters had elevated them. Four of the most prominent and active of these culture heroes were Herbert Marcuse, the neo-Marxist philosopher, Erving Goffman, the sociologist, Gregory Bateson, the cybernetician, and, most importantly from our point of view, R.D. Laing, the psychiatrist turned radical social critic. For those with a pronounced interest in politics Mao Tse-Tung's Little Red Book was much in evidence alongside the tarot cards, the I Ching, the joint and brown rice in many bedsits. Posters and images attested to the revolutionary charisma of Marx, Lenin, Trotsky, Castro and Guevara.

This revolutionary stance proceeded in two directions, outwards towards social action and inwards towards psychological experience. The outer manifestation was political action, perhaps more marked in other Western countries than in Britain – for example, France in 1968. The inner manifestation is summed up in the period's preoccupation with consciousness, a consciousness which was to be 'raised', 'expanded', 'altered', 'changed' or in other ways transformed, above all the consciousness inherited from that generation's parents was to be subverted and replaced with something utterly new. This was accomplished through drugs (primarily hallucinogens of varying strength – cannabis at one end and LSD at the other), through music (rock and roll and 'psychedelic' music) and through a variety of radical or so-called 'Eastern' body practices (for example, bioenergetics, massage, yoga, t'ai chi chu'an, acupuncture and macrobiotics). Above all it was necessary to be thoroughly anti-Western, unless the part of the West involved was patently revolutionary or, as some might think, against reason – Marx, De Sade, Reich, etc.

One way in which it was thought possible to have a spontaneously occurring alternative consciousness was to be mad or schizophrenic. In my view it is arguable that the prominence of schizophrenia in the 1960s was in some senses the equivalent to that which anorexia, sexual abuse and AIDS were to assume in later years. The schizophrenic became a culture hero, the unwitting victim of establishment psychiatry and the previous generation in the form of his or her parents. The schizophrenic's consciousness was raised in objection to the family and to society; to be schizophrenic was to escape the inauthenticity society condemned most of us to, to embark on a 'journey', *à la* Mary Barnes or the hero of *One Flew Over the Cuckoo's Nest* (Barnes and Berke 1971), whose eventual destination might be existential integrity. For those of us who could not achieve this through the pathological resources of our own families, LSD or mescalin offered an alternative route. (Timothy Leary, imprisoned in the United States for his passionate advocacy of LSD, was another culture hero of the time.) Indeed, for a time LSD was referred to in medical language as a 'psychotomimetic'. At Napsbury, LSD had sometimes been prescribed for patients in psychotherapy. One of my patients, a Cypriot artist and friend of the 'Underground Poet' Jeff Nuttall, whose then highly thought of *Bomb Culture* was published in 1968, had himself been admitted to Napsbury, by behaving whimsically with his GP so that he would be thought crazy, in order to carry out an existential experiment on himself. Doubtless the presence of Laing was an inducement to him to choose this rather than some other psychiatric institution. In any case both Laing and another radical psychiatrist, David Cooper, whose schizophrenia research ward, *Villa 21*, was at nearby Shenley Hospital were closely associated with writers and poets in the avant-garde *Sigma* project, which included Nuttall and his Cypriot friend, as well as the artist Yoko Ono before her relationship with John Lennon.

If I've described this period in a somewhat knockabout fashion, this is because the manner is apt. It was an extraordinary period of time in which many and all things seemed possible. It was also, interestingly, the period in which a small group of British artist therapists created an organisation.[7] The British Association of Art Therapists (BAAT) was formed in 1964, and for a time there was some dispute as to whether art therapy would become a 'radical therapy' or be a respectable paramedical profession in the NHS and social services with all its psychodynamic and trade union credentials in order. Right at the outset there was a conflict in BAAT as to whether it should represent psychological or political claims; perhaps inevitably, as time passed, political and organisational interests won the higher stake (Waller 1991). It is extraordinary to recall that the principal speakers I and Rupert Cracknell, one of the other prime movers in BAAT's early days, invited to address our first AGM were James Hillman,[8] David Cooper and the English Surrealist Conroy Maddox. *Inscape*, now the Association's official journal, was created during a discussion in the early hours about Gerard Manley Hopkins in an Islington basement and was intended to be a radical journal appealing to an interdisciplinary readership. In retrospect, the cost of our political respectability might seem to have been excessive, but one had to eat and keep families, and in any case the NHS was where the object of many of our interests, including *bona fide* madness, lay.

Indeed the development of British art therapy had interesting antecedents in both art and psychotherapy. Most of the early art therapists in this country were artists and became therapists via this route. This was as true for me as it was for my predecessors like Adrian Hill, Arthur Segal and his daughter Marianne,[9] Edward Adamson, E.M. Lyddiatt, Jan Glass, Alexander Weatherson and others. During the 1950s and 1960s connections and relationships between art and psychotherapy were a feature of intellectual life. Many artists and critics were impressed with the way in which psychoanalytic theories gave art a psychological meaning and function largely denied it by formalism and Marxism. Some went so far as to submit to analysis themselves. Prominent among these artists and writers were Adrian Stokes (1965), Anton Ehrenzweig (1967) and Richard Wollheim (1970). This was a two-way process, psychoanalysts were fascinated by artistic creativity and the personality of the artist. Art and the artist were, so to speak, more than welcome on the couch. Analysts such as Ernst Kris (1964), Marion Milner (1950, 1969) and Hanna Segal (1955) wrote about art, in the case of Marion Milner about her own personal 'experiments' in art and psychotherapy. In fact it would not be any exaggeration to say that art occupied a much more prominent place in English society during those years than is the case now. Not only did England possess probably the largest and most elaborate art school system in the world, but there were many with influence who thought art rather than science should be central to all kinds and levels of education.[10] Interest in outsider art was also beginning to gather force in the 1960s, and many of the interesting outsider artists were to be found in mental hospitals (Cardinal 1972).

At this time the ideas of C.G. Jung held powerful sway in fields far removed from the province of psychotherapeutic practice. Jung had only recently died in 1961. His influence was to be felt in education (particularly in the education through art movement), in art and literary criticism, and among artists, writers, musicians, as well as eminent scientists.[11] One of the most important figures in the development of art therapy was the Jungian analyst,

Irene Champernowne. In the early 1950s she set up a therapeutic community in Devon, the Withymead Centre, where she put into practice her belief that there could be a therapeutic 'partnership' between psychotherapists and artists of many kinds. She invited painters, sculptors, potters, dancers and musicians to work with her at Withymead (Champernowne 1971; Stevens 1986). Among these were two artists who played prominent roles in the formative years of art therapy as a profession, Rupert Cracknell and Michael Edwards. In the early 1960s she took an active part in creating BAAT.

The fact that Jungian ideas played such an important part in these developments is due to rather more than the happenstance of individual personalities and events. Jung had always valued the image immensely; indeed, he considered the image to be the native form in which the psyche revealed itself. The centrality of the image is a distinguishing mark of Jungian analytical and archetypal psychology in contrast to the Freudian and post-Freudian schools of psychoanalysis which have been more linguistically based. Jung was a talented artist and sculptor himself and from at least the early 1920s encouraged his patients and his associates to use images actively in psychotherapy; that is, actual pictorial work rather than the inner images of our imagination.[12] It is also true that the Jungian tradition has remained close to the German idea of *Geisteswissenschaften* (literally 'science of the spirit') which so characterised German thought and philosophy in the nineteenth and early twentieth centuries.[13] It is also significant, in the context with which I am dealing, that Jung was particularly interested in the mad and the forms in which they expressed themselves. Indeed, it was partly as a result of his early work as a psychiatrist with the insane that he came upon the concepts of the 'collective unconscious' and the 'archetype'. Thus madness uncovered primordial layers of the mind, it was a state in which something vital in our nature revealed itself rather than existing only as a symptom of some psychological wreckage. Jung gave the experience of madness a human and cultural meaning. In recent years this explorative tradition has been developed by James Hillman and other archetypal psychologists associated with him.[14] These two Jungian preoccupations, with the image and with madness, were significant both for the interest of many artists working with the mad as well as in the development of anti-psychiatry. The idea that madness might be intelligible in cultural terms was certainly crucial to both Laing and Esterson, though they were to develop it in a way that differed from Jung's position.

The legacy of all this for psychotherapy and art therapy as they have developed over the past twenty to thirty years is impossible to overestimate. For art therapy it led to the creation of a new profession, and where there were once only a handful of practitioners there are now hundreds working in the health care field. In our current difficult times the wings of this approach to the conjunction of art and psychotherapy have maybe been clipped more than one would have wished. Whereas our original aim was in part to rescue art therapy from the ancillary or auxiliary status in which early National Health Service administrators placed it, through *realpolitik* it has obstinately remained in this position. To some extent, like psychotherapy, it has become increasingly preoccupied with clinical rectitude and other issues of professional practice rather than chancing its arm in the interests of unorthodox innovation. Maybe art therapy is the victim of its own altruism. The socialist beliefs of many members of the profession has led to an intense loyalty to the NHS, but what remains of this once great social experiment hardly permits the degree of imaginative invention in theory and method that might help the psychologically distressed far more than we may at present suspect. Nevertheless, institutions for training are in place that did not exist before 1970. A way has been established for those with an art and arts background to work with psychiatric patients and other troubled clients in particular, and in the psychological domain in general, rather than these remaining the province of the medical and social science professions. I have always believed this is of enormous importance and I trust it will bear fruit in ways I may not be able to anticipate.

ANTI-PSYCHIATRY'S LEGACY

What, then, has the outcome of anti-psychiatry been? What were its essential tenets and how well have they stood the test of time? Have they led to forms of therapy and healing capable of filling the space left in the aftermath of the critique of orthodox medical psychiatry and psychotherapy mounted so dazzlingly twenty and more years ago? We can see how Laing's radical view of things came into being between the late 1950s and the mid-1960s. His position had altered deeply between the initial publication of *The Divided Self* in 1960, and that of *Sanity, Madness and the Family* (with Aaron Esterson) in 1964. In *The Divided Self* Laing is still speaking of pathology from an orthodox even if progressively liberal and sympathetic point of view. The patients he describes with such extraordinarily sympathetic clinical observation are, he thinks, undoubtedly crazy, in need of therapeutic help, and whose experience of themselves is often beyond Laing's ordinary human understanding. In his essay 'R.D. Laing: self, symptom and society' (in Boyers and Orrill 1971) Peter Sedgwick pinpoints the disappearance of the symptom in any medical sense from Laing's account of schizophrenia, in two short passages of writing from the beginning and end of the 1960s. At first Laing writes:

> A good deal of schizophrenia is simply nonsense, red-herring speech, prolonged filibustering to throw dangerous people off the scent, to create boredom and futility in others. The schizophrenic is often making a fool of himself and the doctor. He is playing at being mad to avoid at all costs

the possibility of being held *responsible* for a single coherent idea, or intention.

(Laing 1960: 164)

Four years later Laing and Esterson are to argue that the particular communications of someone diagnosed schizophrenic *are* intelligible, often shockingly so, in terms of the shared communications in the family in which they live. Schizophrenia is no longer nonsense at all. At the end of the preface to the second edition of *Sanity, Madness and the Family* they say: 'Surely, if we are wrong, it would be easy to show it by studying a few families and revealing that schizophrenics really are talking a lot of nonsense after all' (Laing and Esterson 1970: 14).

By now the position of anti-psychiatry had crystallised. It is no longer just that a sympathetic and unprejudiced therapist might come to understand the psychological world of the psychotic – as in *The Divided Self*, and it is now much more than the suspension of belief in the orthodox medical view of madness that predicates Laing's and Esterson's initial approach to research as they state in their introduction to the first publication of *Sanity, Madness and the Family* in 1964:

> That the diagnosed patient is suffering from a pathological process is either a fact, a hypothesis, an assumption, or a judgement.
>
> To regard it as fact is unequivocally false. To regard it as a hypothesis is legitimate. It is unnecessary either to make the assumption or to pass the judgement.
>
> ... The judgement that the diagnosed patient is behaving in a biologically dysfunctional (hence pathological) way is, we believe, premature, and one that we shall hold in parenthesis.
>
> (Laing and Esterson 1964: 18)

Their hypothesis, that the apparently crazy behaviour of the ostensible 'patient' is in fact a sane reaction to an insane family situation, by degrees becomes an implicit assumption and judgement in advance of any evidence that might show this to be unequivocally the case. So strong was their predilection for an anti-family stance they were simply not prepared to countenance any other conclusion than that the family was the pathogenic agent in the development of schizophrenia.

My own experience strongly confirms this. Between 1962 and 1965 I was involved in some of the preparatory work for *Sanity, Madness and the Family*. I, along with a group of several others – psychologists, social workers, therapists and administrators – met either at the Tavistock Institute of Human Relations in London, or at Napsbury, with Laing and Esterson to listen to tape-recordings made by them of interactions between patients from 'East Hospital' and 'West Hospital'[15] and members of their families. Our job, as a cross-section of supposedly informed but impartial people, was to assess aspects of these tape-recordings. In particular this assessment was of the family 'nexus' and the way in which the invalidation of one or other family members might occur. Our task was, on the basis of the recorded interviews, to say whether we thought the mother was putting the daughter in an untenable position, the daughter the mother, the father the daughter, the daughter the father, and so on and so on, through as many combinations of family members as were present on the tape-recording. Though we scored these opinions on prepared forms we all met in one room and our assessments were fairly obvious to the others present, including Laing and Esterson. The pressure to cast our votes in a certain fashion was very clear, to indicate that on occasion one felt a daughter might be being impossible to her mother, for example, was not an easy or popular option within the intimate atmosphere of such a small group where its highly charismatic leader made it obvious that certain opinions were to be preferred to others. I was young and perhaps naive at the time but I remember my consternation at this obvious bias and its distorting influence on what should have been our supposedly impartial and honest assessment.

In fact *Sanity, Madness and the Family* was intended by Laing and Esterson as a first report of their investigation. Not only were the families of a group of male patients to be studied and written up, the authors were at one stage committed to carrying out similar studies of interactions between the members of 'normal' families – that is, where no member of the family had been diagnosed schizophrenic. This was to answer the criticism that the dynamics of the families they had written about might not be so very different from the dynamics of family life generally, and therefore could not in themselves account for one of their members being schizophrenic. This project was never followed up. I suspect that if it had been it may well have partly confirmed this criticism, or at least have shown that family life of all kinds was more complicated than Laing and Esterson were assuming.

The work of Laing and Esterson was part of a wider research initiative into schizophrenics and their social situations being carried out at Napsbury Hospital during the 1960s. Dennis Scott and Tom Fairwell were also pioneering a method of crisis intervention that frequently obviated the need to admit and hospitalise people on the verge of being diagnosed as psychotic. This involved a kind of family narration or account of the 'crisis' underlying the proposed admission of one of their members so that each could see their part in a drama which might, as a consequence of this narration, unfold in a different and kinder direction. Though infinitely less publicised than that of Laing, their work has had a profound and practical effect on community psychiatry in this country.

A close associate of Laing and Esterson during this period was David Cooper. As I have indicated Cooper ran his experimental unit, *Villa 21*, in a hospital very near to Laing, Esterson, Scott and Fairwell. His *The Death of the Family* was published in 1971. I find Cooper's writing an unwitting caricature of one of this period's central themes, a deep suspicion amounting almost to a vitriolic hatred of the family, as indeed it was with Cooper. In Cooper's chaotic and intoxicated prose (literally as well as figuratively) the family is chastised over and again as an 'ideological conditioning device'. He betrays in an exaggerated form the prejudice that underlay much of the anti-psychiatry movement – an intense hostility to ordinary uncultivated human discourse with all its sometimes awkward recourse to commonplace usage. If one reads the family dialogues in *Sanity, Madness and the Family* with a certain attention, one can hear the nervous, abashed, conventional language of many people in distress and put on the spot (particularly being tape-recorded in front of the doctor), and, in the transcripts of these meetings, sometimes being quoted out of context. After all, one can hardly blame these parents for not having read Marx, Sartre and Bateson – and often not knowing where to begin with this kind of thinking, that they were not conversant with the 'correct' concepts, were embarrassed about their family being a focus of psychiatric attention, and were feeling particularly defensive as they sensed there was a thinly veiled suggestion that they were to blame for what had happened to their son or daughter.

The primary theoretical concept underlying Laing's and Esterson's approach to family functioning and the development of a psychosis in one of its members was the 'double bind' mechanism, derived from the work of Gregory Bateson and others involved in information theory and artificial intelligence during the 1950s and 1960s in the United States. Bateson's seminal paper, 'Minimal requirements for a theory of schizophrenia', in which he enunciated the 'double bind' theory, first appeared in 1960 and was later included in an anthology of his writing, *Steps to an Ecology of Mind* (1972). The subject or victim of a double bind is caught between mutually contradictory injunctions. Very often this is in the form of a manifest invitation to behave in a certain fashion which is then undermined by subtle contextual signals, or, contrariwise, an interpersonal context appears to invite a particular behaviour for which the subject is then actually punished. In the so-called 'schizophrenogenic' family one of its members is subjected to double binds affecting quite fundamental things in life over many years from the member's earliest childhood. He or she rarely subjected to physical violence, or indeed to any overt abuse, the attack made upon the member is based upon implicit messages concealed within explicit messages rather, than clearly discernible actions. A merit of this is that it explains why, in spite of many decades of conventional empirical research, there appears to be no conclusive physiological, anatomical or neurological explanation for the existence of schizophrenic symptoms in certain individuals, as well as why they seem to run in particular families.

Furthermore, any explanation of schizophrenia that locates its causes inside the individual is rejected; for example, medical explanations deriving from biochemistry or genetics, or psychoanalytic accounts depending on an individual's psychodynamics. Schizophrenia is a response by one person to an intersubjective situation, the 'nexus' of a family. To try to understand it by examining one individual is bound to be fruitless.

Given such an explanatory stance the therapeutic practices that arose from this work were bound to differ radically from the methods of medical psychiatry or behaviourist psychology, which were often seen as malevolently oppressive, as well as from traditional psychotherapy and psychoanalysis which were seen as misguided and élitist. By and large it was not considered possible to conduct effective therapy in orthodox public service settings, such as psychiatric institutions in the NHS. The anti-psychiatry movement gave rise to a number of organisations and institutions. Among the best known of them were The Philadelphia Association, the loose organisation known as PNP (People Not Psychiatry), Centre 48 (in which I lived and worked), The Arbours Association (which is still functioning as an actual organisation) and Kingsley Hall in London's East End.[16] Apart from Laing, Esterson and Cooper some of the most prominent therapists associated with these bodies were Joe Berke, Sid Briskin, Bill Grossman, Jerome Liss, Harry Pincus, Leon Redler and Morton Schatzman.

It would be difficult to give a comprehensive account of the therapeutic approaches adopted by these establishments, or by the therapists who practised within them, since there were many people and sets of ideas involved. Furthermore, they were continually breaking up and reforming in different subgroups. Nevertheless, most of those involved were united by some basic assumptions and their styles and methods reflected these. The medical idea of schizophrenia being a psychiatric disability was anathema to all of them. Instead it was often held to be a naturally occurring form of psychological healing which, providing its dangers were avoided, offered the possibility of a kind of super sanity. The risks involved were great; if 'nature' was prevented from taking its course the outcome could be a form of existential death – in psychiatric slang, the victim becomes a 'burnt out schizophrenic'. The most common of these risks was that someone entering the early stages of this process might, in that person's relatively helpless state, be treated by psychiatrists. Indeed most schizophrenics in fact were, and they then suffered from the self-fulfilling prophecy of psychiatric diagnosis; if they were not mad to start with, psychiatry usually made them so. According to Sedgwick (1971: 32):

> Psychiatric medicine offered, at best, a mechanistic bungling which would frustrate the lawful progression of this potentially natural process; at worst, it drove its patients insane with its murderous chemistry, surgery and regimentation.

Most agreed that the institutionalised degradation inflicted on patients by doctors and nurses – initial examination, diagnosis and admission, 'mortification ceremonies' as Goffman called them (1961), then subsequent medical treatment and enduring social stigma – actually determined the very illness which psychiatry sought to locate within the individual sufferer. Instead, those in the early stages of the schizophrenic process should be gently initiated and then, according to Laing, '. . . guided with full social sanction and encouragement into inner space and time, by people who have been there and back again' (1967: 10). If fully completed, this double journey could lead to an 'existential rebirth'. Laing attempted to provide such a sympathetic setting at Kingsley Hall, the therapeutic community he founded in 1965, which would help schizophrenics embark on their self-renewal free from medical interference and unsuitable psychiatric institutions.

Perhaps the most famous account of such a 'journey' is that jointly written by the patient and therapist involved, Mary Barnes and Joseph Berke (1971). The events described in their book took place at Kingsley Hall in its brief heyday in the late 1960s.[17] Mary Barnes' transformation through regression and rebirth involved the painting of many pictures. She is now well known as an active, perhaps the most active, advocate, and historical example in person as it were, of the radical therapy which was anti-psychiatry's principal method. One of the problems of anti-psychiatry when it was at its most active was that it had so successfully publicised and politicised its programme, principally through the writings and personal charisma of Laing himself, that it became hard to know who were the patients (as one might know them in an NHS hospital) and who were the ideologically motivated fellow-travellers. A criticism of Laing and others involved in anti-psychiatry is that they made schizophrenia too glamorous. It might have been for my Cypriot 'patient', who acted the part as best he could; it was certainly not so for all of those who suffered, and still do, from the condition itself – whatever its cause may be. None of the patients I knew who were involved with Laing and Esterson at Napsbury was particularly helped by them in any therapeutic sense. It is fair to say that many of those seen by Scott and Fairwell, who were barely known outside the trade, were significantly and at times dramatically helped.

In praise of Laing, however, he trenchantly raised issues ignored by psychiatry and the medical profession. He taught us that madness is more a human than a medical problem, and was one of the main players in the course of events that have altered society's treatment of psychotic patients somewhat for the better. He has had an international influence on mental health policy. One of the most dramatic examples of this has been the creation, through the work of Franco and Franca Bassaglia, of *Psychiatrica Democratica* in Italy. This came about because of the strong impression that Laing and the anti-psychiatry movement made on Franco Bassaglia when he was in England, and the subsequent Italian legislation brought about in 1978 as a result of political work by his widow, Franca, a parliamentary representative. This legislation created Law number 180, which effectively closed mental hospitals in many parts of Italy. At a more local level, those of us working and teaching in Sheffield have until recently had the patronage of an unusually cultured Professor of Psychiatry, Alec Jenner, whose transition from a pharmacological to a social approach to madness could not have happened in the way it did were it not for influence and friendship of Laing. As with many revolutions and their ultimate consequences, it is a case of many steps forward taken rapidly and with great excitement, followed by a lesser number of steps backwards, leaving some abiding change. In recent years, and before he died, Laing himself was somewhat sceptical of the messianic ferment that characterised anti-psychiatry at the height of its activity.

CONCLUSION

Like many of the social upheavals that typified this period, the experiments that took place in the arts and psychiatry have given us a store of experience that underpins many of our current preoccupations. The connections that were established then between art and madness have profoundly psychologised our practice and understanding of art. The formalism that was so dominant in the visual arts over the first decades of the twentieth century opened up to admit some of the living configurations of human experience. The aesthetic forms of dreams, fantasy, madness and personal experience are no longer the exclusive styles of outsider art; psychotic art, or art therapy art, they now characterise much contemporary painting and sculpture. Similarly, while sections of orthodox psychiatry remain rooted in a medical model that is forever trying to eradicate madness as if it were an epidemic that could be excised by medication or surgery, there are now many doctors and therapists prepared to locate a significant portion of crazy experience in personal and social contexts. Insanity becomes a troubling experience that might be understood by the sane, rather than exiled to a mystifying region where it is the subject of medical procedures more appropriate to the body. That this great opening took place was due to a number of artists, doctors and therapists, bold and cultured enough to see beyond the limited confines of their own disciplines, and who saw that quite possibly art has more to tell us about living than the more instrumental forms of science. The last two miserable decades of social life in Britain have seen a reaction against this ethos, including a retreat to older psychiatric attitudes and a retrenchment to market economy considerations in dealing with human problems. One might hope, however, that if and when the social and political pendulum swings back in the direction of what pertained thirty years ago, another period of development can begin that is able to build on what was established then, and that those involved will, in their own fashion, create some of the exciting, sometimes foolish, but rewarding excesses that spiced those years.

NOTES

1 In the years immediately before and after the Second World War insulin-coma shock therapy was a popular treatment for psychotic and depressed psychiatric patients. It was eventually replaced by electro convulsive therapy (ECT), which also involved the belief that inducing a coma was beneficial for many psychiatric conditions.

2 The role of medical superintendents was crucial at this time. They exercised great influence over the treatment philosophy of the hospitals they superintended and had the advantage of being clinicians themselves. Of course this influence depended very much on their orientation; they were able to shape a whole therapeutic environment according to their psychiatric philosophy. In the case of Napsbury this philosophy was liberal and experimental. It was also true that in other hospitals, and depending on one's view, this influence may not have been so fortunate.

3 Not that this work was thought unimportant or superficial, rather that it did not require the radical change of consciousness entailed in understanding the psychological experience of severely psychotic clients.

4 See Lyddiatt (1972) and Thomson (1989). A feature of this approach is to equip an art therapy studio as richly as possible. It is the creative ambience that the therapist offers, both sensuous and workmanlike, which constitutes the therapeutic environment, rather than the person of the therapist.

5 This is most striking when arriving in England for the first time. One could then, and I think to a large extent still can, among other factors such as sex and nationality, map authority and financial reward in English hospitals according to class and accent.

6 *Art as Communication*, The Institute of Contemporary Arts, London, 1964; *Fantastic Art*, Gallery 48, London, 1967; *Art as Therapy*, The House of Commons, 1968 and 1969; and *The Inner Eye*, Museum of Modern Art, Oxford, 1978.

7 These included Edward Adamson, Frank Breakwell, Rupert Cracknell, Michael Edwards, Jan Glass, Diana Halliday, Adrian Hill, Joyce Laing, E.M. Lyddiatt, Michael Pope, Rita Simon, John Timlin, Alexander Weatherson and myself as well as Irene Champernowne, a psychotherapist, and the psychiatrist Stephen MacKeith.

8 Hillman's lecture, 'An imaginal ego', was published in an early number of *Inscape* (1970).

9 Arthur Segal was a Romanian born artist who had worked for many years in Germany where he was a member of the *Blau Reiter* group. He fled to England in the late 1930s to escape Nazism and set up the Arthur Segal School of Art in Hampstead where artists, therapists and doctors studied the psychological principles of form. Edward Adamson was a pupil at the school. The school was temporarily evacuated to Oxford during the war years, and soldiers suffering from battle trauma were actually referred to Segal's school. After his death in 1944 his daughter, Marianne Segal (who I met in 1975), took over the running of the school and brought it back to England's Lane in Hampstead after the war where it continued to function until the 1970s.

10 This position was promulgated by the British Society for Education through Art (SEA) and the International Society for Education through Art (INSEA). One of the seminal texts for the education through art movement was Herbert Read's *Education Through Art*, published in 1943.

11 For example, Jackson Pollock, J.B. Priestley, Herman Hesse, Michael Tippett and Wolfgang Pauli.

12 Michael Edwards has carried out archival research into the several thousand pictorial works resulting from therapy by Jung and colleagues that have been kept in Zurich, although he has not, as far as I know, published anything on this.

13 This has been enormously important in the development of psychiatry; for example, the psychiatric philosophy of Karl Jaspers and the research into the art of the insane carried out by Hans Prinzhorn and Walter Morgenthaler in the years after the First World War. It was Morgenthaler who discovered the art of Adolf Wölfli, perhaps the best known of all outsider artists.

14 James Hillman's work also derives from this period, but in the United States rather than in England.

15 Not the actual East and West hospitals at Napsbury, in their book the terms are used to distinguish between different locations for groups of patients.

16 See Michael Barnet (1973) for a first-hand description of these situations and many of those involved.

17 For a time when I was working with Laing and Esterson at Napsbury I was eager to become a therapist at Kingsley Hall. A combination of financial and, later, other doubts eventually dissuaded me.

REFERENCES

Barnes, M. and Berke, J. (1971) *Two Accounts of a Journey Through Madness*, Harmondsworth: Penguin.

Barnet, M. (1973) *People Not Psychiatry*, London: George Allen & Unwin.

Bateson, G. (1960) 'Minimal requirements for a theory of schizophrenia', *A.M.A. Archives of General Psychiatry* 2: 477–91.

—— (1972) *Steps to an Ecology of Mind*, New York: Ballantine Books.

Boyers, R. and Orill, R. (eds) (1971) *R.D. Laing and Anti-Psychiatry*, New York: Harper & Row.

Cardinal, R. (1972) *Outsider Art*, London; Studio Vista.

Champernowne, I. (1971) 'Art and therapy: an uneasy partnership', in London: *Inscape* 3.

Cooper, D. (1971) *The Death of the Family*, London: Allen Lane, The Penguin Press.

Cox, M. and Theilgaard, A. (1987) *Mutative Metaphors in Psychotherapy: The Aeolian Mode*, London: Tavistock.

Dax, E.C. (1953) *Experimental Studies in Psychiatric Art*, London: Faber.

Ehrenzweig, A. (1967) *The Hidden Order of Art: A Study in the Psychology of Artistic Imagination*, Harmondsworth: Penguin.

Goffman, E. (1961) *Asylums: Essays on the Social Situation of Mental Patients and Other Inmates*, New York: Anchor Books.

Hill, A. (1945) *Art versus Illness*, London: George Allen & Unwin.

Hillman, J. (1970) 'An imaginal ego', London: *Inscape* 2.

Kris, E. (1964) *Psychoanalytic Explorations in Art*, New York: Schocken Books.

Laing, R.D. (1960) *The Divided Self*, Harmondsworth: Penguin.

—— (1967) *The Politics of Experience and the Bird of Paradise*, Harmondsworth: Penguin.

Laing, R.D. and Esterson, A. (1964) *Sanity, Madness and the Family: Families of Schizophrenics*, Harmondsworth: Penguin (second edition, 1970).

Lyddiatt, E.M. (1972) *Spontaneous Painting and Modelling*, London: Constable.

Milner, M. (1950) *On Not Being Able to Paint*, London: Heinemann (reprinted 1973).

—— (1969) *The Hands of the Living God*, London: Hogarth Press.

Musil, R. (1930–42) *Der Mann ohne Eigenschaften* (English trans., *The Man Without Qualities*; trans. E. Wilkins and E. Kaiser, 1954), London: Secker & Warburg.

Nuttall, J. (1968) *Bomb Culture*, Harmondsworth: Penguin.

Read, H. (1943) *Education Through Art*, New York: Pantheon.

Sedgwick, P. (1971) 'R.D. Laing: self, symptom and society,' in Boyers and Orill (1971).

Segal, H. (1955) 'A psychoanalytical approach to aesthetics', in M. Klein, P. Heimann and R. Money-Kyrle (eds) *New Directions in Psycho-Analysis*, London: Tavistock.

Stevens, A. (1986) *The Withymead Centre: A Jungian Community for the Healing Arts*, London: Coventure.

Stokes, A. (1965) *The Invitation in Art*, London: Tavistock.

Szasz, T. (1961) *The Myth of Mental Illness*, New York: Secker.

Thomson, M. (1989) *On Art and Therapy: An Exploration*, London: Virago Press.

Waller, D. (1991) *Becoming a Profession: The History of Art Therapy in Britain 1940–82*, London: Routledge.

Wollheim, Richard (1970) *Art and its Objects*, Harmondsworth: Penguin.

Chapter 10

The forgotten people

Claire Skailes

INTRODUCTION

This chapter illustrates how art therapy was used to help patients, who had lost the ability to communicate, to find a voice. The work took place in an old psychiatric hospital in Gloucester over a period of three years from 1975 to 1978. It was at this time that art therapy was becoming recognised nationally as a profession.

There had been two psychiatric hospitals in Gloucester: the older one, Horton Road Hospital, was built within the city; the other, Coney Hill Hospital, was a large rambling Victorian building built on the outskirts of the city. In January 1995, Coney Hill Hospital was closed and demolished, and a new psychiatric unit, very different in quality from its predecessors, was opened. It had been built on land close to Horton Road Hospital. Though this hospital closed in 1988, the building itself is still standing, as it is a listed building. It is of Georgian architecture and has a fine façade, but internally it is like a rabbit warren of stairways and passages. Since its closure no use has been found for the building. It now looks sad and desolate, its beautifully proportioned windows boarded up. The fabric of the building is slowly crumbling away, rather like its former inmates – the crumbling façade, the confused interior. The former inmates were the forgotten people of the title of this chapter.

BACKGROUND HISTORY OF HORTON ROAD HOSPITAL

Horton Road Hospital was built in 1823 originally to house 120 patients. The building had been designed by a Glasgow architect who was considered 'experienced and knowledgeable' – 'yet the form he chose was a crescent, the most expensive and the worst for supervision he could have adopted', according to J. Curtis Hayward writing in the *Gloucester Chronical* in 1869 (Hollingsbee and Morris 1988: 2). The building was enlarged in 1856 to accommodate 600 pauper patients, but it was still 'found barely sufficient to meet the increasing claims of lunacy in this county' (Hollingsbee and Morris 1988: 1). During the 1860s plans were made to build another asylum on what are now the outskirts of Gloucester. Coney Hill Hospital was opened in 1883, and was intended to replace Horton Road Hospital; it did not. Horton Road Hospital remained open until 1988, being used mainly for chronically ill psychotic patients and patients with what was then described as senile dementia. The hospital survived despite its inappropriate and inconvenient building. Throughout its existence it seemed to engender in those who worked in it feelings of affection, pride and care of the patients. In 1860 it was written: 'The asylum, from being one of the earliest and in its construction, one of the most inconvenient and faulty of the County asylums, has become remarkable as one of the most cheerful and agreeable' (Hollingsbee and Morris 1988: 12). There was dancing, magic lanterns, an organ in the chapel and patients formed a choir. A band of musicians was organised comprising patients and attendants; not far away Elgar led a similar band in the hospital in Worcester. Over half the patients were involved in work making all the clothes and shoes that were needed; the women did needlework and worked in the laundry. 'Employment is, and always has been considered in this asylum, a matter of first importance and treatment, and amusements are added as they can be reasonably afforded' (Hollingsbee and Morris 1988: 14).

But maybe it was too cheerful and agreeable, as in 1863 there is a comment: 'many chronic and harmless quiet patients who scarcely appeared to require the expensive accommodation of the County asylum but who could not be sent back to the workhouse. Tried to get them into suitable accommodation in other workhouses, but no good' (Hollingsbee and Morris 1988: 12). However, as places were not found for the patients they remained in hospital. Up until the 1930 Mental Health Act it was very difficult for a patient to be discharged from the hospitals. I quote from a letter found in an attic of a local workhouse. It was dated 15 October 1930 and was written to the super-intendent of the workhouse from a patient who was pleading to be discharged from the hospital: 'I have no friends or relatives outside to claim me out and the Doctor has given good account of me and says I can go out as soon as someone will come and claim me out, or sign the papers for me.' This patient died in hospital in 1976. Discharge was still difficult after 1930 as many of the patients were in a similar situation to the writer of the letter, and there would be few that would have been prepared to give them a home. Even those with relatives did not get discharged, and later in the 1970s there was much resistance to the establishment of Group Homes in the community, as people did not wish to live next door to 'those mental patients', even though they could be described as 'quiet and harmless'.

Early in the century both hospitals fell into decline. There were 'complaints about lack of treatment, poor and overcrowded accommodation and that the hospital (Coney Hill) was not keeping up with current practices' (Severn NHS Trust, Special Supplement No. 2: 3). From 1930 onwards considerable work was done to bring Coney Hill Hospital up to date, but Horton Road Hospital continued as before. In 1949 it was described as being 'entirely obsolete in structure. It seems almost impossible for the staff to provide a satisfactory home for the patients who are for the most part of the chronic type – a considerable number of patients sitting about doing nothing' (Hollingsbee and Morris 1988: 28).

Though the building remained obsolete, attempts were made to improve the quality of life for the patients. In 1960 it was quite a self-sufficient unit; all that was possible was produced by the patients and staff. There were tailors' and cobblers' workshops, and at Coney Hill there was a large farm. Many of the patients did meaningful and purposeful work within a very secure environment. In 1962 it was recommended that the farm be closed, and industrial occupational therapy was introduced. It was unfortunate that often the few contracts that were available brought work for the patients that was repetitious and sometimes destructive; for example, there was one where the patients had to break up old telephones in order to retrieve a piece of metal that had value. In Horton Road Hospital a small department was set up for the less able patients, and the work there was mainly very monotonous.

In 1975 I began working in the department at Horton Road Hospital doing two sessions of art therapy a week. My employment as an art therapist was probably very typical of most art therapists working in psychiatric hospitals at that time, as art therapy was in its infancy as a profession and was just struggling to survive. Diane Waller in her book *Becoming a Profession* (Waller 1991) describes how art therapy came into being out of certain conflicts and confusion of identity. Difficulties arose because there was a wide range of people with very different professional backgrounds using art as therapy. They differed in their ways of perceiving art in therapy. For the purpose of this chapter, I shall concentrate on art therapy in the treatment of the mentally ill. Diane Waller describes the work of two founding members of the profession and shows very clearly how they differed in their way of perceiving art therapy. Adrian Hill had found art to be essential for his own recovery from illness and enthusiastically worked in hospitals with patients enabling them to find a means of recovery through being actively involved with art work. 'Hill used his skills as an artist, his love of teaching and his desire to make art accessible to all as a basis of his work' (Waller 1991: 50). Many other artists came into hospitals and encouraged patients to paint and work with clay. My predecessor in the hospital was such an artist. She formed painting groups with the patients which was seen to be therapeutic.

Waller shows another way of perceiving art therapy in the work of Irene Champernowne, who was a Jungian analyst who encouraged her patients to be creative in painting, modelling and writing. She and her husband Gilbert founded the Withymead Centre where there was a meeting of therapy and the arts (Stevens 1985). Irene Champernowne made a distinction between the art therapist and the psychotherapist. 'The art therapist would help the patient produce the pictures but it was the psychotherapist who would enter into the deeper meaning of the work with the patient. She was inclined to refer to the art therapist as a "midwife" in the process' (Waller 1991: 63). Edward Adamson (1984) working as an artist in the Netherne Hospital was certainly a 'midwife' for his patients' paintings. He generated a therapeutic atmosphere which enabled patients to work freely and spontaneously, but it was the doctors who made use of the artwork in their treatment of the patients in attempting to interpret or find some meaning in the pictures.

Art therapy was struggling to establish itself as a profession at this stage. Using Adrian Hill's model could easily have led to being absorbed by the occupational therapy profession, as occupational therapists felt they could do the art activities. However, taking the view that image-making or free expression could be valuable within the psychotherapeutic process, the art therapists, who wanted to be working with the pictures rather than just be the midwife, needed to be specifically trained to enable them to be engaged appropriately with the work. The art therapist would need to be well developed and experienced in his or her own creative work – a visual arts graduate who had personal maturity and who could be trained as a therapist. This gave the art therapist an identity which would differ considerably from that of the occupational therapist. Art therapists employed in psychiatric hospitals working within occupational therapy departments would often find themselves being treated little differently from aides and working in very poor situations. They did it because they cared about the work they were doing.

In 1975 I was working in five different areas within the health authority. I shall describe each of these settings. A day hospital, a unit for the severely subnormal, a unit for chronically physically disabled, an adolescent unit, and Horton Road Hospital for the chronically ill psychotic patients. Each client group presented a different setting and perception of the work of an art therapist. In the day hospital I was in the midst of the occupational therapy department providing for my patients an alternative afternoon activity to ping pong. In the unit for the severely subnormal, my work was received with enthusiasm by patients and staff. I was interested in channelling this enthusiasm to aid developmental skills and combined my work with a speech therapist, through which the patients were pleased to name, and talk about, their images because they had made them. The work in the unit for chronically physically disabled centred around clay and here I worked with a physiotherapist. The movements that were made in the clay were physically beneficial to the clients as well as giving them an opportunity to express the unspeakable feelings of the experience of their relentlessly deteriorating bodies. The adolescent unit was the only place where I had a suitable room and found my work to be understood. Here the young people had a facilitating environment and, through play, began to discover themselves out of their confusion. Waller writes of the 'sense of mission' that is noted by Bucher and Strauss (1961), that 'it is characteristic of the growth of specialities that early in their development they carve out for themselves and proclaim unique missions' (Waller 1991: 190). At that time I was enthused by a 'sense of mission'; it was important for me to let people know how I, as an art therapist, worked.

ART THERAPY AT HORTON ROAD HOSPITAL

I was required to work in the small occupational therapy department in Horton Road Hospital. It was run by two nurses who had great experience of the patients and who genuinely cared for them. The work the patients had to do was very repetitive: some of them cut up nylon stockings into tiny pieces so that they could be used to stuff the door-stops knitted by some of the women out of nylon yarn in awful colours and texture; others cut the yarn into three-inch strips to be used by the more able patients in the group to make rugs. There were some who were not able to settle for any length of time and they would spasmodically unravel bandages and attempt to roll them up, but these bandages were never used and were there merely to be unravelled and rolled up as something for these patients to do. As the patients worked, they were not looking at what they were doing but fixed their gaze into some vacant spot, where their eyes remained throughout the session. Sometimes they muttered or moved their lips as if engaged in some private dialogue in a totally different space from the nurses and myself. When they arrived and went back to the wards at lunch-time, and at the end of the afternoon, they moved slowly and in a very mechanical robot-like manner. They would eventually arrive at their destination but it did not feel as though it really mattered whether they arrived or left; the world as I knew it seemed not to matter to them at all. They were totally cut off from it and lived in their own private isolated space due to the psychosis that had originally taken them away from the world, the treatment that they had received dulling their senses, and the effects of the institutionalisation.

When I entered the room, I was utterly appalled by what I saw; this vacant mechanical world which seemed totally unapproachable and the terrible ugliness of the work they were doing. Britta Warsi describes how, for the institutionalised patient,

> The real former self may have been withdrawn altogether so that all that remains is a dehumanised shell. The institutionalised self has been stripped long ago of all the previously taken for granted privileges of living in the outside world. His decisions are no longer his own, there can be little sense of autonomy or freedom, he is a faint surname on a large, bulky, and impersonal case history file.
>
> (Warsi 1975: 6)

These patients were described as being chronically ill psychotics, but this description would probably cover a wide range of conditions from those who had been highly disturbed, manic and a definite danger to others to those who acted in rather odd ways but were harmless. There were also what was then described as the 'simple-minded'. Scattered among the group in the room were soldiers who had broken down in the war over thirty years before. Had they lost a limb or been blinded they would have been seen as heroes, but they lost their minds and, in a way, their lives. Also in the room were a few patients that came from countries in Eastern Europe; they, too, were left over from the war and were lost in an alien culture. The actual psychosis from which they had suffered had become blurred which, combined with the medical treatment they had received and their living an institutionalised life, had left them in a state that was often described as being a 'burnt out case'. Psychosis is a disturbance of the patient's perception of the normal everyday world which is often viewed from a distorted perspective; the ego is thin, and may be fragmented. Bion (1967) states:

> that its contact with reality is masked by the dominance in the patient's mind and behaviour of an omnipotent phantasy that is intended to destroy either reality or awareness of it; and thus to achieve a state that is neither life nor death.
>
> (Bion 1967: 46)

Whether because of their psychosis or the way they were living, they were in a world in the hospital that was totally cut off from reality, and their existence was a state that was neither life nor death. I saw them as the walking undead.

I was expected to work with a group of patients in the room where they were doing their occupational therapy. E.M. Lyddiatt, who had worked for many years in hospitals, stressed that 'in a hospital there must be a workroom where the painters belong and where they can feel at ease. They should come to feel that this is their domain, to be looked after and valued: a safe place where dreams and imagination live' (Lyddiatt 1971: 14). I had then to decide what would be most helpful for these patients. I could have followed Adrian Hill's model and considered that the painting would be a pleasant occupation. I could have drawn pictures for them to colour, or given them some pictures to copy. Some probably would have been able to do this quite well and might have gained some pleasure in being occupied in such a way. However, I thought they had other needs and that it would be essential for these patients to be able to do something of their own volition. This meant that I would take a non-directive role; I would provide the materials, paper, crayons and paint and then stand back and allow the patients to discover for themselves what would happen when they picked up a crayon or a brush and made contact with the paper. For the work to proceed, I needed the co-operation and understanding of the two nurses. I realised that my presence was experienced by them as an intrusion into their well-managed space and the idea of the patients making their own marks might have seemed at first to be a pointless exercise, and perhaps threatening. I needed to explain how precious it was for patients to make marks on the paper of their own volition, to make a spontaneous gesture. It was important that we did not intrude on what was occurring, but waited and allowed it to happen; also not to make any judgemental comments or critical remarks. At the beginning I had no idea what might occur. It was in a way an experiment, but I drew on my experience of working with the severely mentally subnormal and my earlier work with children who could not communicate.

I worked in the department for three years. I believe a facilitating environment is essential for the work to proceed. Physically the room was not facilitating, as too much was happening within it and there was no privacy for the work. I had to provide the facilitating environment out of myself and to do this I needed to have certain qualities which would enable the patients to experience consistency, continuity and a certain sameness of experience. It is these qualities that Erikson describes as being necessary for a sense of trust which, when developed by a mother in her care for her child, enables him to feel safe and secure; and in such a way I could enable the patients to feel safe.

In order to give the reader an idea of the situation, I shall describe my first session in the department. A few patients sat at the table; I gave them paper, placing a choice of crayons and paint before them. The response of the patients was very varied; two immediately picked up the crayons and used them quite energetically on the paper, making marks, circles and crosses, then after a few minutes put the crayons down and rested. Another man picked up a crayon and moved aimlessly back and forth over the paper, his head turned away, occasionally stopping and remaining very still, and then starting the aimless movement again. One man picked up a pencil and with great intensity began to make very small lines, close together – he continued making his lines until the end of the session when he had covered about a third of the paper. Two men made use of paint, one appeared quite thirsty to use the paint making bold scribbles and using several pieces of paper. The other man covered a sheet of paper with a very pale wash.

Two people picked up pencils and began to make representational drawings, but the way they used their drawings was very different. One of these patients was the only woman in the group; she was nearly 60 and had entered the hospital at 19 following the birth of her illegitimate baby. Her baby had been taken from her and, in a way, so had her life. She was neat, very well behaved and appeared to live in a totally bizarre fantasy world. She seemed to find the introduction of the art therapy sessions a wonderful relief, and came regularly to the sessions, gaining in confidence to express her own ideas. This women painted her fantasies and dreams and later, as the months and years passed, she was able to communicate how she felt about herself and her life.

The other person who drew representationally, drew a river, two ducks, a tree, a fence and a stile, and I could have been justified in thinking that this had some potential had it not emerged that this was the only picture he ever drew. He did not become a regular member of the group, coming occasionally, sitting down and making the exact same drawing – it never changed in any detail whatsoever. Similarly, if one were to meet him walking around the hospital, he would stop and have quite a long conversation; afterwards, one might feel that it had been an interesting conversation and, perhaps, question what he was doing in the hospital. However, if one met him at any time of day, month or year, one would have exactly the same conversation. It appeared that he held on to these pockets of reality, fearing to change them, and he lived the rest of his life in an unreal world which was impossible for others to reach.

Earlier, when I mentioned a patient appearing to be quite thirsty to use the paint, I was referring to the quenching of such a metaphorical thirst which I consider to be a particular asset of art therapy. The patients in Horton Road Hospital appeared as if they had spent many years in a desert, experiencing dryness to such a degree that the mouth was no longer able to be exercised through speech, allowing no means of communication. When, in later years, I was working in Coney Hill Hospital with the acute admission patients, I found that patients in the early acute stages of psychosis would seem to experience their art therapy sessions almost as if they had found an oasis. This thirst was the desperate need to find a place which could hold some of the inner confusion of disconnected thoughts, images and words. The patients would come in a wild, frightened and alienated state, yet as they made contact with the clay or paint and the images began to flow, they appeared to enter a state of peacefulness and quiet reflection. Though they did not communicate directly with me, there may have been a certain sense of being in the presence of another which, to some degree, was containing and allowed them relief.

Initially, my aim had been for the patients to make moves of their own volition. The work progressed slowly and hesitantly, but gradually patients began to get more confident in using the materials and the marks began to form images which, to the patients, could be a means of communication – at first with the patient, looking at what he or she was doing and reacting to it, then later, sharing with other patients or myself.

By the third year of working in the department, I had a regular group of about fifteen patients and, as the weeks, months and years passed by, I was able to get to know them as individual people. To show how art therapy was able to help these patients to communicate I shall now give brief verbal sketches of two patients, both of whom had found themselves in hospital following their harrowing war experiences.

Cyril

Whenever I spoke to Cyril he seemed to be quite startled as if surprised that he had actually been spoken to. His eyes almost popped out of his head and he would make an utterance in a high-pitched squeak. He often appeared to be very frightened. I think initially he had been trained to be a carpenter and then had been called up to fight in the war. From his experiences in the war he broke down mentally, and had been in hospital from the time the war had ended – when I met him it had been over thirty years. Cyril began his work in art therapy by carefully covering a piece of paper with a thin blue wash and, for several sessions, continued to do this. In one session, whether by chance or intention, when he had covered half the paper with blue, he changed the colour to yellow: the finished painting was divided in half – blue and yellow. Cyril noticed the difference. The next session he started his work with the yellow paint, quite boldly painting a yellow circle in the middle of the paper and surrounding it with blue. Cyril gained some confidence and gradually became a very fluent painter.

There was an area that caused some difficulty for Cyril; this was, I believe in figure/ground perception. He would make lively drawings but when he started to paint them, the drawings would be lost as he used one colour, which usually was brown. There seemed to be a difficulty for Cyril to see colours as differing from one another. There was also an apathy – not bothering to change the colours – as it didn't matter. It seemed to illustrate the experience of the institutionalised patient for whom, in truth, there was no differentiation between figure and ground – their world was monochrome and featureless. Cyril began to appear sad at the loss of the drawings yet helpless to do anything about it. I felt that help could be given through stimulating the environment of the room. I brought in objects that could be handled and looked at. Fresh flowers and plants were provided by the nurses and I borrowed stuffed wild animals and birds from the local museum. The latter helped Cyril; he loved drawing the animals, painting them and then he created his own background which was very different from the animal in the foreground. He became more confident and really enjoyed his art sessions, and allowed his imagination to flow. He loved drawing pictures of cowboys, of scenes of action about to take place.

As Cyril became more confident of being with me, he drew pictures of his childhood, his family and shared with me his terrible fears of going to bed at night, not knowing what was lurking in the wardrobe. When he drew figures that related to his childhood they would appear as being distorted, very different from the cowboys he liked to draw. The psychosis emerged from a very bleak and alienated childhood, yet it was this frightened man who had been sent to fight in a war. He painted scenes of his war and was able to talk to me about the events he was recalling. Cyril had found a way of expressing what had been for many years unspeakable, and through the images on the paper they were contained. His fears lessened, and he appeared to be not so startled. The squeaky monosyllabic voice lowered in tone and he began speaking, using whole sentences.

Janek

Janek was Polish, one of a group of Poles and Ukrainians in the hospital, somehow left over from the war. They spoke very little English. Janek probably suffered from a manic depressive illness; it was doubtful whether there had been any real communication with him to discover the nature of his illness. In fact, his not being able to speak English was little different from Cyril who did not speak, but Janek was very different from Cyril in his approach to art therapy. At first Janek was reluctant to begin; he sat solemn and silent for a few sessions, then he picked up a brush and began to paint. He needed and wanted to communicate.

Janek painted a red eagle which pleased him. He called me to him, touched the eagle and made it very clear that this was Polish. He was to paint the eagle many times and as he gained in confidence he was able to select coloured paper which enabled him to paint the eagle white. The white eagle is the national emblem of Poland. The first paintings where the eagle was coloured red might have been appropriate as this colour may be connected with an experience of pain and rage. Janek very quickly showed how needy he was for the paper and paint. He would paint about eight pictures during the session, mainly scenes of the village in which he had been brought up. I got to know that village so well, the countryside surrounding it, the farms, the people who worked in the fields, the different houses and shops and the events that took place in the village. Unlike Cyril, I believe his childhood was loving and secure. Scenes of the marriage, the birth of a child, the death of an old man, gave Janek such joy to paint.

Later he painted pictures which illustrated his war experiences. Clearly Janek had been made to work in a concentration camp; he painted the most horrifying scenes of German soldiers shooting the Jews, the gas ovens and the crematoria. They were painted in black and red and as he painted them the tears rolled down his cheeks. I sat beside him and felt that it was helpful for Janek to paint these pictures, that they could now be placed and shared rather than caught up and held fast within him.

One of the pictures that Janek painted and that moved me was of a donkey that had a large tear under its head (Figure 10.1). Janek pointed to the tear and to his eyes; he, too, cried. Once he became so depressed that he was not able to leave his ward, so I went down and worked with him there. I had been told by one of the other Poles that he was really worried about Janek as he was not attending Mass. Normally, even when he was sad, he still attended Mass. Janek seemed relieved to be able to paint and painted a church. He

Figure 10.1 Janek: the donkey has shed a large tear

placed his hand over it and turned to face me, looking with such appeal in his eyes. They were very dark eyes. I felt that I had the message and suggested to the charge nurse that a Polish priest should be found. A week later the other Polish patient told me that Janek was again attending Mass. It appeared that Janek had been fearful of dying without making a proper confession.

As the work with Janek developed I became aware of how his moods and emotions, which swung from being very manic and heightened to being almost immobile in depression, were reflected in the subject matter of his paintings. When he was excitable and manic his painting became nationalistic and the Polish eagle and other emblems would dominate; when he was sad and depressed he painted pictures of the concentration camp, and on the days when he was on an even keel he painted the pictures of the village. What was revealed in this work was the irreconcilable conflict that had torn this man apart for over thirty years. A man who had been proud to be Polish had been made to do what was utterly degrading and despicable to him. In later years when I was working with acute admission patients in Coney Hill Hospital I was to find that the quality of the extreme states of the manic depressive were rarely recognised and understood; the medical model of treatment was to bring the patient into the central area of being on an even keel through medication, leaving the two extremes still in opposition.

The further development of art therapy at Horton Road Hospital

Manic depression and schizophrenia are both forms of psychosis, but, unlike the schizophrenic who views other people with a distorted perspective, often finding them persecutory, the manic depressive is mainly concerned with how he or she is viewed by others. Manic depressive patients need to perform well to gain positive regard, and to protect other people from what they experience as an unacceptable self-image. As the level of self-esteem plays a crucial role in their well-being it is likely that particular life events would deeply affect the course of their illness. It is to be hoped that now, in the 1990s, those who find themselves in similar situations as experienced by Janek and Cyril, would have the opportunity to receive appropriate therapy or counselling.

The sessions gradually became established; they took place on Monday and Friday mornings and lasted from 9.30 am to 12.00 noon, with a short break for coffee. As the months went by more patients joined the group until the group settled. My original aim was to facilitate these patients in making moves of their own volition; to be able to make marks spontaneously. This they were able to do, some very slowly and hesitantly, but gradually as they became more confident and their periods of concentration improved, the marks became stronger and more purposeful, transforming into shapes and forms. They began to make pictures. Usually the pictures depicted memories of childhood as if one part of the psyche had remained undamaged keeping these memories intact. Most of the patients had come from country areas and the pictures showed all kinds of activities taking place in the countryside. They became interested in what they were doing and gradually became aware of the pictures of the other patients and sometimes they talked to each other.

What I am describing might appear as rather innocent childlike images and not the images that might be expected to be drawn by chronically ill psychotic patients. Ernst Kris (1974: 77), writing just before I was working in the hospital, found the drawings of psychotic patients to have certain characteristics in common with dream imagery. The drawing was likely to have a weird quality due to condensation – the bringing together of two or more images to make one complete picture. There were gross distortions, particularly of the human body, and the use of symbols was very much in evidence.

This description would fit the work that I was later to see when working at Coney Hill Hospital with patients in the early, acute stages of psychosis; usually I found that as the medication took control, so the artwork lost its bizarre quality. I illustrate this with two pictures painted by a woman (Figure 10.2 and Fig 10.3). The first picture has a bizarre quality; the colour is strong and vivid in marked contrast to the patient's very controlled behaviour and dull affect. There is a strong feeling of strangulation which might have connected with the early maternal relationship. The patient had been treated for depression, but as she began to hallucinate and her speech became disorganised, her medication was changed. Her second picture, painted

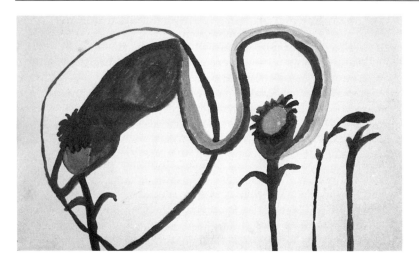

Figure 10.2 The effect of medication: the painting of a patient being treated for depression

Figure 10.3 The effect of medication: the same patient a week later. There had been a change of medication to treat psychosis

Figure 10.4 The patient sat in her chair, surrounded by blue space, with the natural world outside

the following week, is very different. The colours are duller and with the single meal placement there is a suggestion of her loneliness; it has a stronger connection with reality. The patients in Horton Road Hospital were all heavily medicated and I believe that all the pictures were of scenes remembered prior to the onset of the illness. Janek's stories ended with the end of the war. Cyril's cowboys were from films he had seen before the war.

One woman painted a picture of herself in her chair surrounded by blue space with the green natural world outside (Figure 10.4). The picture shows her utterly alone and isolated, and this was probably the only one that was really connected with the experience of being in hospital. The period of time spent in hospital by the patients seemed to be obliterated, almost as if they themselves had not existed; this was true as they had no sense of self, they only had memories of what they had known. The woman sitting in her chair was probably the only one who knew that she was a person who sat in her chair, cut off and isolated from the outside world. It was quite likely that she was not actually psychotic – she was one of a number of women who came into hospital following the birth of illegitimate babies. The others had no sense of being someone at all.

The art therapy sessions became a haven for these patients; they were able for a period of time to make some impression on something external. Through making marks and images they were causing something to happen that had not occurred before, and only *they* were doing it. They were able to make decisions about what they did, how they did it and were able to find that it was acceptable and not treated as meaningless rubbish. After years of silence they discovered that they could communicate to an other and be understood. When Janek placed his hand on the church he had a sense that I was there and was able to receive his communication. The sessions became markers in the patients' week, giving them some sense of rhythm – a session would end, there followed a gap and then another session. Gradually they learned to know when the sessions were beginning, which gave a certain shape and purpose to their lives. There was a sense that some of the patients were just beginning to come alive, and this affected the department as it became a livelier place to be in.

During the time I was working in the hospital I also did two sessions a week on a ward. I had felt the department to be grim but the ward was even grimmer. The ward was the last locked ward in the hospital; it was locked because a number of the patients were restless, wanderers and needed safe containment. The ward was set apart from the rest of the hospital. It had been built as an extension, and was reached by a long, featureless corridor and a covered alleyway which I remember very clearly as it had a beautiful tiled floor, and there was a door to be unlocked with a very large key. Nothing could have prepared me for my first visit to the ward. It was 1975, yet it was unlikely that any change had taken place for many years. In the hospital it was referred to as the 'snake pit' and my first impression was that this was what I imagined Bedlam to be like. On stepping on to it I was hit at first by the terrible smell, predominantly of human urine. Then the general horror of the place really shook me. The ward was very long and narrow; I first came across people sitting immobile in armchairs, staring at a blank wall. Beyond this the ward opened out where more people would be sitting very still and here was the ward staff office. Further on there would be the sleeping quarters. Most of the patients sat immobile, but there were a few patients who were constantly on the move, never resting, often shouting or screaming. I had been asked by the staff to come and work with patients, but as I stood in the centre of the ward I thought there was no way I could contemplate working there. But the staff encouraged me – they really wanted me to be there and it was refreshing that they did have some understanding of art therapy. I was always impressed by the gentle, caring quality of these nurses. I remember seeing one young student nurse shaving a male patient with such care and gentleness. I believe that it was because of the quality of the staff that I began to work on the ward.

I was offered a room that would be private to work in, but after a few weeks I chose to work in the main area of the ward. This was because I did not feel entirely safe and the patients were not comfortable. It is not surprising that the patients needed considerable persuasion to get out of their chairs and go to what was for them a strange room to work with a person they did not know.

If it had just been these rather immobile patients, they probably would have got used to coming to the sessions and the room might have developed into a place that could be safe and secure, but it was the restless, active patients who frequently came into the room and were very disturbing and, I was aware, could also be dangerous. I needed to keep my eyes on them and, while I did, the patients that had been so difficult to prise out of their chairs had been able to return to them with remarkable swiftness. It was with some reluctance that I gave up the room. However, one of the main qualities of a room in which art therapy can take place is safety and this one did not feel safe. I moved into the main body of the ward where the patients who had begun to work with me appeared more relaxed and willing to remain at the table.

I found it helpful to draw on my experience working in the severely subnormal unit where I was using the art therapy sessions to help develop the patients' periods of attention and concentration. I had also worked with a few patients in the general hospital who had suffered brain damage following strokes or road accidents, and the aim of the work with these patients was also to help gain attention and develop concentration. I considered that it would be in these areas that the art therapy session would be of most use on the ward. I was to find a very different attitude in the way that patients approached their work. In the subnormal unit the patients were very enthusiastic; the difficulty was stopping them at the end of the session! The patients in the general hospital were usually very well motivated as they really wanted to improve their situation, but the patients who were on this locked ward had no motivation to do anything at all. They sat looking at blank walls or charged around mindlessly. It was not a place for enthusiasm.

When patients came to the table I would sit with them. There was paper and paint on the table. I talked quietly to them, and though I never had any response from them I felt it was helpful for them to hear the sound of my voice. At the beginning I would need to give each patient a paintbrush loaded with paint. I did not have to force it into their hands – they would take it and hold it quite readily. Often they would hold the brush about six inches above the paper; then they would turn their heads away and look into some distant corner of the ward and remain utterly still and would probably have stayed there until tea-time. I needed to get their attention, yet I did not want to force them or push them into action. I would wait beside them for a few minutes (sometimes ten minutes) then call them by name and, occasionally, they would respond. Sometimes I found tapping a rhythm on the table or gently clapping my hands would help. This would bring them back and they might look at me, at the paper and sometimes they would let the brush drop and touch the paper making a mark. Then their eyes would widen as if noticing the effect of the mark they had made. Then very carefully they would put the brush down beside the paper. We would then go through the whole, extremely slow process again. Most of the time I would just sit and wait; if any action took place it lasted only a few seconds, I would reinforce it and then we would have to wait again.

When I had been working on the ward for about six months, I was able to look back and see that there had been some improvements. The patients now came readily to the table and were able to pick up a brush themselves and put it into some paint and usually make a mark on the paper straight away. It was important that they were now able to choose for themselves the colour with which they wanted to work. It seemed to matter what colour they used; if they had red they would put the brush down almost as soon as they had made a mark. If they used blue or green they would keep the brush working on the paper enlarging the mark, working the brush back and forth until the paint had run out. I found it much easier to gain their attention and the periods of concentration were now beginning to form. At first it had been only a second or so, then a minute and now they could be looking at what they were doing and painting for up to five minutes.

At the end of the first year there was quite a change, the most exciting development being that the patients were now able to join the marks up together to form shapes. The marks had been quite aimless at first, scattered over the paper; but the shapes now had some purpose. The patients could work with some sense of intention; they could choose what they would do with them and the work became much more individual. They could follow through their own ideas. They began making patterns. They might fill the shapes with solid blocks of colour and were able to add lines to a round shape to form 'primitive tadpole figures' (Kellog 1970). It was hardly necessary to call them to gain their attention as they were now able to attend to what they were doing themselves. As they became interested, they were able to concentrate for periods of up to ten minutes. I now had a little group of about six patients working with me and I felt they were gaining some pleasure from the sessions. They were still not able to talk.

During my second year of working on the ward a new consultant took charge, and her arrival brought about quite a change. She spent time with each patient, looking at their histories which were particularly sad, and observing their behaviour to gain some understanding of its nature and cause. Most of the patients appeared totally apathetic and immobile, while a few were constantly on the move, always restless; they were confused, their behaviour bizarre and crazy. Often they stripped all their clothes off and frequently urinated on the floor. The psychotic patient uses very primitive forms of communication which are mainly non-verbal. Non-verbal communication takes place in a number of ways, through simple behaviour, gesture, posture and other bodily movements and facial expression. Time was needed to be spent unravelling the havoc that had been wrought in these patients by the psychosis, and the diverse attempts to treat it. Most of the patients had been in hospital for over twenty years, and had been given an indeterminate number of electric shock treatments (electro convulsive therapy, ECT) leaving them severely confused. The medication for most of the patients was changed, which meant that the patients who had been so immobile became a little more alert and a behavioural psychologist was brought in to help with the management of the restless patients. In a few weeks the ward gradually became a more pleasant and certainly fresher place in which to work. The doctor regularly gave her support to the staff and talked to the patients; for me her arrival was a great joy because she was really interested in the work that I was doing and it was good to have her support and encouragement. The work continued to develop. There were patterns in a wide range of colours, but still the blues and greens predominated; the tadpole figures developed their own bizarre characteristics. Some patients suddenly began painting representational images freely as if they had awakened a former talent. Then gradually the patients began to talk; at first simply, naming the images they were painting, then later making comments as if the image might have triggered off a memory.

I would like to give an example of how the work developed for one of these patients. Dennis had echolalia, which meant that he copied and fed back, parrot-fashion, anything that was said to him. I hoped that with the artwork he would be able to develop his own speech. Once Dennis had begun to use the paint freely, which was about the end of the first year, he began painting very colourful patterns. Then he developed an interesting series of tadpole figures: a circle with lines for limbs and usually some marks inside to indicate facial features. Over a period of six months, these tadpole figures developed and Dennis became very excited about drawing actual people. About this time Dennis was having some treatment with the psychologist and had been taken out on shopping trips in the town. He happened to be a very large and slow-moving man and, as his life had become more eventful, this was reflected in his drawings, which had become quite delightful. He was beginning to say what they were about, he was now talking on his own, no longer parrot-fashion. Quite suddenly, in one session, he started to paint as he had done at the very beginning – making haphazard marks. I was quite alarmed and could not imagine what had happened to him. I wondered, had he been doing too much? Was there too much stimulation? At the end of the session I told the charge nurse what had occurred. The following session the charge nurse told me that Dennis had been put on some medication to help lessen his appetite to help him lose some weight. This medication interfered with the other medication he was already taking. Dennis's general behaviour had not indicated that anything was wrong. It was the art therapy that had revealed this problem. The charge nurse had thanked me, because had no contra-indications been observed, the change in Dennis might have caused a problem which could have been damaging to him. The medication was changed and Dennis returned to painting pictures of his favourite nurses.

The last Christmas that I worked on the ward we made a reindeer out of *papier maché*. It had been quite fun to make and the nurses had helped the patients, who seemed to enjoy working with the *papier maché*. On completion it did have something of the look of a four-legged animal which had antlers.

One of the patients became eager to make a harness, and when it had been made, another patient, Albert, volunteered to put the harness on the reindeer. Albert was a small, bony man who complained bitterly about his bad knee; whenever one saw him all he ever said was 'I've got a bad knee', and screwed himself up with great pain. As Albert put the harness over the reindeer's head, he stood still holding the sides of the head between the palms of his hands. In a moment he appeared transformed; he seemed to relax in his body, no longer screwed up in pain. Clearly the action of putting on the harness over the head was one he had performed hundreds of times in his youth. Albert started to talk about the horses that he had used in ploughing, and also talked about the fields and the farm. It was as if suddenly he had come alive. For a few weeks he continued to talk about his memories and then very suddenly he died.

ART THERAPY AT CONEY HILL HOSPITAL

My three years of work in Horton Road Hospital came to an end when I left for a year's secondment to do an MA in art therapy. I found it very hard to leave the patients, particularly as it was difficult to make them understand that I was leaving. When I returned following the secondment, I was required to work in Coney Hill Hospital with acute admission patients in an occupational therapy department. There was no suitable room for the work to take place, nor was there a suitable referral system; most of the patients that I saw were those who did not settle in occupational therapy, and although some did engage in art therapy they would frequently be discharged without my knowledge, which meant that the work was very frustrating.

Though there had been considerable progress in the development of art therapy as a profession, it was slow to reach the old psychiatric hospitals in the country where it was still considered that the occupational therapists were able to do all that was necessary for the treatment of the patients in terms of diversional and meaningful activities, including art and crafts. At the time, 1980, there was 'much emphasis on "normalization" of the patient through the provision of activities, diverting "destructive energy" through tearing paper and wedging clay' (Waller 1991: 152). Adrian Hill's model for art therapy would have fitted well into an occupational therapy department. Art therapy itself was beginning to be viewed 'as a "radical" element in the treatment of psychiatric or emotional disturbances in that it encouraged patients to make choices, to feel that they had power to change, to take some responsibility for their own "cure"' (Waller 1991: 147).

The original intention of my MA thesis was 'to find a way for art therapy to be recognised as having its own identity and role to play within the hospital which would not be confused or seen to be part of the occupational therapy department' (Skailes 1984: IV).

By the end of the study I was able to look to the future with a certain degree of optimism. This was because I had joined the teams of two consultants, one of whom I had met earlier on the ward at Horton Road Hospital. This meant that my work could flourish as I was given suitable referrals, was able to be present at discharge meetings and often it was suggested that I should continue working with a patient following their discharge for as long as it seemed necessary. It was now recognised that my work was professional and concerned with the development of a long-term relationship and was not seen to be a diversional activity. Also, after years of struggling around the hospital with my cardboard box of materials, my dream became reality as an art therapy department was established at Coney Hill Hospital. I was given two good sized rooms which were highly suitable for the practice of art therapy as they were the only two rooms on a first floor which allowed them to be private and apart from the rest of the hospital. 'Here the patients [would] find a place where they could discover and explore their own potential. A place where they could BE' (Skailes 1984: 75). The art therapy department was opened in 1985 exactly ten years after I started work in Horton Road Hospital. No longer was I the only art therapist, as three more art therapy posts were created. Now, in 1995, there are six art therapists working in the area which shows how, in twenty years, art therapy has expanded as a profession.

I never forgot the work that I did at Horton Road Hospital, and I believe it influenced me considerably in the way I approached my work at Coney Hill Hospital, particularly with young patients suffering their first psychotic breakdown. I was able to offer for them a facilitating environment where they could develop emotional maturity and, for some, there was a real hope that they would not come back into hospital. I also provided space during the week for the increasing population of long-term psychotic patients who were now in group homes or supportive lodgings. They valued the regular containing sessions of art therapy. Over the years I got to know them very well through their artwork as they rarely spoke, and this knowledge was found to be of value. Once I noticed that a rather bizarre element had entered a patient's drawing. I felt uneasy and informed the community nurse. I was told that there were no problems at the group home, but the nurse would look into the matter. He did and later told me that the patient had stopped taking his medication. In the present day, there are many similar patients out in the community. They, too, need a containing space where they can work with someone who is experienced and knowledgeable. Such a person is able to pick up the slight deviation from the norm which could indicate that all is not well. Art therapy can be a very effective early warning system.

CONCLUSION

I left my work in Coney Hill Hospital in 1989 as I needed to develop my own work away from the hospital. Also, I was fully aware that the hospital itself would be demolished in a few years' time. I felt that it needed someone new with fresh energy to develop art therapy out in the community in Gloucestershire. It is to be noted that when Horton Road and Coney Hill Hospitals closed they did not empty the patients out into the countryside. It was a gradual process. When I was still at Horton Road Hospital in 1978 the work had begun to assess and rehabilitate the patients. Suitable accommodation was found for them in group homes, supportive lodgings and, for the very vulnerable, small hostels which were run by nurses. Some patients were able to make the transition well and others found it difficult, but there has been much care taken in the closure of the hospitals although it has been a very painful process. There has been an outcry about the hospitals closing; perhaps a shadow has been aroused in people who would feel better if these patients could return to the institutions where they would not be seen but left to be forgotten. In my opinion the idea for these patients to be in the community is probably a good one, but the resources are not available to enable it really to work.

REFERENCES

Adamson, E. (1984) *Art as Healing*, London and Boston: Coventure.

Bion, W. R. (1967) *Second Thoughts*, London: Karnac.

Erikson, H. (1971) *Identity*, London: Faber & Faber.

'Coney Hill Hospital', in *Special Supplement No. 2*, Gloucester: Severn NHS Trust (April 1994).

Hollingsbee, I. and Morris, C. (1988) *Gloucester's Asylums 1794–1988*, Gloucester City Council.

Kellog, R. (1970) *Analysing Children's Art*, Mayfield Publications

Lydiatt, E.M. (1971) *Spontaneous Painting and Modelling. A Practical Approach in Therapy*, London: Constable.

Kris, E. (1974) *Psychoanalytic Explorations in Art*, New York: Schocken Books.

Skailes, C. (1984) 'A place to be – a study of the development of art therapy within a psychiatric hospital', unpublished MA thesis.

Stevens, A. (1985) *Withymead: A Jungian Community for the Healing Arts*, London: Coventure.

Waller, D. (1991) *Becoming a Profession. The History of Art Therapy in Britain, 1940–1982*, London: Tavistock/Routledge.

Warsi, B. (1975) 'Art therapy – a way to self-knowledge', London: *Inscape* 14.

Chapter 11

Where words fail: a meeting place

Sue Morter

As far as we know, the unconscious has no vocabulary in our sense; although words exist in it, they are neither more nor less than any other object representation; they do not possess the overriding symbolic function that they will acquire in adult language. They are mainly pictures, images and sounds which, without much ado, change their meaning or merge into one another.

(Balint 1968: 97)

During the late 1980s, I was working in a large psychiatric hospital as an art therapist. The hospital was in its final phase of closure, with escalating pressure to 'resettle in the community' patients whose community had been the hospital for many years. The atmosphere was often tense due to the frequent sudden decisions that were made. Morale of staff and patients alike was low as the date for closure was given, then changed again, month by month. These disruptions made the continuity of the work difficult to maintain. I was part of an established team of art therapists working within a busy department, where we offered treatment for referred patients, on a sessional basis. Where possible we continued to treat patients, who were already in art therapy, within their new settings. Outside constraints at times made this impossible and much of my work during this time involved dealing with endings.

I shall discuss a period of working with a young man who was severely psychotic. I intend to explore the way I used my own art as part of the therapeutic relationship. This can offer a non-verbal dimension to patient–therapist interaction. Words can be important to clarify this process but, at times, may feel inadequate to express or be received as expressing intense emotional experiences. Psychotic states may involve a regression to very early pre-verbal phases. Harold Searles (1965) suggests that in long-term psychotherapy with chronic schizophrenics, various symbiotic phases are worked through. He believed that the failure to negotiate these normal developmental stages in early mother–infant relationships formed an aspect of the roots of schizophrenia. Harold Searles worked at Chestnut Lodge, and his work with psychotic patients often lasted up to fourteen years. Searles was receptive to communications contained within long periods of silence in his interactions with these patients. He felt these silences to be necessary, particularly in the early stages of treatment.

Searles discusses how 'the therapist's face has a central role in this symbiotic interaction' (1965: 645–9). He felt that facial expressions made in response to these patients provided a kind of 'mirroring' similar to the reflection given by the mother's face to the infant. This he felt could help patients in the same way to recognise their own 'aliveness' through the emotional responses of the therapist. He describes the importance of the need to move from this way of relating to a more neutral approach during the same or different sessions. In this case, I shall explore the use of my own art as part of the 'empathetic mirroring' which was integral to my approach.

Part-identifications with the therapist's creativity by the patient can be a necessary stage in therapy. The making of visual art objects requires the patient to take some form of action, and how the art therapist responds to the method used, and resulting images, will have an effect. The psychotic patient is especially sensitive to non-verbal responses. Interventions, such as the use of the therapist's own art within sessions, could be experienced by the psychotic patient as intrusive or seductive. Envious feelings may be evoked that could be felt as overwhelming for a patient whose self-esteem is poor.

I shall describe a five-year period of hourly individual art therapy sessions with a patient, who I shall call Darren. After the first year, he attended twice a week. In retrospect, I think my work was influenced by Melanie Klein's play technique (1955). Klein developed this method of working with very young children with disturbed behaviour. She incorporated her observations using toys through which the children could explore the therapeutic relationship with her, into her work with adults. Both Searles and Klein were acutely sensitive to feelings communicated through actions and qualities of silence with children or adults, working through pre-verbal developmental phases. My technique of 'empathetic mirroring' involves giving back to the patient, both verbally and non-verbally, responses to what I think he or she may be communicating through artwork. Essentially this also includes the patient's method of working and feelings expressed through gesture, facial expression and other body language.

Art is an acceptable form of play for adults. In essence it can address both the adult and 'child within' simultaneously. Symbiotic developmental phases replay mother–infant relationships and therefore involve emotional ways of being together without the use of words. Psychotic patients are often relating in a similar way, evoking feelings of fusion and merging. Separateness for psychotic adults evoke extreme anxieties. This is further compounded by the physical and intellectual developmental stage of the adult patient. The art process gives access to both the child and adult developmental stages. Tension and balance between the verbal and non-verbal is a struggle that I, as an artist and therapist, engage with in my work, particularly in dealing with psychotic processes.

My usual approach in working with psychotic patients includes refraining from engaging in any artwork myself. I might make interventions in relation to the patient's own artwork when called for, in terms of suggestions, comments or technical help. The timing of these is aimed at aiding further expression for the patient. On many occasions a patient will invite me to paint or intervene in some way with his or her work, but it is only after exploration of the meaning of this that I would decide how to respond. When verbal exploration is impossible the therapist has to trust in the process of the work. Darren told me he did not 'talk much' and words for him had 'different meanings'. I think painting with, for or alongside Darren within the sessions, at times provided a way of containing and communicating feelings, when words felt impossible or inadequate. I shall explore the tension I experienced in this case between non-verbal and verbal ways of relating in art therapy with a psychotic client.

FIRST MEETING

I had been for some time part of the team on the Unit for Young Schizophrenics, set on the outskirts of the hospital. This villa housed fourteen patients of mixed sex and ethnic backrounds. Each week we met to review the progress of the residents and assess new patients when space became available. There was an atmosphere of sadness at the team meeting on the day I first met Darren when he came to find out whether he had been accepted for the unit. We had heard his case history. He was abandoned at birth, and was now 20 years old. There was a long history of repeated and traumatic separations from unsuccessful fostering placements and long periods in children's homes from which he often ran away. He had no contact with natural relatives except with a sister who was two years his senior. When he was 3, an aunt had cared for him with this sister for a short time. We heard that he was a bright but solitary child at school and spent much of his time listening to music or watching television 'at home'.

Prior to arriving with us he had spent two years in an acute psychiatric unit in which he was placed from a children's home the day after his eighteenth birthday. He had been diagnosed as suffering from 'paranoid psychosis' and believed himself to be attacked by 'aliens'. Feelings of despair and anger were expressed through his 'suicidal ideas'. There was a resigned note in his voice as he agreed to come to another institutional 'home'. It was particularly difficult for the team as the continuity so needed by him was ultimately not to be found due to the uncertain future of the hospital.

After a few months the 'compassion' of the team grew to despairing frustration. Darren did not appear to be settling in any way. He was stubbornly refusing to fit into the ward programme, which included weekday attendance in the occupational therapy department as well as groups and activities on the unit. When it was time to go, he would mysteriously lose his shoes, and he would arrive late for meals. He was seen wandering around outside the unit or standing gazing up at the sky with arms outstretched. He seemed to evoke hostile feelings, particularly among the other patients. He appeared lost, frightened and remote. It was for these reasons that Darren was referred for individual art therapy. When asked if he might try art therapy, in a team meeting, he turned to face me and asked, 'Will you *be* there?' The importance of the meaning of this question was explored throughout our working time together.

The art therapy department was at this time in a two-storey, converted coaching house quite close to the unit. It contained a large studio within which there was space to work privately or in a group. There was also a smaller room used for individual art therapy work. A corridor linked these two areas to an office used by the art therapy team and a kitchen used by the patients for tea-making. Upstairs there was an office shared by a drama therapist and dance and movement therapist. There was also a room used for closed groups and a now redundant darkroom. As part of the initial six-week assessment period, it was agreed with the patient the working area that was to be most appropriate, and this could be reviewed again during treatment.

TENTATIVE BEGINNINGS

Our first meetings in the art therapy department gave ample space for Darren to wander and explore his surroundings. He was continually 'getting lost' or coming on the wrong day or time. He would verbally agree to something but show that he also held opposite feelings. He would pick things up and casually break them, or pace restlessly around the inside or outside of the building in a detached manner. If people or objects came into his path he knocked into them with surprise. He stirred up an unsettled atmosphere with the other studio members. His behaviour reminded me of Searles' description 'Out-of-Contact' (1965: 525–31). After five sessions he asked to work in the small individual studio and remained there for the duration of his treatment. He agreed, after many frustrating months, that in his 'getting lost' and leaving his belongings tossed around the department, he was pleading to be 'gathered up'.

He was on neuroleptic medication at this time and this may have increased his hyperactivity. Periods of activity were followed by periods of extreme withdrawal. I reflected on the work of John Bowlby (1973: 21–44), who studied the behaviour of infants in situations where they experienced separation from attachment figures. Darren's ways of dealing with anxiety and loss seemed to be in keeping with these studies. Findings from these studies showed that infants often clung to attachment objects or figures, and kept them under great scrutiny for fear of further loss. At first Darren behaved in this manner, which felt disconcerting considering his adult size. He sent me repeatedly to fetch art materials, books and 'kits'. It felt uncomfortable to stay with him, but if I left he followed or watched me closely. His asking 'Did I have. . . .?' became later a beginning of a request we could smile at. He insisted 'he could not draw' but seemed to delight in finding 'gimmicks' and ways to play with the materials.

A MEETING PLACE-THE ROOM

The small studio in which the work took place was a private room within the art therapy department. As well as the painting, drawing and modelling materials there were expanses of walls where paintings could be worked on or looked at. There were shelves where individual work could be stored, an electric fire, a window out into the grounds, and a mirror. Other objects Darren used included particular books and comics, a blanket, a camera and cassette machine. Initially, and at later times when particularly anxious, he would leave the room to pace up and down along the corridor outside. He seemed gradually to come to trust that I would be there on his return. The way he used the space and the objects helped me to think about his inner world and his relationship to me. Despite the long periods of silence there seemed to be a lot going on in the space between us. While writing this I read Case's paper on 'Silence in progress' describing her art therapy with children. She writes:

> It is possible that when we lack the word we inhabit the silence imbued with the affect we are unable to express verbally. The silences of our patients then become available to be understood through the counter-transference in a similar way that we might understand images in the quality that they arouse in us.
>
> (Case 1995: 26)

The silences aroused in me feelings of excited anticipation, followed often by disappointment, hopelessness and despair, which I think reflected Darren's feelings. At times there was a quality of remoteness as if there was a huge chasm between us – a void to be filled. I was aware of his persistent efforts to fill this void as he searched for ways to paint, draw and model with clay and plasticine. He asked in a childish way, 'What *can* I do?' Images were sought to copy. His own were often 'spoilt', 'messed up', or deemed 'no good' and screwed up.

MAKING A MONSTER

The struggle he went through in making images was highlighted by a succession of sessions when he engaged in creating 'a monster' out of clay. He had been attending for four months and had been searching for something to work from. He had found an existing fired model of a reclining figure built in small pieces. He attempted to replicate this by covering it with slabs of wet clay, but seemed to get lost in the process and in exasperation exclaimed 'it didn't work out!' He was about to abandon the project, as he so often wanted to, so I suggested he might take the pieces and try to make a figure of his own. He picked up a further fired figure of a baby with a broken arm to look at while he struggled reluctantly to form parts of a body. He said this was to be 'a monster'. He took enormous care over 'the features', squeezing, thumping and pressing the red clay into the head and legs. In the following session he formed the arms, spending a great deal of time detailing the long fingers, and going back to working on the toes. He then had the problem of how to bring the parts together. He looked across the table where we were working and asked, 'Can you make me a body?' and then said, 'I want to make a body like there hasn't been before.' I resisted his requests to provide him with a ready-made body, and he snatched back the clay, indignantly exclaiming 'I'll do it!' Biting and sucking at a pen top furiously, he pushed and jabbed at the clay to squeeze it into a wasted torso. I was aware he was looking across at my torso while doing this (Figure 11.1).

After minimal help on how to 'keep it all in shape' he managed to press the bits together on this 'body' and there was some relief for both of us when he announced that 'it's finished!' and turned it around for me to see. He looked at my face and asked, 'Do you like it?' As I gently held it I felt the fragility of this beautiful but ugly 'monster'. He asked to look at it in many subsequent sessions. We shared the anxieties about its vulnerability when putting it into the 'cooker-heater thing' to be fired. Many weeks ensued before he would entrust me to put it in the 'cauldron'. Eventually I did so, and he asked to watch it hardening. Once it was fired he wanted to make it scaly, spraying it fluorescent green and gold to make it 'outstanding'. The holding of the process felt vital. He was later to name it 'the creature from the lagoon', a predatory character which came from one of the many stories Darren had incorporated into his inner world.

CHANGING WORLDS

In his solitary life it seemed that Darren had spent long periods reading comics, or watching television and films, which seem to be experienced as real. In many of the silent sessions he sat by me looking at science-fiction books, and comics full of monsters and superhero figures. At times he might look up and ask me to explain something in the pictures or tell me he liked something or not. He became very absorbed in a way I sometimes found frightening and I encouraged him to discuss the feelings aroused by the images. He would go over and over the same pages with a quality of panic.

After a year he increased his sessions to twice weekly at his own request. His attendance improved immediately and the intensity of feelings increased

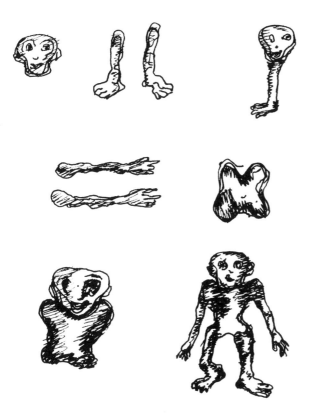

Figure 11.1 'I want to make a monster'

as he became more focused in the sessions. He said there were two worlds which he called Earth 1 and 2. His voice took on a dream-like quality as he described people who changed into demons or mutants. He gouged the wet paint to make powerful images of these. Multi-limbed, twin-headed witch-like figures were set down using black or white strokes, later to be scribbled over with forceful movements.

I thought that during this phase he was experiencing me as Searles describes as 'the Bad Mother' (Searles 1965: 533). He made many portraits of me which were entitled 'pictographs'. They had disembodied faces and eyes which felt cold and penetrating to me. There was a contemptuous mocking in his executing these and sense of triumph as he simply said 'That's you!' His body-language seem to echo his ambivalent feelings towards me. He often began the sessions with his back to me. He would turn around slowly after I suggested he may be letting me know how it feels to have someone turn their back on them. He laid his head down on the table. His long fingers then would stretch out to dip into the palette of paint between us. He said he felt himself to be one of the 'untouchables' with 'humanoid skin' and complained of feeling 'frozen'. He made an image of frozen landscape separated from a red hot sun by a huge empty void. He filled this with a 'whirlwind' in the last minute of the session. I felt extreme opposites of emotions. Moments of punishing rejection changed to fearful longings for closeness and back again. I struggled with the unanwerable question of how to speak within the 'whirlwind' atmosphere between us.

Darren arrived one day and expressed his ambivalent feelings through making a large image on a door-sized sheet of paper fixed to the wall. It began as a stick figure of 'the Saint', a good detective character from an old TV series. He used a decorator's wide brush to make this life-sized figure and then proceeded to obliterate it with layer upon layer of thick red paint. He wanted to know if I had limitless supplies of paint and asked if I liked it. I took some time to answer as it was difficult to know what he was really asking. I had been feeling sickened by the apparently sadistic pleasure in the process. He squeezed out the contents of the tubes of paint and overflowed the palette, which seemed to delight him. I thought of milk and then of blood as he stirred the paint and it ran down the paper onto the floor. I asked whether he liked it and said I felt it had stirred up some strong feelings, reflecting how the saintly figure was now covered by the paint. I also pointed out the real limits to the paint supplies and what the surface could hold, and I helped him remove it from the wall. In doing so I was aware of feeling the actual as well as emotional weight of this piece. He seemed to look to me for response through his image for his conflictual feelings to be contained.

Feeding became a concrete issue in the sessions. Repeatedly complaining of feeling 'hungry' or 'thirsty' in a demanding tone, he began to bring armfuls of food and drink which he proceeded to eat in front of me. I said it felt as if he was showing me how hungry he was, and also how he felt he had to do his own feeding. I was to hear from a rare conversation between his key worker nurse and sister how she had kept him from starvation at one of his fostering placements with stolen chocolate bars. After compulsively consuming vast quantities of cake, crisps and coke he would demand a cup of tea with three sugars! He then threw down the empty packets and crushed can. I made an image of one these crushed cans, emptied, rendered useless and discarded (Figure 11.2). This image seem to express how he often made me feel.

I encouraged him to express through the art materials his distress when he had 'churned-up', 'broken', 'head buzzing' feelings. He talked of dreams and nightmares which at times were 'too frightening' to put on paper. The staff on his unit, with whom I met regularly throughout the treatment, witnessed his climbing into bed with other patients when he was upset at night. Gradually over the years he became able to reach out to those nurses he trusted, and they would sit with him holding his hand until his night terrors subsided. He often came to his early morning sessions with these terrors still

Figure 11.2 Crushed can

very real. Invaded by his 'alien' voices, it took him some time to come into our world within the room, and then he would ask me what planet I would go to if I was invaded. At these times I experienced him as a very confused and frightened child who was unable to differentiate between his internal and external worlds.

GRAFFITI: 'A MEETING PLACE'

> *Kids write graffiti because it's fun. It is also an expression of the longing to be a somebody in a world that is always reminding you that you're not.*
> (Chalfant and Prigoff 1987: 7)

Darren found a medium for expressing himself using spraycan paints. He made many associations through this process. The youth culture of 'hip-hop' music, rap groups at school, graffiti images he had seen in Covent Garden were intertwined with his monsters and superheroes. He made large images, moving around the room on sheets of paper stuck to the wall. They seemed to show part-words and images that he found difficult to verbalise. Often they seemed to hold elements of my name or his, sometimes combined. He seemed to really enjoy this medium and for the first time admitted to liking the results.

Within this process grandiose themes of creating and destroying, defining and diffusing seemed to emerge. The danger of using spraycans required that we wore masks, and opened the windows. The edges of the paper gave a concrete boundary to his freestyle marks. He became fully involved with the process until drawing back he would as always ask 'Do you like it?' and admit that he liked it. His need for my response seemed to me to be saying 'This is what I can do . . . do you like me?' Using thick markers he would then return to redefine areas of the work. Together we would stand back and view the finished pieces, often made over several sessions. This looking together at his creations, often without words, seemed important.

Graffiti is a powerful means of expression, whereby calligraphy and pop art images come together. Made on a large scale, often in public spaces, the resulting images are often beautifully rich in colour and shape. I am interested in how, as an artistic expression, it came to connect different cultures as a universal language. As an art form it originated as a type of street protest in the disaffected communities of New York. Darren had spoken at different times of feeling he would 'fit in' in America where there was 'more space'. The food and drink he chose to cook and eat were American, the limited clothes he managed to acquire that he liked were American and worn streetstyle. Hooded sweatshirts, sloganed jackets and jeans expressed an identification with American culture. He loved music and as he worked on his 'pieces' the rhythms of music, as yet inside his head, seemed to carry his movements. He sprayed the rich colours and I think that the process gave him a safe outlet for his inner protest.

Gradually more of our time together became enjoyable. The frustrations when the 'cans' ran out did not seem to spoil the pleasure he derived from working with this medium. Over three sessions he was to create a 'piece' around a word which I did not know. It seemed to be like the secrecy of the special language used by the street artists. Eventually, after some exploration, inferring that I would not understand, he said it meant a 'club or meeting place'. I felt like I was privileged to be invited to enter such a meeting place, one of a different generation or culture, where a mutual language existed to include or exclude. These artworks allowed some sense of being apart and then coming together within the 'meeting place' in art therapy.

PAINTING AND PLAYING TOGETHER

The fragile trust growing between us was constantly tested, and this was highlighted in any changes to his routine. After I had to cancel one of his sessions, he arrived for the next art therapy hour, very angry and restless. I suggested there were some difficult feelings perhaps about the missed session. I added he might more easily express these on paper. He picked up a piece of charcoal and shot two parallel lines across at me. I said I thought these lines came at me like some kind of weapon. He smiled. Then he made two further parallel lines across the first two, looked me in the eyes and invited me to play 'noughts and crosses' with a look of challenge. Up to this point I had refrained from any direct engagement in the art process. He put down a cross defiantly in the centre. After I added my nought, we played several games, where, if he won, he showed triumphant pleasure. We took turns in winning and losing until we ran out of space on the paper, and he drew a circle around the first game where he had won. I said I felt he had found a safety in the game where he could enjoy 'beating me'.

Many previous times Darren had showed that he wanted to play with me or by me. When we had exceptionally cold weather, he had asked 'Have you got gloves and boots?' He wanted to go out in the snow and play. By remaining in the art room he was able to gather long icicles from the roof, through the window. He delighted in spraying them in bright colours in a tray. After unsuccessful attempts at trying to preserve them by different printing methods he threw them out to stand up in the snow outside. We took a photograph of them and he later called this image 'kryptonites' from a superman story. I felt quite guilty initially to enjoy these pleasurable sessions, after so many intensely hateful periods.

Gradually the guilty feelings subsided and the ever-present silences became to feel more comfortable. Sometimes it felt as if he created a womb-like atmosphere. In the warmth of the fire, he yawned and made sucking sounds, stealing the odd glance as if to check that I was still there. The portraits that he continued to make of me seemed to possess more human qualities. Despite the fact that he appeared not to look at me, he accurately portrayed a sense of my face and clothing, and sometimes I was even given a body. In some we appeared to be merged, as elements of our skin colours or clothing came together, in watery semi-abstracted images. He invited me to draw him and then covered his face. I drew this repeated posture. He would then look at it with me, and compare it to what he saw when he looked into the mirror. I think that the use of the portraits he made of me gave an opportunity to express and explore both his self-perceptions and our relationship. The portraits I sometimes made of him helped me to *be* with him without the need for words. As a way of 'empathetic mirroring' they were a way of affirming he was there with me.

He asked me to do a picture of a character from a Batman comic called 'Nightwing'. Previously I had asked him if he might like to try this when he had seemed to be locked in to staring at these graphic illustrations. When I suggested he might like to draw this for himself, he insisted 'I want you to do it for me for a change!' The statement implied he felt he had to provide for me. He seemed, also simultaneously, to be asking me to show him what I can do and to do something for him. I copied the figure while he sat and watched every mark intently. He followed my progress, comparing my drawing with the original. He wanted to know why it was 'all squashed up?' and why the figure was so 'muscley'. I explained that the original illustrator exaggerated the body features to make the figure appear strong. I added that I wondered also if he might be thinking of his own body (which in reality was thin and less than muscley). He whispered 'I am Nightwing'. He said that 'Nightwing is good' and he thought my drawing was 'magnificent'. He asked me if I was an artist and said 'I never knew you could draw like that!' He wanted to take it for a poster 'for his room'. I said it seemed that he wanted to take something good from me to keep by him, just like it seemed he wanted me to keep him in mind when he asked me to get things for him between sessions. Having acknowledged this I gave him the picture. It got 'lost' as the occasional tapes that I had made for him got 'screwed-up, lost or stolen'. I think he had wanted to see if I would give him what he asked for, but it seemed that these things always got lost or spoilt. The importance in this interaction seemed that he could repeat this process. It highlighted his desires for and difficulties of hanging onto anything good. The other patients constantly complained how they gave to him and he was unable to give anything in return. He did start giving in his interactions with me, in a concrete sense, by offering me some of his food. It seemed important to him that I was not only able to give, but also to take from him.

Mildred Lachman-Chapin (1979) in discussing 'Kohut's theories on narcissism: implications for art therapy', talks about the different ways that art therapists can use painting with narcissistic personalities. In Darren's development his narcissistic needs had never satisfactorily been met, because he had had so many changing parenting figures in his early years. I thought about his surprise and delight when I drew for him the Nightwing figure. I felt I was an idealised figure, much as Nightwing was for him. For example, he asked for my autograph. He could somehow share in my magical powers as an artist and he referred to me as a 'sorcerer'. In the following session he tried to emulate my technique and, though a little distorted, he managed to copy a figure of Catman from his comic. He expressed a wish to draw like me and we were able to explore his feelings of lack of self-worth through this. It could be argued that by painting with patients in this way their already low self-esteem is further damaged. However, on this occasion, I think that this process opened opportunities to explore the damage that was already there, and helped to name it.

MERGING AND SEPARATING

Through the painting, both separately and together, art therapy was able to offer ways of working with the symbiosis which had developed. At times we sat opposite each other painting on the same sheet of paper covering the large oak table. Images of thrusting and receiving echoed the intercourse between us. Looking at our joint work, he now began to speak of the existence of an Earth 3 where there was 'one person and one time and you don't need anything'. I suggested that this sounded like how a baby might feel and he agreed. Then he spoke of 'Caesar – a destroyer and chaos'. His words seemed disjointed and took on again that dream-like quality. I found it hard to make sense of what he was telling me. I said it seemed as if he may have some sense of a timeless place where only he existed, but also a sense of something destroying this place. He looked again at our separate paintings on the same sheet of paper. He looked at his painting and then at mine, saying my painting made him 'happy' and he wanted to keep them together.

In the later period of treatment separation was inevitable due to the reality of the escalating closure of the hospital. He would come and ask why various resources were closing. There was a lot of uncertainty around; staff and patients were leaving and ward moves were a regular occurrence. The art therapy department did not escape the moves. There were unspoken feelings of loss which intensified in the sessions. Amidst this there were feelings of loss which reminded me of those which Searles discusses in 'The phase of resolution of the symbiosis' (Searles 1965: 543). This he describes to be when patient and therapist strive, at different times, for individuation with ensuing feelings of apartness. At this point, Searles suggests that the therapist acknowledges that the patient has a choice whether to recover, and realisation that the therapist is not the only person able to assist the patient in this recovery. With this recognition comes the accompanying feelings of loss that change brings. I felt that Darren was realising that I lived in a world outside of him. He asked if I had a husband and did I know how to create someone? He asked 'could a boy be God?' It seemed he was questioning his own capacities to be a husband or father. When I left the session he was lingering on after it finished, and he asked, 'Are *you* going?' There seemed, expressed in this, an awareness of our separateness.

He appeared highly anxious throughout many sessions, circling around me in our now changed room. He was able to draw less and less, and asked 'Why *can't* I draw any more?' In the last year he made few images and seemed depressed. I had heard he may be going to a hostel in the community. In the sessions I began to address the real anxieties around the move that combined with the issues of merging and separating already alive within the relationship. He spent many of the sessions listening to tapes of music. He listened to the same tracks repeatedly, rewinding it back to the beginning to start again. This is similar to the way he looked at his stories, over and over again. He brought a blank tape to record a favourite 'hip-hop' tape and he sat beside me to paint. While the music played we both painted. He painted layers of watery colours merging into a rainbow which he put in front of me like a gift. Then he added what he described as 'galoshing' in form of the 'sparkle' with pink paint onto my moving circular form (Figure 11.3). His interactions of giving and touching, through the artwork, seemed to be intimate both childlike and adult. They felt charged with a sexual quality. I thought of Searles' descriptions (1965: 429–42) of the unresolved yearnings for infantile gratifications that become enmeshed with emerging adult feelings.

Figure 11.3 'Galoshing'

I acknowledged that there seemed a lot of energy around both in the music and in the images today. Also that he seemed to want to give me something in the form of 'a rainbow' and by adding to my painting. I asked him what he meant by the word 'galoshing'. He said it was similar to 'swords clashing, when a shooting star met something or like fireworks'. He seemed to be describing a sexual climax. I felt and said that there had seemed a lot of contact between us today. He left happily taking his tape.

LAST MEETINGS

In the final months of treatment, I found it hard to address the final time for our actual separation. It had been decided that he was not now suitable for the hostel to which most of his fellow patients on the unit were to go. However, I had also decided to leave the hospital. I felt a mixture of sadness and guilt at leaving Darren, as well as other patients I had known for many years, especially as they were experiencing many losses. I knew that it was important to give Darren as much notice as possible but only had a few months to give him a definite date. When I told him I was leaving he reacted with silence, turning away again from me into apparently painful, hurt feelings. There were hopeless, despairing feelings of 'crying inside' which seemed to move between us. At other times he reacted angrily, turning up the volume of hard rap music, as if to block me out. He refused to leave after the sessions and came between sessions, seemingly reverting to his original lost state.

As the real separation approached I felt acutely aware of his feelings of abandonment and loss. Words were inadequate to express the conflictual feelings around. I thought of an abandoned child who had been left, when words were not available to ask 'why?' It seemed impossible to find the words to so many unanswered questions, yet I felt this separation was an opportunity to understand earlier separations. I expected, as the time drew near, he might have stopped coming as he had often done in earlier times around holiday breaks. However, he did keep coming, even for his final session. We were able to work separately to create together a copy of one of his favourite images from the *Spraycan Art* book (Chalfant and Prigoff 1987). He then asked if he could look at his previous graffiti work, and we displayed it around the room. He ran his hands across his images and said 'Did I do that?' He wanted to take with him the image we made together, but I persuaded him to take it only when our work together ended.

Some months before, when I had suggested he might like to review his work with me, he had agreed reluctantly, and showed his ambivalence by lighting a match and holding it to his folder. He had on many occasions tried to set fire to his bed and cooker on his unit. Matches were kept in the room used for his art therapy sessions to enable him to light his cigarettes. I had on this occasion interpreted his ambivalence, and decided not to pursue reviewing his work at this time. We were shortly to move department and I felt that the timing of the review with this change was making him more anxious. His need to set fire to things seemed to be his way of relieving tension. By attempting to destroy his work it seemed he was letting me know how he felt now that his safe space was being destroyed.

Three months before we finished working together I told him when I would be leaving. He had arrived for his session very early and when I told him he went away to buy a box of cakes. He proceeded to eat them one by one at the start of his art therapy session. He seemed especially anxious and agitated. I knew that he had been bullied on the unit by another patient in the past week, and had needed to sleep on another ward for his own safety. Darren had acted out very violently twice in my time of knowing him but often evoked verbal and physical threats from others. Now he chose a tape to listen to and paced around the room. I moved to a position to sit behind the table, feeling threatened. I felt bullied both through the aggressive sounds from the music and Darren's movements. He looked as though he was punching at an invisible aggressor, while restlessly pacing around. I turned the music down, and said that it seemed he was experiencing some difficult feelings. He eventually sat down and I suggested it might be helpful to put some of these feelings down using the art materials. He sat looking down away from the table, controlling the volume on the tape-machine. He asked me if I could

Figure 11.4 Two horses

sing that, and said he thought he could. I commented that it seemed he was identifying a lot with the singer and words of the song today. I had started to paint an image that developed into two horses (Figure 11.4) The pair of horses seemed to be identical, with one the aggressor and the other cowed down under the attack. I was feeling stirred up and needing to find safety behind the table and in painting. I said it felt as though I was expressing some of the feelings around today, and doing the painting for him. He responded by coming over and painting a sheet of paper with purple.

During a quiet moment, I told him I now had a leaving date and when our last session should be. He responded by turning up the volume of the music, and sat with his back to me to lay his head against the wall. I said that he may have feelings about finishing his art therapy sessions with me and my going, and we had twenty-four more sessions to explore these together. Amidst the feelings of rage there was an almost unbearable sadness between us. After several minutes of silence, I went across to turn the fire and tape machine off, and his eyes were watery. After a brief look at the paintings he left to go to the bathroom, and did not return until it was time to finish the session. I told him I would see him for his next art therapy session, and he left slamming the door. Another therapist passed him on the way back and said she had fantasied his 'murdering' her.

In view of our real separation, it is difficult to know the stage that Darren had reached in terms of what Searles referred to as 'the Late Phase' (1965: 551–8). Searles discusses how this evolves when the symbiosis is resolved, and the psychotic patient is able to gain strength from part-identifications from the therapist and other present figures in his or her life. Similarly, he suggests that these patients are able to be selective about what to relinquish and retain from figures from the past. Searles thus describes the patient 'much like a naive little child who doesn't know anything, and who therefore needs to be taught all over again, and correctly this time, how to live' (Searles 1965: 552).

Darren presented himself so often in this way, particularly in the last months of treatment. Increasingly, he asked questions about history and creation, that I suggested he seemed to be trying to create a history for himself. He wanted to know how I felt in relationship to him and expressed wanting to know me more fully. This seemed poignant in the knowledge of his never being able to fully know his real mother or form adult relationships.

CONCLUDING THOUGHTS

When words fail to be reliable, the sound and intonations of the therapist's voice can help to let the patient know that someone is there. Painting with the patient may also offer a way of being there when words feel insufficient. Art is an accepted medium for adults to access the needs and feelings of the 'child within'. Artists I think are able to express their feelings held from childhood through adult artistic expression. In working with severely psychotic patients, these areas of the personality can be linked through words and images. By using my own art I was aware of the possible intrusion into his space with my own inner world, but felt it to be a valuable means to aid the therapeutic relationship.

My relationship with Darren was both rewarding and challenging. The approach I used developed after trust was built up over many difficult months. He appeared to have little reason to get well, but seemed to want to make sense of his bewildering experiences. Over time he did show some improvements. He was able to gain some understanding of his 'changing worlds' while integrating, through his experience in art therapy, positive and negative aspects of himself. His ability to express himself increased, and he was able to participate more fully in the programme on the unit, including contributing positively to a drama therapy group which ran for two years. He surprised other members by his perceptive comments in the community meetings, and his attendance at the occupational therapy department improved greatly. He still responded best to individual attention, enjoying especially his individual cookery sessions and outings that involved eating. I met up regularly with the other team members to discuss his progress, and despite the climate of uncertainty within the hospital we attempted together to provide as much continuity for Darren as possible. I was aware that art therapy was the most continuous treatment he received, and it seemed to be very important for him. He was able to experience a relationship where he could '*be*', and so begin to develop a sense of his own identity. His initial question to me, when asked if he wanted to try art therapy, had implied the importance of his need for me to '*be*' there for him.

All patients, and especially psychotic patients, require that the therapist learn their language (Balint 1968: 92–8). Art therapists may adapt their way of working to the needs of each patient. Skills as artists and therapists may be used in different ways. The technique of painting and playing with Darren developed a safe space whereby intense and often conflictual emotions could be expressed.

REFERENCES

Balint, M. (1968) *The Basic Fault, Therapeutic Aspects of Regression*, London and New York: Tavistock.

Bowlby, J. (1973) *Attachment and Loss*, Vol. 2, London: Hogarth Press and Institute of Psycho-Analysis.

Case, C. (1995) 'Silence in progress' in London: *Inscape* 1: 26–31.

Chalfant, H. and Prigoff, J. (1987) *Spraycan Art*, London: Thames & Hudson.

Klein, M. (1965) 'The psycho-analytic play technique: its history and significance', in *New Directions in Psycho-Analysis: the Significance of Infant Conflict in the Pattern of Adult Behaviour*, London: Tavistock.

Lachman-Chapin, M. (1979) 'Kohut's theories on narcissism: implications for art therapy', *American Journal of Art Therapy*, 19: 3–8.

Mitchell, J. (1986) *The Selected Melanie Klein*, London: Hogarth Press, Institute of Psycho-Analysis and the Melanie Klein Trust.

Searles, H. (1965) *Collected Papers on Schizophrenia and Related Subjects*, London: Hogarth Press.

Chapter 12

Art psychotherapy and psychiatric rehabilitation

Terry Molloy

What are days for?
Days are where we live.
They come, they wake us
Time and time over.
They are to be happy in:
Where can we live but days?

Ah, solving that question
Brings the priest and the doctor
In their long coats
Running over the fields.

(Larkin, 1982: 357)

'What are days for?' This is surely a question central to the process of integrating previously institutionalised psychiatric patients into the community. These patients often give accounts of days that are experienced as long, empty and boring; days that provide fertile ground for the growth of depression, anxiety and paranoia. Day-care facilities for psychiatric patients in the community do exist, although the level of provision has certainly not kept pace with the rate of institutional discharge and closure. A media cliche, that is nevertheless true, is that hordes of patients who have been 'rehabilitated into the community' can be found aimlessly wandering the streets and shopping precincts of that community after being turned out of their sparse bed-and-breakfast accommodation for the day.

Public concern about the disturbed conduct of these ex-patients centres around a belief that they are singularly unable to answer the question 'what are days for?' for themselves; they are seen as people that are mad, bad, volatile and unpredictable, people about whom 'something must be done'. The worst cases find their way into the newspapers and onto television screens; questions are raised and answers are demanded from the professionals involved. Consequently the 'caring professions', like the priest and the doctor of the poem, come running to proffer advice upon what days are for and how they should be filled.

In areas where adequate resources exist, patients, or 'service users' as they are now referred to, may be offered a wide variety of activities that seem to address most essential aspects of daily life. Common headings for such activities include life skills, daily living, recreational therapy, social skills and assertiveness training. Practice runs to supermarkets are made, meals are cooked and eaten in groups, social conversation is rehearsed in focused exercises and the concept of stringent weekly budgeting is introduced to adults who have frequently never had more than the equivalent of a child's pocket-money at their disposal. However, despite the best efforts of workers in these programmes, there is a high level of failure to translate what is rehearsed into real-life situations and there is often a low level of client attendance at many day-care facilities. Frequently cited causes for this failure or rejection are severe damage stemming from years of institutionalisation, basic personality disorder and non-compliance with prescribed medication. Although these factors are clearly important and it is probably impossible for community services to attract and cater for all cases, it seems insufficient to locate all causes of failure within the personalities of the 'user'; if the customers, to use current health service parlance, are not buying, then it may be necessary to examine the relevance and quality of the product.

It often seems that existing rehabilitation services address themselves to the question, 'what are days for?', on a somewhat basic level, one that does not really accommodate all the complex needs of the whole person. Work, food, shelter and social functioning are the aspects of life towards which most programmes are directed. While these are obviously things that need attention, something frequently neglected is that aspect of 'days' embraced by another line of the poem; 'They are to be happy in'. As well as needing a job, enough to eat and a roof over their heads, people also need to find something in their lives that goes beyond the practicalities of day-to-day living, something that caters for inner emotional needs. To many professionals in the field, this aspect of life is seen to lie outside the brief covered by psychiatric rehabilitation. However, it is within this area that many patients founder and become unable to make use of the practical skills they have been taught. People are not simple components that can be reprogrammed and replaced into the machine; they are complex, mysterious and unpredictable individuals whose difficulties must be approached in a much more comprehensive and sensitive manner if they are to be helped at all.

An adequate service of psychiatric rehabilitation must, therefore, contain elements that respond to inner emotional needs; one of these elements can be art psychotherapy. It is the purpose of this chapter to consider the various ways that art psychotherapy can be of help to people trying to recover from a period of mental breakdown and to examine the problems involved in incorporating it into existing psychiatric rehabilitation services.

WHY ART PSYCHOTHERAPY?

What can be achieved by an integrated programme of art psychotherapy and rehabilitation? It would be unrealistic to expect that people will emerge from such a programme devoid of symptoms and problems and ready for a trouble-free life. To use Freud's phrase, perhaps all we can say to a patient is 'much will be gained if we succeed in transforming your hysterical misery into commonplace unhappiness' (Freud 1974: 393). It is difficult to find objective proof of the efficacy of any particular form of treatment in the field of mental illness and it is certain that no method of treatment, including art psychotherapy, can be looked upon as a universal panacea. Nevertheless, I feel that it is a particularly suitable treatment method for certain specific problems faced by people attempting to adjust to normal life following a period of mental breakdown. In this chapter I shall consider some of these areas. They encompass problems experienced by many patients who have already undergone periods of hospital treatment and rehabilitation and who have great difficulty in surviving in the community. Each of the following sections is prefixed by a quote from a survey that I shall refer to several times in this article, so I shall provide some background for it here. It is a project that was completed some twenty years ago, but still has relevance today.

The survey, published as a book entitled *Not the Same as You*, or 'The Salford Project', as it will be referred to in future, was a research project set up in 1975 to investigate the possibility of a 'Continuous Care Register'. The purposes of such a register would be to monitor ex-psychiatric patients in the community, identify and locate instances of breakdown and provide a centralised service of intervention. The sample for the survey consisted of 190 people who had all suffered from some form of psychiatric illness for several years. The diagnostic categories covered the range of illnesses usually found in the average psychiatric hospital; psychotic, neurotic, mixed disorders and short-term problems of a recurring nature. The people in the sample were asked, by means of questionnaires, to provide information about most aspects of their lives. The results were tabulated and conclusions were arrived at by the author (Korer 1975). However, one of the most illuminating aspects of the survey was the extensive use made of the subjects' actual words in describing their feelings. It gives a valuable insight into the way that they assessed the quality of their lives and I feel it throws some light upon the results of existing methods of psychiatric rehabilitation. Although the sample could be said to be relatively small, some of the feelings expressed will be recognised by many people who have worked with patients undergoing rehabilitation.

CHILDHOOD MEMORIES

As a child, I felt I just couldn't fit in. I remember standing on a hill when I was eleven, feeling very different from every one else.

Many psychiatric patients can remember feeling unhappy as children, as can many people with no record of mental illness. Nevertheless, many psychiatric problems are part of a long history and clear connections can often be seen between past and present difficulties. For example, the feeling of being 'different' or solitary is one that can be carried from childhood through to adult life, where it is added to the burden of anxieties.

Spontaneous artwork can recreate childhood memories in a most vivid and evocative manner. Fragmentary and vague recollections that are difficult to fuse into a coherent verbal narrative can find expression through subtle shades of colour, textures or direction of line and movement. Self-consciousness can often melt away when people become engrossed in creating images from their past. I have seen houses, gardens, pets, mothers and fathers, all depicted without a care for proportion or perspective; the picture becomes such an evocative link with the past that it attains rules and conventions of its own. I once watched an elderly female patient create a scene of Thames paddle steamers from many years ago. The style of drawing indicated a child of 7 rather than a woman of 70, but this did not concern her. The drawing drew other patients to her in a flood of shared local memories – an important event for a woman who had rarely spoken to others on the ward up to this time.

Patients can also use the medium of art psychotherapy to recall unpleasant memories. Such memories may have been repressed for many years and making contact with them is both difficult and frightening. Again, coherent verbal description may prove too elusive, but with paint or clay, past monsters and ghosts can emerge from formless beginnings. Some memories are so threatening and unpleasant that they can only be expressed in a very messy, shapeless way to begin with. Art psychotherapy can offer a patient an opportunity gradually to develop a personal language of symbolic expression that also offers symbolic containment and resolution. Obviously, simple catharsis is not enough. Once such material is produced, however, a skilful and trained therapist can use it in a way that will help the patient incorporate its meaning into his or her present life. The original trauma cannot be eradicated, but it can be vividly confronted as an image in paint or clay. In this way, some fears can be conquered, especially in the atmosphere of a sharing and supportive group.

Consistent work in art psychotherapy can also enable a patient to re-construct his childhood with some degree of continuity. A collection of pictures can provide a confused patient with a more reliable and meaningful record than a series of partly remembered, partly forgotten conversations. Many patients find that looking back through a series of images can draw together hitherto fragmented aspects of their past life and can provide an invaluable starting point for further work. The formation of some sense of continuity regarding childhood was seen by Freud as a central task of therapy: 'In psychoanalytic treatments we are invariably faced by the task of filling up the gaps in the memory of childhood' (Freud 1973: 237). For the patient who is emerging from a psychotic breakdown, the sharing of concrete imagery and the joint consideration of its symbolic content can provide a much needed objective island in a sea of over-intensified subjectivity and fragmentation.

Art psychotherapy, by means of attention to fantasy and imagination, can provide another link with childhood: that of play. Many people with a history of psychiatric illness speak of being lonely, isolated and excluded from school as children and it is thus likely that they will have been deprived of many aspects of creative play. It may be of great value to them to lose some of their psychological 'stiffness' and to become involved in work that allows a spontaneous sense of fun to develop. Art psychotherapy can provide an ideal setting for free-flowing imagination, games and nonsensical fantasy and a skilful therapist can use such situations to enhance his work with patients. Indeed, such an attitude is seen by many to be one of the basic requirements of therapy. In the words of Winnicott: (1971: 63)

> The general principle seems to me to be valid, that psychotherapy is done in the overlap of the two play areas, that of the patient and that of the therapist. If the therapist cannot play, then he is not suitable for the work. If the patient cannot play, then something needs to be done to enable the patient to become able to play, after which psychotherapy may begin.

Generally, art psychotherapy can be a means of forging links between childhood and present life and can thus enable a patient to see the events of childhood in the context of current life. These events, good or bad, cannot be denied without risking inner discontent, and confrontation with them can do much towards resolving the conflicts and stresses of rehabilitation.

EMPTINESS OF LIFE

I wish I could have these last six years different from what they've been. Everything's missing from my life. There's nothing really happy. I've felt like this for quite a few years now. I've tried to commit suicide twice. Sometimes I still want to.

People are never totally satisfied with their lives or everything they have done, and some people with no background of psychiatric illness would echo some of the sentiments expressed above. However, such feelings are often present to a very intense degree in those patients who have recently been discharged from hospital, or who are working through rehabilitation. The process of adjustment to normal life often becomes too difficult and they come to believe that the coming years will have no more to offer them than the past. Further examination of such feelings will often reveal that many patients feel totally disconnected from the progress of their lives; they feel that things just happen and they are powerless to influence such happenings.

A paralysing sense of emptiness begins to penetrate their lives and they are unable to make use of the practical rehabilitation that is offered to them. It is probable that there will be those who cannot be helped to overcome these difficulties and find some meaning in their lives. However, if we are to find any solutions, we must examine some of the things that patients are offered as meaningful pursuits and see if they are likely to prove acceptable.

One of the elements that is highly valued in rehabilitation programmes is work. It has been said that 'work is the cornerstone of rehabilitation' (Morgan and Cheadle, 1981: 8). Much is said about the value of work and activity: if you work you will feel good, if you stay active you will stay well. For some, this may well be true but for others it is so often not. Many patients commence jobs but do not continue with them and many others positively reject the whole concept of employment. The Salford Project showed that nearly half those asked were not even attempting to look for work (Korer 1975: 12). Although work and gainful employment are clearly important aspects of life, it is unrealistic to expect that the whole of a patient's life can be filled with activities that are exciting and fulfilling. Ex-patients find themselves on the bottom rungs of the employment ladder when seeking work, and they will probably be forced to accept the most boring and mundane jobs in order to survive independently. If their lives can also contain activities that foster creative growth and provide psychic nourishment, I feel that their other work will be made more bearable and their lives will be less empty and stressful.

I worked with a young female patient in an adolescent unit who had reached an astounding state of inner emptiness. Offers of help and opportunities for progress were all around her; psychotherapy, group therapy, medication, help from her family, education, careers advice and social skills programmes. She rejected all of these and remained inactive, staring into space and communicating only rarely. With a great deal of persuasion, she began to attend open art therapy sessions. At first she always sat in the same seat facing a wall and began painting a picture of that wall and the paintings on it. She then moved to a seat facing a window and painted the view from it, including the window frame. Over a few weeks, she continued in the same fashion until she had painted the view from all the windows in the art room. She then painted a picture of me. Over a period of several weeks, she gradually moved out of the art room and painted various interior scenes around the unit. Other patients and staff took an interest in her work and they began to appear in the paintings. In the later stages, she painted views of the unit from the outside, the final paintings from a viewpoint some distance away. These changes in her artwork were accompanied by changes in her behaviour and attitudes. She began to take more part in group psychotherapy and her social interactions with staff and other patients became more meaningful. Expressions of extreme anger, hatred, sadness and affection became possible.

In spite of these many changes, her story was not an entirely successful one. She did manage to leave the unit and start work, but setbacks occurred.

She still suffered much unhappiness, but she became reconciled with her family and managed to cope with life reasonably well. I think the important thing that art psychotherapy offered her was an opportunity to make a gradual but nevertheless concrete and continuous progress; a form of inner creative reconstruction. This inner process was connected to the outside world by permanent and personal images which engaged her in relationships with others. She effectively painted her way through, out of and away from the institution, both making and breaking connections with its physical and social content as she went.

Herein lies one of the great powers of art psychotherapy. Elinor Ulman (1975: 13) has described it thus:

> Its motive power comes from within the personality; it is a way of bringing order out of chaos – chaotic feelings and impulses within, the bewildering mass of impressions from without. It is a means to discover both the self and the world, and to establish a relation between the two. In the complete creative process inner and outer realities are fused into a new entity.

The inner emptiness described by many patients may well be a total splitting-off of unbearable thoughts or feelings. It may also be as described above: a psychic paralysis resulting from the terrifying confrontation of two worlds, one of inner personal needs, fears and shadows and the other of public demands and consequences. In such cases, no amount of practical training in coping with work and the realities of life is likely to be of much use. Art psychotherapy, by providing a safe symbolic container for trauma and accumulated psychic chaos, can help to break through the emptiness and, as rehabilitation progresses, can support a patient's return to some form of compromise with reality.

INABILITY TO PREVENT INNER NEUROSES FROM INTERFERING WITH EVERYDAY LIFE

I was retired from work because I was always late and crying and unfriendly to customers.

The above is a reflection of what must surely be one of the most common experiences of psychiatric patients who are attempting to master the effects of their disturbance and get on with normal life. I feel it gives further indication that the rehabilitation process needs to contain far more than work training and practice in the tasks of daily living. Unless attention is given to underlying emotional conflicts, they will simply force their way through and render practical progress impossible.

A way of considering the nature of these lurking forces is to recall Jung's concept of the 'shadow'. In her book about Jung's work, Frieda Fordham has described it thus:

The shadow is the personal unconscious; it is all those uncivilised desires and emotions that are incompatible with social standards and our ideal personality, all that we are ashamed of, all that we do not want to know about ourselves. It follows that the narrower and more restrictive the society in which we live the larger will be our shadow.

(Fordham 1966: 50)

People with a long history of psychiatric illness usually find themselves living in a prescribed and more restrictive world than the rest of us, in terms of opportunity, social freedom and financial stability. Their 'shadows' will thus loom larger. Add to this their emotional wounds caused by successive breakdowns and their decreased sense of independence caused by periods of institutional care and a picture will emerge of a person who will experience great difficulty in confronting his or her more unacceptable aspects. Of course, it is quite impossible for anyone to be in total control of their unconscious mind and always able to confront their 'shadow'. But if a patient is to function even reasonably well in everyday society, then he or she is likely to need consistent help in this area. The 'shadow', or personal unconscious, is an elusive and amorphous force to deal with. Many patients, in verbal psychotherapy, are unable to find descriptions that will adequately communicate the nature of the frightening and sometimes bizarre thoughts that are interfering with their life. They feel that a coherent explanation is necessary, but such an explanation is often not the best way of describing emotions that may be transient and fragmented. Art psychotherapy, with its use of fantasy, symbolisation and visual free association, is often more suited for the task.

I recall a middle-aged female patient who once depicted herself as a mermaid carrying a fish on her head. She told me that this image came to her whenever she approached her discharge from hospital, a process that she had undergone many times. She was a patient who did not usually communicate many deep feelings to ward staff, but most of them could remember her talking about this image prior to previous discharges. This had often been met with amusement from both staff and other patients. The patient herself acknowledged that she became embarrassed by the thought and she was unwilling to pursue it further on a verbal level. However, when she incorporated this image into a picture she painted in a ward art psychotherapy group, the response she encountered was very different. Her picture was seen as an imaginative and artistic creation; what seemed out of place in everyday conversation seemed perfectly natural in the setting of a creative art group. With support the patient was able to reveal that, as she approached discharge, she began to feel like the mermaid; a creature that became helpless once it left its own environment. She felt that once she left the protective hospital environment she would be helpless and would need to be carried. At first, she claimed that this was what she wanted and said that her husband should support her more. However, subsequent examination of particular elements of the picture revealed more; she saw the fish on her head as her husband. Although she desired more support for herself, she was also very ashamed of needing it and felt that she should be able to support her husband more with his difficulties.

Through her painting, this patient confronted her 'shadow' and its attributes: weakness, shame and despair. She spoke of trying to work but soon becoming overwhelmed by feelings of hopelessness, of being unable to cope with even small setbacks and of eventually giving up. Many other patients in the group were able to share these feelings and she thus became less alone with her anxieties. The discussion that followed enabled her to go some way towards realising that it was possible to separate trivial daily anxieties from deeper and more permanent ones.

This example illustrates how vague, but nevertheless extremely disturbing, emotions can be reached by a form of therapy that encourages fantasy and the use of symbols. Subtle shades of meaning can be expressed by subtle changes in image content. If the art therapist can help the patient to 'stretch' the image, different levels of meaning can be revealed. Mysterious impulses and indescribable conflicts that are interfering with the progress of normal life can be examined and linked with current realities. If such feelings, instead of being expressed, are constantly repressed, then successful rehabilitation will not be possible. To quote again from Frieda Fordham (1966: 51):

> While some repression is a necessity of social life, the danger of repressing the shadow is that in the unconscious it seems to acquire strength and grow in vigour, so that when the moment comes (as often happens) when it must appear, it is more dangerous and more likely to overwhelm the rest of the personality, which otherwise could have acted as a wholesome check.

Repression of the 'shadow' can thus lead to increased neurosis and possibly to complete breakdown. It is also likely inwardly to separate a person from the strong emotions that are needed for survival. Jung came to the conclusion that the 'shadow' also contained 'good and useful qualities, such as normal instincts, appropriate reactions, realistic insights and creative impulses' (Jung 1951: 266). This concept can sometimes be sensed in a patient's artwork. Often, following the production of a series of images that express deep feelings of shame, guilt or badness, a patient's work will take on a new vitality and power of expression. Once the bad aspects of the 'shadow' are confronted and accepted, the creative aspects can also be reached and utilised for growth.

Art psychotherapy also offers an opportunity to exercise self-discipline, an attribute that will be of great value to a patient who is attempting to adjust to the pressures of a changing life. Anyone who has struggled with the demands of creative artwork will know that it is insufficient to produce a simple cathartic flood; impulses and emotions must find symbol, image and form if they are to be usefully expressed and communicated. Edith Kramer has described this:

> The process of sublimation constitutes the best way to deal with a basic human dilemma, but the conflicting demands of superego and id cannot be permanently reconciled. In the artistic product conflict and form *is* contained but only partly neutralized. The artist's position epitomizes the precarious human situation; while his craft demands the greatest self-discipline and perseverance, he must maintain access to the primitive impulses and fantasies that constitute the raw materials for his work.
>
> (Kramer 1977: 6)

Most ex-patients who are attempting to work and lead a normal life are only too aware of their primitive impulses and fantasies; it is an inability to contain them that eventually leads to breakdown. Experiencing a good and consistent programme of art psychotherapy will give them many opportunities to confront this problem and will go a considerable way towards helping them cope with it in the outside world.

REHABILITATION AND DRUGS

I want to get off these injections and drugs and solve my problems for myself.

When I was very ill and things got nasty and unbearable seeing these visions, the drugs got rid of it and that's a fact. They didn't get rid of my unhappiness but they got rid of that. I think they were wonderful for stopping me seeing visions and things.

These two quotes, both from the same survey, illustrate the conflicting attitudes of patients towards drug treatment; the same conflicting attitudes can often be found in staff responsible for their rehabilitation. Many patients have great faith in drugs and would reject any proposals to limit their use, while others reject them and desire some other form of solution to their problems. Although there are patients who would be seen as unable to function at all without drugs, it is also clear that drugs are often used as a substitute for inadequate resources in other areas. Many doctors and nurses in the rehabilitation field freely acknowledge that the use of certain drugs could be considerably curtailed if more time and money was available for consultation, counselling and the provision of a variety of supportive therapies.

Quite naturally, if drugs are freely offered as a mainstay of a rehabilitation programme, people will accept them and come to rely heavily on their effects. Many drugs produce a rapid change in mood and quickly relieve acute symptoms. This is understandably attractive to someone who is suffering greatly. It would be clinically dishonest to deprive a patient of information regarding drugs which can be used to control symptoms. Equally, it is just as dishonest to deprive patients of other facts about drug treatment: that their mental and physical functioning will be impaired, that the initially attractive feeling of instant relief will lessen with time, that physical and psychological dependence may occur and that eventually many patients become dissatisfied with such passive treatment. It is also dishonest to deny them access to various forms of psychotherapy and art psychotherapy by developing programmes of rehabilitation devoid of such treatments. For many psychiatric patients, a series of mental breakdowns followed by long-term reliance on drugs has resulted in considerable damage to their self-esteem. I feel that consistent art psychotherapy can repair some of this damage and can lead a patient to take a greater part in the management of his or her own treatment.

Many rehabilitation workers would say that chronic patients cannot cope with the demands of psychotherapy. In some cases this is probably true although it is an opinion that is often too readily applied. In verbal psychotherapy, a patient may be in a situation that he or she has experienced only too often; sitting with another person and being unable to start a conversation. The silence grows from embarrassment to fear and then to absolute despair and the therapist may find this an impossible barrier to successful work. This process can be the result of a patient being totally unused to taking an active part in his or her own treatment.

In art psychotherapy, similar difficulties can occur, but it is a less familiar situation for the patient. Creation of personal imagery can take place gradually and most patients can be encouraged to make a start somewhere, even if initially it is only at the level of decoration or playing with materials. In these early stages, conscious symbolic content may be at a low level while enjoyment or diversion may be paramount. A skilful and sensitive therapist can draw out themes from unconscious content and feed these back to the patient, thus increasing insight, awareness and communication. Gradually, as each image or series of images builds up, the patient creates a personal world in an active, constructive way. Such a collection of concrete expressions, coming from a person who is normally the passive recipient of medication or instruction, can mark the beginning of real movement towards change. Edith Kramer has noted this process in her work with disturbed children:

> In psychotherapy the child's activities are varied. He may talk, play, draw or model, do any number of things. The only constant factor is the therapist's presence. The child may remain isolated, unable to relate to him for long periods of time. Art activities, on the other hand, invite the creation of a world that is egocentrically organised. Each element in the child's work contains part of himself.
>
> (Kramer 1973: 32)

This symbolic, personal world is the meeting place for the patient and the therapist. With treatment by medication, the doctor gives and the patient receives. In art psychotherapy, images are created which draw the patient and the therapist together; a common ground of active participation is established. Rehabilitation workers frequently use the term 'self-care', meaning the degree to which a patient looks after his or her physical needs and overall well-being. A person who is a mere recipient of a passive form of treatment will not be encouraged to take an active interest in his or her overall well-being; reliance on such treatment will surely lead that person to leave more and more to others. Art psychotherapy can help patients to increase the degree of active participation they take in their treatment. This can lead them truly to believe that they have some control over their future. Once the beginnings of such a belief are established, the patients will be more inclined to direct energies towards making real changes in their lives. This is true and meaningful self-care.

ART THERAPY AND REHABILITATION: PROBLEMS OF INTEGRATION

After outlining some of the ways in which art psychotherapy can be used in a programme of integrated rehabilitation, I now wish to turn to the problems that will face art therapists who wish to work in this area. There may be some institutions where few problems exist and where a variety of therapeutic opportunities are available to patients. Conversely, there seem to be many institutions where very little is offered in the way of treatment or therapy and where there is not much more available than work training, non-qualified counselling and medication. In this sort of system, the art therapist will experience great difficulty in ensuring that the service offered is of maximum benefit to patients. All workers in a team must obviously be prepared to 'fit in' and modify their approaches to accommodate the needs and demands of the institution. Therapists can become too single-minded and rigid in their philosophy and thus engender hostility and isolation. On the other hand, if therapists are forced to modify their work to a degree where its very nature becomes distorted, they are unlikely to serve the patients' best interests. The following examples cover some of the main areas of philosophical and practical difficulty that art therapists may have to face when working within a rehabilitation system.

Rehabilitation: general atmosphere and staff attitudes towards therapy

As previously mentioned, an art therapist operating within a rehabilitation system may be working with staff who are more interested in practical training than in a psychodynamic or psychotherapeutic approach. The department's atmosphere may place great emphasis upon apparent activity and pay little attention to deep and lasting change. An idea of this atmosphere can be discerned in the following extract:

> The most important single ingredient in rehabilitation is an atmosphere of stimulation. One tries to convey to patients that things need to be done as quickly as possible, as promptly as possible and as much as possible. One is looking for an increase in their alertness, energy and speed of movement. Standards matter, personal appearance matters, timekeeping matters, output matters, sociability matters.
>
> (Morgan and Cheadle, 1981: 6)

Although one can understand, to a degree, that such elements may have a place in a work training programme, it is difficult to see how they can create an atmosphere that would be anything but harmful to the concept of art psychotherapy. Staff with these attitudes, considering the work of an art therapy group, would value briskness, output, neatness and punctuality. Slow and hesitant work, messy work, inconsistent output and poor communication would be judged as undesirable qualities to be quickly eradicated. I feel sure that an art therapist would also consider the items in the quote as important aspects of a patient's personality and would endeavour to understand them in terms of the therapeutic relationship. However, it often seems that rehabilitation staff are more concerned with simply changing such behaviour than in understanding it. The art therapist will need to make constant efforts to show how much such aspects of a patient can give valuable insights into individual and social pathology and how such insights, once gained, can be used constructively to help the process of rehabilitation.

This atmosphere also affects the patients' attitudes towards activities which are offered to them within an institution. Many of them are afraid to make a messy painting, to produce only a small amount, to paint a 'weird' picture, lest staff should think they are not working constructively. Such fears can be sensed in rehabilitation departments, but it is difficult to persuade patients to acknowledge them. Nevertheless, bringing such anxieties into open discussion is an essential part of establishing art psychotherapy as a useful form of treatment. It is an area where the therapist must tread carefully, as many rehabilitation staff frown upon an activity that encourages patients to criticise the system. However, therapy may only reach a very superficial level if this problem is not very firmly dealt with.

Because of the orientation of many rehabilitation departments, therapy is often looked upon as an activity that is esoteric, abstract and unrelated to 'real-life' tasks. Staff may be unwilling to change their attitudes sufficiently to enable their participation in the art psychotherapy programme to be useful. Indeed, if they have been selected for personal qualities that are suitable for a traditional rehabilitation regime, it may be almost impossible for them to adjust. Carl Rogers (1951: 21) has said:

There are also many whose concept of the individual is that of an object to be dissected, diagnosed, manipulated. Such professional workers may find it very difficult to learn or to practice a client-centered form of psychotherapy.

If this attitude does prevail in staff it is a great pity, as I believe, ideally, that art therapists should attempt to draw other staff towards their work and extend that way of thinking into the institution. However, it may be virtually impossible for an art therapist to have a great deal of influence on the general atmosphere of a rehabilitation department. Many such departments are run on very traditional lines with medical superiority and a strict nursing hierarchy. In spite of this, I feel that art therapists should constantly be trying to make themselves heard and should be speaking out on all policy issues. As well as being an effective method of treatment, art psychotherapy can act as a powerful general creative force that can bring about radical changes in attitudes towards psychiatric rehabilitation.

Respect for the boundaries of the therapeutic situation

Throughout the time that I have spent conducting art psychotherapy sessions in a psychiatric hospital, I have been struck by how difficult it often is to establish and preserve what would be considered the most basic requirements for therapeutic work: a separate room, a set time, consistent staffing, a stable patient group and freedom from interruptions. If these elementary criteria are not met, psychotherapeutic work becomes extremely difficult if not impossible. The therapist has to spend so much time dealing with the effects of interruptions, staff changes, room changes and variations in time, that the individual pathology of the patients or the inner dynamics of the group are pushed into the background. Respect for the work is lost and its strength diminished. When faced with such difficulties, it is very easy for a therapist to become extremely angry and to feel that deliberate sabotage is taking place. This may not be a paranoid fantasy; people can become professionally threatened by forms of treatment that challenge the status quo. However, another reason for this apparently careless and insensitive attitude may be simple ignorance of the basic principles of psychodynamic therapy.

I remember conducting an individual art therapy session with a patient in the side-room of a rehabilitation ward. The patient was engrossed in his painting when two men from the hospital works department walked in saying 'excuse us'. They then made a brief inspection of the plumbing. As they were leaving one of them, who recognised the patient, came across and said, 'Hello Bill – doing some sketching? That's nice.' The whole incident was over in less than a minute, leaving me angry, distracted and wondering if I would ever be able to get reasonable boundaries established, as this sort of casual interruption had happened many times before. In actual fact, a useful session followed as I took the event up with the patient and we did some fruitful work about lack of privacy in institutions and how this related to his family background. Nevertheless, persistent interruptions of this sort can be very destructive. Afterwards, I began to consider the incident in greater depth; at whom, or what, should my anger be rightfully directed? The men themselves? The ward staff? The institution? Myself? I came to the conclusion that it would probably be unjust to blame the workmen or the ward staff. With regard to the workmen they had probably never had the experience of being refused entry to any other form of art session in that institution; they were just following their normal procedure. With regard to the ward staff, they were probably also following a system that had always prevailed; when maintenance work needs to be done it is done, regardless of what the patients are doing.

This is why it is so important to get psychodynamic work and thinking into rehabilitation departments. Until staff have experienced the power and depth of such work, they will simply not believe in the effects that seemingly casual actions can have upon it. Art therapy is particularly effective for demonstrating this. If staff can witness how, from a very basic image, a rich fantasy world can be created and developed, then they will begin to believe in the significance of everyday events. If they are allowed to see the uncanny, almost telepathic, lines of connection between images in group art therapy, then they will begin to pay greater attention to mood and atmosphere on the ward and will understand the part they play in it to a greater degree. If they can follow a series of paintings and see how a patient's internal world is deeply affected by the intrusion of seemingly trivial events, then they may begin to become more sensitive in their interactions.

To many art therapists, these comments may seem over-optimistic. I shall acknowledge that there will always be staff who are insensitive, inconsiderate, even downright destructive. However, attitudes are not going to change without intervention. I feel that art therapists need to be constantly making such interventions: stressing the importance of consistent boundaries, pointing out relevant dynamics and sharing the excitement and the power of their work with other staff. People really need to understand the damage that interruption can do, even if it is preceded by 'excuse me'. This 'spreading the word' is particularly important in the case of art psychotherapy. In psychiatric institutions generally, and in rehabilitation particularly, art activities have a long history of connection with diversion and recreation. This can only be changed by a process of consistent and precise definition.

Rewards and punishments

Rewards and punishments are very direct terms for processes that are often clearly in evidence in psychiatric rehabilitation departments. They may not be referred to in such an obvious manner; terms such as 'positive or negative reinforcement' and 'therapeutic disapproval' are much more common. Many would say that such elements form an appropriate part of a rehabilitation programme and that they are aspects of daily life that patients must accept. This is a debatable point with which I do not intend to become involved here. What I do wish to consider is the effect of a judgementally oriented atmosphere on the process and practise of art psychotherapy. Jung (1938: 338–9) has said:

> If the doctor wants to guide another, or even accompany him a step of the way, he must feel with that person's psyche. He never feels with it when he passes judgement. Whether he puts his judgements into words, or keeps them to himself, makes not the slightest difference.

Sensitive art therapists will attempt to accompany patients on a journey through the psyche and will be guided by the images produced. They will be seeking to maintain a delicate balance between understanding, interpretation and investigation and will be aided in this task by subtle changes in the overall pattern of process and imagery. If a therapist pauses to pass judgement or to adopt the stance of a director, the flow of unconscious material will be interrupted and thus ground in gaining a real understanding of the patient will be lost.

Within the atmosphere of many psychiatric rehabilitation departments, the art therapist may find this course difficult to follow. The very fact that patients have arrived at such a department or have been selected for discharge introduces the concept of reward; it is a form of promotion from other, more 'chronic' environments. Places in the more attractive community projects are often few and far between and are usually awarded to patients whose manifest behaviour has shown steady improvement. I have found that patients are sometimes extremely cautious about what they reveal to staff about their true feelings in these circumstances. They are afraid that they may incur disapproval and thus slip back down the promotion ladder. Added to this is the fact that 'positive' behaviour is rewarded and 'negative' behaviour is frowned upon. This would, perhaps, be less of a problem if it was not approached at such a superficial level as is often found.

During my reading of the literature on psychiatric rehabilitation, I listed two sets of adjectives that were used to describe patients and their behaviour. The following words, from the first list, were used to describe patients whose performance was considered unsatisfactory: INERT, FLABBY, SCRUFFY, LAZY, DULL, APATHETIC, CHILDISH, DEVIOUS, BORING, INEPT, UNSKILLED. The words from the second list were used to describe patients who were considered to be making progress ENERGETIC, BRIGHT, ENTERPRISING, CLEAN, MOBILE, POLITE, JAUNTY, HELPFUL, OUTGOING. This method of describing patients' personalities and progress concerns, almost entirely, their outward behaviour. It pervades the attitudes of rehabilitation staff to a very high degree and it is not only applied to patients. It produces an atmosphere that encourages the simplistic seeking of rewarding or positive experience and the avoidance of painful, disappointing or punishing experience. I feel that this atmosphere is detrimental to the formation of meaningful relationships between staff and patients and it is certainly damaging to the practice of art psychotherapy.

With regard to rewards, 1 feel that staff will seek immediate gratification; they will be more impressed by images of an obviously expressive nature and will be less moved by more subtle, quieter imagery. Weight and power in painting will be valued more than real content or latent potential. In the same way, patients may seek rewards by presenting images that have 'expressive punch', colour and energy; images that shout rather than whisper. This sort of work is common in newly formed art psychotherapy groups in psychiatric institutions. Broken hearts drip blood, gravestones and aspirin bottles abound. The underlying feelings are genuine, but the expression is motivated by external factors. Patients may also expect art therapy sessions to give them immediate and concrete rewards in the same way that they have been rewarded for good behaviour. When this does not happen, or when they do not receive praise from the therapist, they may lose faith in the treatment as a potential source of help.

With regard to punishment, this may be seen in staff attempts to avoid disappointment. The usual theme of rehabilitation is one of steady and measured progress towards change in behaviour. In an atmosphere ruled by rewards and punishments, lack of apparent progress can be experienced by staff as a deliberate act on the patient's behalf – a form of attack. This may find outlet in direct anger or irritation with the patients, or it may emerge in a more subtle way in the form of a desire to force progress, a wish to speed things up. This may influence staffs' attitude towards artwork. They may be led into making hasty and ill-considered interpretations of patients' work in an effort to produce results or to 'see' a coherent pattern of symbolic meaning that may not really exist.

Furthermore, the actual perception of images may be distorted; positive aspects may be magnified, negative aspects diminished. Patients may seek to avoid punishment or disapproval by conscious concealment of images or ways of working that they feel may be frowned upon. If they are surrounded by an atmosphere that has reward and punishment as its main motivating factors, they may also develop an unconscious 'censor' that prevents the emergence of certain material in their work; free association, an important factor in art psychotherapy, will be impeded. Fear of punishment can also lead to the natural progress of artwork being diverted or distorted. Patients in rehabilitation departments can often be heard to say, about paintings: 'Is it alright? What should I do now? Should I carry on with it?' The reasons for such anxieties are obviously complex and multi-determined. However, it is possible that they are caused by the patients looking at their paintings and seeing the emergence of elements that they fear may lead to disapproval. Free expression is checked and instead of a patient being liberated by the painting, he or she is trapped by it.

I feel it is clear that a rehabilitation regime that has reward and punishment of behaviour as a central element of its philosophy will present the art therapist with great difficulties. It may be possible to change such an atmosphere by frank staff discussion, emphasising the detrimental effect such an atmosphere has on treatment. Some discussion of the difference between real and apparent change will also be necessary. If reward must play a part in the system, let real psychic change be what is approved of, not change in behaviour. Even this, of course, is not a desirable state of affairs and can be damaging to real therapy. Failing success along these lines, it may be necessary for art psychotherapy to become an 'island' in the system, where different rules apply. However, this must be looked upon as a last resort as it will probably be ineffective. Patients will carry the prevailing climate of the department with them and will find difficulty in letting go of it. Overall I feel the art therapist must attempt to be an agent of change, for isolation within a treatment programme may only be of limited benefit to patients.

Interpretation

Interpretive work in art psychotherapy can be an invaluable asset to those involved with the problems posed by psychiatric rehabilitation. However, it is also an area where great misunderstanding can arise when the art therapist tries to familiarise other staff with his or her work. Nurses, doctors and other professionals will often point out a piece of artwork and say, 'What does it mean?' They seem to see art psychotherapy as a means of diagnosis, a short cut to the unconscious, or a way of sorting patients into categories. There seems to be a popular opinion, outside the art psychotherapy profession, that there are universal interpretations that can be applied to artwork regardless of individual pathology. People talk about 'schizophrenic art' or 'psychotic art' and seem to feel that a single painting can confirm the diagnosis of such conditions. The art therapist is seen as the person who can unlock the secrets of a patient's pictures in an esoteric and magical way.

Of course, it is true that a patient's artwork may have many shades of meaning and, also, that it can provide insight into his or her current state of mind at both a conscious and an unconscious level for both patient and therapist. But such meanings are personal and particular rather than universal, even when familiar images and symbols are employed, and their exact significance can only be ascertained by consistent therapeutic work with an experienced art therapist. This symbolic individuality can be clearly seen if one listens to patients in an art psychotherapy group discussing their work; a single image will provoke many different interpretations and each person will be drawn towards meanings that relate to his or her own pathology or position in a group. It is the task of the art therapist to enable a patient to arrive at a meaningful and useful interpretation of his or her own work. Ulman has expressed it thus;

> Treatment depends on the development of the transference relation and on a continuous effort to obtain the patient's own interpretation of his symbolic designs. The images produced are a form of communication between patient and therapist; they constitute symbolic speech.
>
> (Ulman 1975: 4)

Once such interpretations are obtained and confirmed, they can provide rehabilitation staff with a way of understanding and responding to patients' needs. However, staff must realize that patience is required; an ill-considered comment based upon interpretive understanding can mystify, confuse and frighten a patient and can be very destructive to a programme of careful work. The art therapist must help other staff to adopt a sensitive approach by explaining various aspects of symbolic content in artwork. If they can see how symbolic meaning can change with time and mood, how unconscious meaning can gradually emerge from a series of paintings, and how different interpretations within a group are related to both group dynamics and individual pathology, then they may become more able to make useful comments.

Staff also need to realise how their own pathology affects their perception and interpretation of patients' artwork. When we look at a picture, we are looking at a patient's attempt at some form of communication; but we cannot receive that communication without being emotionally affected by the images used or without being influenced by our own past and present symbolic perceptions. This is obviously not a barrier to understanding. Indeed, it is a process that is utilised by the art therapist in his attempts to understand the patient's work in terms of the therapeutic relationship. Experienced and trained therapists are familiar with the necessity of taking these factors into account when considering patients' artwork and they are assisted in this by professional supervision. However, the understanding and acceptance of concepts such as transference and countertransference is rare in traditional rehabilitation regimes and the art therapist may experience difficulty with many staff. Not only are these concepts difficult to grasp, but they are also of a nature that may be considered a threat to prevailing attitudes in rehabilitation; to staff who have become used to operating in an atmosphere of 'the helper knows best', they may be completely alien.

At worst, interpretation can be used as a subtle means of control within an authoritarian regime. Staff can come to believe that their interpretation of a patient's behaviour or a piece of artwork is the true and valid one and that patients are unable to perceive unconscious meaning in their own work because of the limitations imposed by their illness. This can reinforce a system of superiority and the patient is thus denied opportunities fully to understand, through a process of personal enablement, all the levels of meaning in his or her work. Staff's opinions about a patient's work can obviously help that patient to consider it in a wider sense and may enable him or her to approach different levels of meaning in it. However, it must be realised that, as well as being a valuable aid to understanding, interpretation can be frightening and persecutory if it is used in an ill-considered and insistent manner. I feel that art therapists working in rehabilitation departments must be constantly trying to help staff understand this, for not only will such understanding give them a better grasp of art psychotherapy, it will also give them greater insight into the dynamics of all their interactions with patients.

Another aspect of interpretation that is surrounded by misunderstanding is that of what can be expected from a patient when he or she is confronted with interpretative comments. Interpretation is often seen as a magical key that, once turned by presentation to the patient, will instantly unlock some sort of binding and imprisoning force. Most experienced therapists will know that this is far from the truth. Anthony Storr (1979: 32) has said:

> Thus, one function of interpretation is to make the incomprehensible comprehensible. This seldom immediately abolishes any neurotic symptom, but it does have the effect of relieving any anxiety which the patient may have about his sanity; and also converts the symptom from a shadowy, unknown adversary into a more clearly identified problem which can be worked at.

I think the important phrase is 'which can be worked at'. In the case of art psychotherapy, interpretation of an image to the patient is only a small part of a continuous process. An interpretation should only be made when the therapist has become fully familiar with a particular patient's work and symbolic approach. After it is made, it may take some time for it to have any effect and for it to trigger further images; indeed, it may have no effect whatsoever. The art therapist needs to tread a careful path, maintaining a delicate balance between intervention and silence.

In many ways it is understandable why some rehabilitation staff are drawn into making inappropriate comments about patients' artwork. Many patients display their work in the department or show it to staff and invite opinions. Faced with this situation, staff may be tempted to comment in what they consider to be a therapeutic way, by making an interpretation. I feel that the art therapist must make every effort to convince staff that direct interpretations are best kept within the boundaries of art therapy sessions and that it is more useful to encourage the patient to talk about his or her work in a general way, while giving support, encouragement and understanding. The art therapist must also emphasise that symbolic meaning can only be truly understood by reference to individual pathology and the overall pattern of a patient's work.

CONCLUSION

Doublethink means the power of holding two contradictory beliefs in one's mind simultaneously, and accepting both of them.

(Orwell 1990: 223)

Nineteen eighty-four has been and gone and I feel sure that it has left art therapists struggling to master the art of 'Doublethink'. The two contradictory beliefs that they are trying to accept are, firstly, that it is possible to practise art psychotherapy and, secondly, that it is possible to do so within the state mental health services. Although this is an obviously pessimistic conclusion, it is one that I am inevitably drawn towards after consideration of the questions posed in this chapter.

However, I still feel it is possible for therapists to make a valuable contribution to the rehabilitation of psychiatric patients, but to do so they will need to find considerable emotional strength. The philosophical basis of traditional rehabilitation is radically different to that of psychodynamic art psychotherapy and much opposition, even hostility, will be encountered. Nevertheless, if art psychotherapy is to survive as a valid treatment process, this hostility must be faced and met with sound clinical reasoning. In fact, more is at stake than a method of treatment. If art therapists do not take up this challenge, mental health services will be deprived of a whole way of thinking: one that focuses attention upon emotional problems in depth rather than at a superficial level and one that accommodates the human need for more than material success in life.

At times, it seems grossly unfair that art therapists should have to strive so hard for acceptance, in addition to doing a very demanding job. Those who make policy decisions in mental health would probably reply that they are not inclined to make radical changes in treatment policy to accommodate the philosophy of a comparatively new discipline that has no proven benefit. The examination of 'success' in psychodynamic therapy would require more space than I have here and would require the questioning of certain basic definitions. Very few methods of treatment can provide reliable long-term proof of their efficacy. What is certainly true is that many patients who are discharged from mental hospitals return time after time. This pattern has become so familiar to mental health workers that it has acquired a name: 'the revolving door syndrome'. In some ways, it seems to have become an accepted aspect of society. Jacky Korer, the author of 'The Salford Project' has commented on this:

It seems to me, from the results of this study, that in some ways we are guilty of leaving the patient 'high and dry'. Present low levels of functioning in the community seem to be acceptable to us even if the patient himself is unhappy with his situation. Thus we are guilty of wasting a valuable opportunity to consolidate the advantages we have gained in the treatment of mental illness by stopping short at the control of symptoms, instead of going on to create a dynamic and therapeutic environment for those patients who are as yet unable to bridge the gulf between social isolation and social integration.

(Korer 1975: 21)

It is clear that, in spite of the efforts made by many workers, the present system is failing badly. By all means let us look at every factor in order to find solutions and in order to see what additions are necessary to achieve improvement. But let us also give some attention to the questioning of existing methods of treatment and rehabilitation and see if they are counter-productive.

Psychodynamic therapy is one method of treatment that has been given virtually no chance to show how it can help. A survey carried out in Camberwell in 1965 revealed that, for a population of 175,000 people, fifteen hours a week of psychotherapy were offered by the National Health Service (Varma 1974: 275). Therapists working within the service will know that things are not much better today. Art psychotherapy is certainly in a similar, if not worse, position. This appalling rejection of a treatment method could be understood if it consisted of a dubious remedy offered by unqualified 'quacks'. It is not; it is an established therapeutic discipline practised by trained and qualified professional people. It is often the only form of psychotherapeutic service offered to many psychiatric patients, especially those diagnosed as psychotic. The very fact that art psychotherapy still exists at all is a tribute to the professional integrity and personal dedication of its practitioners. It is time that this profession was allowed to put itself to better use in the service of psychiatric rehabilitation.

REFERENCES

Fordham, F. (1966) *An introduction to Jung's Psychology*, Middlesex: Pelican.
Freud, S. (1973) *Introductory Lectures on Psychoanalysis*, Middlesex: Pelican.
Freud, S. (1974) *Studies on Hysteria*, Middlesex: Pelican.
Jung, C.G. (1951) 'Aion', in *Collected Works*, Vol. 9, Part 2, London: Routledge & Kegan Paul.
Jung, C.G. (1951) 'Psychotherapy and religion', in *Collected Works*, Vol. 11, London: Routledge & Kegan Paul.
Korer, J. (1975) *Not the Same as You*, London: The Psychiatric Rehabilitation Association.
Kramer, E. (1977) *Art Therapy in a Children's Community*, New York: Schocken.
Kramer, E. (1973) *Art as Therapy with Children*, New York: Schocken.
Larkin, P. (1982) 'Days', in *The Faber Book of Modern Verse*, London: Faber & Faber.
Morgan, R. and Cheadle, J. (1981) *Psychiatric Rehabilitation*, London: National Schizophrenia Fellowship.
Orwell, G. (1990) *Nineteen Eighty-Four*, London: Penguin.
Rogers, C. (1951) *Client Centred Psychotherapy*, Boston: Houghton, Mifflin.
Storr, A. (1979) *The Art of Psychotherapy*, London: Secker & Warburg.

Ulman, E. (1975) 'Art therapy: problems of definition', in E. Ulman and P. Dachinger (eds) *Art Therapy in Theory and Practice*, New York: Schocken.
Varma, V. (1974) *Psychotherapy Today*, London: Constable.
Winnicott, D.W. (1971) *Playing and Reality*, London: Penguin.

Index